GRC De

A Business Leader's Guide to Cyber Security

Jason L. Rorie
C|EH, CISA, CISM, CCSP, CISSP

Copyright © 2024

All rights reserved. No part of this book may be reproduced in any form or by electronic or mechanical means, including information storage and retrieval systems, without permission in writing from the publisher, except by a reviewer who may quote brief passages in a review.

ISBN: 9798871457924

Dedication

To my dear Mother, who always wondered if my passion for writing was just a phase. Surprise, Mom! I wrote ANOTHER book! To my amazing family, thank you for putting up with my late-night typing symphonies and endless rants about cyber security GRC. You proved that even when faced with cryptic acronyms and sleep-deprived ramblings, you can still love me.

To Maddie and Mason, Daddy loves you! Always know you can accomplish anything you want. Look at me! If I can write a book, you guys can definitely do anything! I'm so proud of the young people you have grown up to be. You two are truly a blessing in my life.

To Paola, you were the light at the end of the tunnel. You believed in me when I was at the bottom. Because of you, I rose and embarked on a new journey. With you and our furbaby, Cross, by my side, I feel like I have my grove back! Our future is bright, and I can't wait to watch the sunsets on the Corpus Christi bay!

Acknowledgment

Embarking on the journey of writing this book has been a rollercoaster of challenges and triumphs, and it's with immense gratitude that I acknowledge those who made this venture possible.

First and foremost, my heartfelt appreciation goes to my mother, Patricia. As an accomplished author herself, your wisdom and guidance transformed this daunting task into a joyous adventure. Your love is my greatest inspiration.

To my better half, Paola, your unwavering support and cheerleading have been my anchor. You've not only saved me from writer's block but also from countless coffee emergencies. Thank you for being my rock.

To my children, this book is a testament to the idea that dreams are achievable. You inspire me every day, and I hope this journey encourages you to reach for the stars.

To my Veteran friends, your enduring friendship and support in the ever-evolving IT landscape mean the world to me. Our shared experiences have been a source of strength and camaraderie.

A special shoutout to the fantastic team at Triad Resource Group. Your hard work and dedication have propelled our business to new heights. I am honored to have you as part of my business family, and I am continually amazed by your passion and commitment.

To our clients, your trust and partnership have been the driving force behind our success. Your appreciation for our work fuels our determination to be the best in the business.

This book is a collaborative achievement, and I am profoundly grateful for the collective efforts of my family, friends, staff, and business associates. Here's to the power of teamwork, the strength of connections, and the endless possibilities that unfold when we support and believe in each other.

About the Author

Jason Rorie's journey from a small Mississippi town to the pinnacle of the cybersecurity and technology industry is a testament to unwavering dedication, resilience, and a passion for excellence.

A proud veteran of the United States Navy, Jason honed his technical and security expertise while also cultivating invaluable leadership skills, a strong work ethic, and an unwavering commitment to integrity. Transitioning to civilian life, he brought the same fire and determination to his endeavors.

After an honorable discharge from the Navy, Jason pursued higher education, earning a degree in Computer Network Engineering and a Bachelor's in Management of Technology. In 2006, he planted his roots in Houston and founded Superior IT Solutions. Through relentless dedication to both his employees and clients, Jason propelled his company to become a trusted technology services provider in the Houston area.

His strategic vision and commitment to excellence led to the recognition of Superior IT Solutions companies on the Houston Business Journal's Fast 100 and Houston's Largest Cyber Security Companies, a testament to the company's rapid growth and success across industries. In 2016, Jason was honored as one of Houston's 40 Under 40, showcasing his leadership prowess and impact.

Always thirsting for knowledge and growth, Jason pursued a Master's Degree in Cyber Security | Network Defense, fortifying his expertise in the ever-evolving landscape of cyber threats. In 2018, he extended his influence further by founding Cyber Security Insurance Group, LLC, a specialized insurance agency focusing on cyber security insurance for small and medium businesses. His commitment to cyber security stems from a genuine desire to help business owners safeguard their enterprises, clients, and reputations.

Beyond his professional pursuits, Jason finds fulfillment in giving back to the community. Actively involved with veteran organizations, he channels his experience to coach and mentor veteran entrepreneurs. In his cherished moments of leisure, Jason enjoys family time around the water, completing the portrait of a multifaceted individual whose achievements echo far beyond the realm of business.

Preface

Hey there, fellow small business owner! Do you ever think cyber stuff is too complicated for your enterprise? Think again! I get it – it's easy to believe that cyber-attacks only happen to big shots. But truth bomb: size doesn't matter in the cyber world. Your business is just as tasty to hackers, whether you're big or small.

So, welcome to "GRC Decoded: A Business Leader's Guide to Cyber Security" – a guide made just for you, in plain English. No tech gibberish, promise! I've been around the block and seen small businesses hit by cyber trouble. The "it won't happen to me" idea? Yeah, let's kick that to the curb.

In this book, we'll chat about Governance, Risk, and Compliance (GRC) – not as scary as it sounds. From keeping your data safe to dodging cyber baddies, we'll cover it all. It's time to be the superhero your business needs. No more crossing your fingers and hoping for the best. Let's dive in because being clueless is not cool in the cyber world. Ready? Let's roll!

Table Of Contents

Dedication 3

Acknowledgment 4

About the Author 6

Preface 8

Table Of Contents 9

CHAPTER 1 11

INTRODUCTION TO GOVERNANCE, RISK, AND COMPLIANCE (GRC) 11

CHAPTER TWO 38

UNDERSTANDING GOVERNANCE 38

CHAPTER 3 59

DEMYSTIFYING RISK 59

CHAPTER 4 76

NAVIGATING COMPLIANCE 76

Chapter 5 133

THE CYBER SECURITY TRIAD 133

CHAPTER 6 160

GRC AND RMF FRAMEWORKS 160

CHAPTER 7 281

CYBER SECURITY CONTROLS 281

CHAPTER 8 377

IMPLEMENTING A GRC PROGRAM 377

CHAPTER 9 409
   SUSTAINING YOUR GRC PROGRAM 409
Chapter 10 419
   GRC IN ACTION 419
   CONCLUSION 434

CHAPTER 1

INTRODUCTION TO GOVERNANCE, RISK, AND COMPLIANCE (GRC)

Over centuries, the concept of Governance, Risk Management, and Compliance (GRC) has become deeply ingrained in the idea of how an organization ought to operate. Despite not being formally acknowledged as a known solution, it has been implemented at all levels inside every company. A GRC framework encompasses all policies, laws, regulations, company codes of conduct, and business risks, even if they were not explicitly named as such. Business risk calculation and controls, bookkeeping, financial reports, company policies, and cloud-based procedures and technology were typical practices before the advent of the digital age. Due to the tragedies that have rocked modern society, Forrester declared in 2002 that GRC is becoming an increasingly important tool in the market as technology and the market grow.

After 2002, GRC systems began to be regarded as a marketable commodity, allowing businesses to manage their commercial processes digitally. At the time, this was sufficient to run a business. Modular solutions let practitioners view a specific section of their business simultaneously, with less data to manage. However, when the regular requirements changed and the need to manage businesses increased, so did the time required to analyze the data in the GRC software. This trend has only angered cybersecurity specialists and regulatory compliance teams who use GRC solutions to grow and operate their security activities.

GOVERNANCE, RISK MANAGEMENT, AND COMPLIANCE (GRC)

GRC stands for Governance, Risk, and Compliance. Organizations use the system to organize administration, risk management, and adherence to regulations. The idea is to coordinate and coordinate an organization's risk management strategy and compliance with laws. Amplifying and rationalizing these processes may improve business performance and decision-making in Corporate Governance Boards.

The OCEG coined the term "GRC," officially defined in 2007 as "the collection of skills that allows an organization to achieve goals with confidence, deal with uncertainty, and act with integrity." As the name implies, the discipline comprises three major components: risk management, compliance, and risk management. Each of the three components will be explained individually.

1. GOVERNANCE

Firstly, Governance is the collection of laws, policies, and procedures that ensure an organization's activities align with its goals. Ethics, resource management, accountability, and management controls are all part of this.

Governance also guarantees that top management can drive and influence what happens at all levels of the organization and that business units are aligned with the needs of customers and broader corporate goals.

Effective management creates an environment where employees feel valued and behaviors and resources are controlled and organized. One management goal is to balance the interests of the company's various stakeholders, such as upper management, employees, suppliers, and investors.

To maintain this harmony, the government can ensure that agreements between the company's internal and external stakeholders are in place to provide a fair distribution of responsibilities, rights, and benefits. It also includes procedures for resolving competing interests among parties and practices for ensuring supervision, control, and data flow function as a control and balance system. Control over facilities and infrastructure, such as data centers, is provided by management, as is oversight of applications at the board level.

Before, governance was used to hold people accountable for their actions and outcomes. Establishing ethical business practices and corporate citizenship standards can help control behavior. Jobs business lines in good Governance define that jobs people are evaluated based on results rather than obligations.

2. RISK MANAGEMENT

Risk management detects, assesses, and controls an organization's financial, legal, strategic, and security risks. To reduce risk, an organization must devote resources to reducing, monitoring, and managing the effects of adverse events while encouraging positive ones. Risk management is a collection of people, procedures, and technologies that enable an organization to align its goals with its values and risks.

A business risk management program seeks to achieve corporate objectives while limiting risk and protecting value. Giving priority to the parties' expectations and providing reliable information is part of this task. A risk management program also identifies and plans to mitigate cyber security and information security threats, including software vulnerabilities and improper employee password habits.

The program must assess system performance and efficiency, evaluate old technology, identify operational and technological flaws that may affect the primary business, and monitor infrastructure risk and potential network and computing resource failures.

A risk assessment program must adhere to legal, contractual, internal, social, and moral goals and monitor newly implemented technology regulations. By focusing on risk and dedicating the required resources to control it, a firm will insulate itself against uncertainty, decrease expenses, and raise the possibility of business continuity and success.

3. COMPLIANCE

Compliance entails adhering to the rules, policies, standards, and laws established by businesses and government agencies. It is possible that failing to do so will have a negative influence on an organization in terms of poor performance, costly errors, fines, reprimands, and demands.

Regulatory compliance includes industry laws, regulations, and standards that apply to businesses. Corporate or internal conformity refers to the standards, regulations, and internal controls established by a particular company. The internal compliance management program must be integrated with the external compliance requirements. The integrated compliance program should be based on creating, updating, distributing, and monitoring compliance policies and employee training on them.

Organizations must identify high-risk areas and focus their resources on them to create an effective compliance program. Following that, policies must be developed, implemented, and communicated with employees to address risk areas. It is necessary to create an orientation to facilitate policy compliance.

PRINCIPLES OF GOVERNANCE, RISK, AND COMPLIANCE

Governance, Risk, and Compliance is a business strategy to manage a company's overall Governance, enterprise risk management, and regulatory compliance. GRC is a structured method for integrating IT (people and operations) with business objectives while effectively managing risks and meeting regulatory requirements.

Businesses must adhere to this environment's best practices and procedures to meet their goals and maximize their profits. GRC exists to reduce threats to productivity and enterprise value by developing standards, regulations, and policies. Even more importantly, GRC helps to build trust in the organization. This confidence results from increased efficiency, improved communication, employee trust in information sharing, and commercial performance.

GRC assists businesses in developing a value culture by educating all members of the organization and education on how to protect the company's value, reputation, and decision-making process.

THE CRUCIAL ROLE OF GRC IN CYBER SECURITY

Organizations must align people, systems, and technologies with business objectives to establish solid and successful cyber security. Everyone must be alert and take appropriate precautions when carrying out their responsibilities; it is all about awareness and knowledge.

Governance, Risk, and Compliance is the finest tool for developing an integrated system that focuses on achieving goals while addressing risks and operating with integrity. GRC is important because:

- It supports vital cyber security activities, such as standardizing best practices to ensure everyone acts with integrity and security.

- It improves communication by delegating roles and responsibilities to businesses and users.

- It assists in the execution of data processing procedures.

- It gathers the vocabulary of the divisions and teams.

- It encourages ongoing control monitoring and supports internal audits.

- It assists in reducing risks both inside and outside.

- It encourages meeting industry and government regulations.

Furthermore, GRC provides a framework that integrates security and privacy with the organization's overall goals. It enables businesses to make informed decisions about the risks associated with data security while lowering the risk of compromise.

THE TECHNICAL ROLE OF GRC IN CYBERSECURITY

1. **THIRD-PARTY SUPPLIER SELECTION:**

Many organizations use a third-party scorecard to get basic information about potential vendors. This information includes the company's reputation, financial data, network security, cyberattack history, and geographical location. A solid GRC model would assist IT and security teams in selecting and verifying potential third-party suppliers. More importantly, GRC can support the development of preventative measures and supplier evaluation.

2. **RISK MITIGATION:**

IT can utilize GRC to determine the scope of cybersecurity and document the present security program's strengths and flaws. The GRC enables organizations to describe and act on various sorts of data.

3. **REGULATION COMPLIANCE:**

GRC is critical for maintaining compliance when new regulations emerge worldwide. Furthermore, it quickly brings these altering changes to the security team's attention, allowing them time to plan and respond. Finally, GRC will assist in developing and overseeing policies, regulations, and standards to respond to regularly changing commercial and industrial laws.

4. **AUDIT SUPPORT:**

Companies today have expanded their procedures and protocols to provide evidence and audit papers to their auditors. It will be evident that the house is organized if the policies and best practices are well documented. Critical audit material may include responses to events, cybersecurity training, internal control test results, cybersecurity compliance reviews, and other initiatives.

GRC assists in creating and maintaining a single source of truth for compliance, allowing everyone to be on the same page. GRC assists firms in staying on top of the ever-changing world of privacy requirements by allowing the IT staff to guarantee that the necessary safeguards, logging, geographic storage, and so on are in place to protect consumers' and employees' data.

5. VISIBILITY:

The comprehensive approach of GRC helps businesses to have visibility into all aspects of their security compliance procedures. This is critical because it allows various units, managers, and staff to view the overall picture and make data-driven and educated decisions.

In summary;

- A well-planned GRC program enables firms to gather and keep high-quality information and improve decision-making.

- Encourage teamwork and accountability

- Create a strong culture

- Improve your efficiency and agility.

- Promotes visibility

- Reduces costs by promoting appropriate investments

- Boost integration

- Keep the company's assets and reputation safe.

GRC AND CYBERSECURITY:

Why do companies need an integrated approach?

Integrating GRC and cybersecurity is critical for firms seeking a long-term, sustainable security strategy. Aside from improved communication, consistent metrics, collaboration, and decision-making, combining GRC with cybersecurity has several other advantages.

An integrated strategy reduces manual input and the possibility of human mistakes, lowering expenses and providing businesses more time to add value to the company.

More importantly, a good integration allows the board to see the organization's security posture clearly and thoroughly. Business leaders can deliver better security stories to consumers and empower workers by knowing the cross-functional stance.

To summarize, GRC and cybersecurity work in tandem toward a lower-risk future and value generation — they cannot exist apart. While cybersecurity (from a technical standpoint) attempts to secure systems, networks, and data, GRC conveys the best methods and practices.

Organizations that use an integrated approach will:

- Improve efficiency
- Improve your security posture

- Increase leadership support by increasing overall visibility
- Avoid fines for noncompliance or regulatory violations
- The IT and security teams set the tone for the entire organization

GRC METHODOLOGY FOR EMPOWERING CYBERSECURITY

The OCEG created this Capability Model (Red Book) as an open-source methodology that combines the sub-disciplines of Governance, risk, audit, compliance, ethics/culture, and IT into a single approach.

Organizations can adapt this standard to accommodate specific conditions ranging from small projects to large-scale rollouts.

Here are several examples:

- Anti-corruption initiatives
- Continuity of operations
- Third-party administration

The model is critical for structuring discussions on GRC capabilities with the board of directors, senior executives, and managers. Organizations may also utilize this GRC Capability Model with other functional frameworks, such as ISO, SOC2, HIPPA, CMMC, NIST, and others.

The GRC Capability Model encourages businesses to document best practices to:

- Unify terminology across fields
- Define common elements and components.
- Define everyday information needs.
- Standardize policies and training processes,

The Capability Model is divided into four sections:

1. Learn

The fundamental aim here is to identify the organization's business culture, stakeholders, and business practices to steer their goals, strategy, and objectives properly.

As a procedure, it would be as follows:

- Learning about business plans and objectives
- Understanding strategic goals

- Being aware of existing and upcoming compliance initiatives

- Making contact with crucial stakeholders

2. Align

This level is concerned with connecting strategy to objectives and actions to plans. The goal is to create an integrated approach involving senior leadership and supporting the decision-making process.

Simply put, this procedure requires:

- Align corporate goals with strategy.

- Align CEOs' expectations with those of stakeholders.

- Align planning for resource allocation with objectives.

3. Perform

It is now time to put your business goals and objectives into action. This step entails setting suitable controls and regulations, preventing and mitigating undesirable risks, and monitoring to spot problems immediately.

4. Review

As a final phase, assessing the present strategy and activities' design and operational performance is critical. More importantly, this step encourages firms to examine goals to improve integrated GRC efforts continuously.

This approach aims to create a continuous and integrated improvement process to achieve optimal performance and create value for the firm.

BENEFITS OF A GOVERNANCE, RISK AND COMPLIANCE STRATEGY

When used correctly, Governance, risk, and compliance can lead to an organization's success. This technique promotes educated decision-making, aiding in risk mitigation and preventing reputational and financial losses.

It can also protect against compliance violations, data breaches, and other consequences of poor decision-making. GRC also encourages ongoing collaboration and improves a company's ability to respond to threats strategically. GRC is also helpful in driving business success for many firms.

Here are some other advantages of GRC services:

1. TRANSPARENCY IN THE BUSINESS WORLD

Governance, risk, and compliance can assist firms in creating a more productive and efficient environment in which all components contribute to a single purpose. GRC can also aid in the detection and avoidance of common risks.

When GRC information is correctly integrated, management can make more informed decisions quickly. Improved decision-making can help firms develop with fewer disruptions and lower the frequency of errors.

GRC also aids in aligning their aims with the organization's mission, vision, and values, resulting in increased business confidence and superior decision-making abilities.

2. PROCESS IMPROVEMENT

Governance, risk, and compliance are crucial for identifying and prioritizing resources on key business process elements. Businesses can learn how to minimize non-value-added processes from their routine operations while streamlining value-added activities through GRC.

This can help organizations save time and money while avoiding undesired deviations. Manual preventative controls, for example, are replaced with automated detective controls to improve traceability and overall efficiency. Over time, GRC can also help to improve business performance while lowering audit costs.

It only takes one error for a company's reputation to deteriorate quickly. Governance, risk, and compliance can assist firms in more successfully managing risks and protecting their brand. Governance, risk, and compliance services can help save a company's reputation and brand in various ways.

GRC data can also manage crises professionally and effectively while defending the firm, its board members, and executives.

3. REDUCED COSTS

Cost reduction is one of the numerous advantages of Governance, risk, and compliance. GRC assists in the elimination of duplicate and divergent processes, resources, and tools that waste money and time.

GRC can assist firms in better defining their business rules, reviewing controls, and visualizing future growth, resulting in cost savings. Governance, risk, and compliance can help firms address cybersecurity concerns more effectively.

Cybersecurity is a growing problem in practically every industry; strategizing how to control digital dangers and reduce financial losses is critical. Businesses must always have a plan to cope with cyber-attacks and safeguard necessary data. Companies can save money by being proactive about cyber security and data privacy.

EVOLUTION OF GRC

Manual processes were standard in the past, with wire and fax being the most commonly utilized modes of communication. As a result, risk management was also focused on business management strategies. With the introduction of the internet and online business, transactions began to be conducted online and consistently. Administration training has also evolved, with a greater emphasis on internet-related risk. Experts learned new cyber skills and abilities to maintain stability during the wave.

The emergence of data-related innovations is an issue that experts in data security risk constantly address. Because organizations must manage the daunting obstacle of collecting their royal gems while adhering to legal and administrative regulations, more effort is needed to raise employee knowledge. On the other hand, staff members must be more vigilant than ever before.

Another essential concept that deserves further thinking is significant consistency. Consistency may be viewed as little more than a plan to follow, yet this viewpoint undermines the ultimate aim of consistency. The emphasis should be on balancing administrative processes with consistency needs, focusing on ongoing improvement. Because risk specialists are generally viewed as counsels by the board, they are frequently under pressure to be educated about innovative trends in the corporate working environment.

While risk specialists are not expected to be experts in innovation or business, they must comprehend the business cycle and the hidden gamble. Risk specialists should enlist the help of appropriate, competent authorities to map out the world of gambling. According to the experts, the GRC calling has a long way to go and is centered on growth, with innovation as the primary agent for company empowerment. It forecasts that emerging technologies focusing on information security and protection will continue to pose challenges for risk professionals.

FATHER OF GRC

We must remember the GRC's inventor whenever we debate it. This GRC is the brainchild of Michael Rasmussen, a pioneer in education, research, analysis, and consulting services. He monitors challenges and trends influencing corporate Governance, enterprise risk management, and workplace compliance duties (GRC).

Michael is known as the "Father of Governance, Risk, and Compliance" since he was the first to discover and model the GRC market at Forrester in February 2002. His goal was to create a GRC process for the organization that was clear, efficient, consistent, and long-term.

HISTORY OF GRC TECHNOLOGY

Pundit Michael Rasmussen coined the term; "Governance, risk, and compliance" about 20 years ago. GRC has since expanded to include various issues, such as risks, controls, and other areas of an organization's operations
.

GRC 1.0 was primarily concerned with Sarbanes Oxley (SOX), which enhances the quality and reliability of business disclosures required by securities regulations, among other things. As technology advanced, more firms transitioned from GRC 1.0 to GRC 4.0.

- GRC technological stages are as follows: GRC 1.0 - SOX Captivity (2002 to 2007):

When it was first described and modeled, GRC technology at Forrester in February 2002 characterized it as a comprehensive and integrated perspective of objectives and the risks, controls, and policies related to those objectives. Unfortunately, Sarbanes Oxley was implemented in 2002, and the first focus of GRC was SOX compliance and internal controls over financial reporting. It propelled and enhanced market solutions but hindered them from becoming the more extensive GRC solution that was envisioned.

- Enterprise/Integrated GRC 2.0 (2007-2012):

After corporations resolved SOX, it was time for GRC technology to return to its original purpose: an enterprise perspective of corporate objectives and the risks, controls, policies, and issues associated with those objectives. The notion of the Enterprise Integrated GRC platform gained traction, implying that many departments may manage risks, control, policies, compliance, audits, assessments, and incidents using a shared information and technology architecture.

However, solutions had strengths and weaknesses, and no person could handle everything. The final Forrester Wave before departing Forrester at the end of 2007 contained four separate Wave images to demonstrate the merits and flaws of a solution from various perspectives of risk, compliance, audit, and overall.

- GRC Architecture (2012-2017):

As the organization's usage of GRC technology grew, it became clear that only some platforms could solve all of the GRC concerns. It required integration as enterprises sought to employ best-of-breed risk, compliance, and control solutions when appropriate while also integrating with an overall risk aggregation, normalization, and reporting platform. There was frequently still a single hub for GRC management, but it no longer tried to do everything and interaction with other business systems and highly focused GRC solutions were required.

- Agile GRC 4.0 (2017-2021):

This is the current GRC technology stage. There is a requirement for highly adaptable technology that engages the entire organization in GRC from front to back office. Citizen development is agile technology that is modifiable without advanced credentials and experience (however, this can get out of hand and cause issues if not monitored and regulated), where things did not fail upon upgrades due to highly tailored coding.

The production of very intuitive and engaging GRC interfaces that were contextually relevant and easy to use for the job that was using them. Interfaces with a solid visual and interactive component. Many older GRC solutions attempt to adapt to Agile by repainting the user interface, while the underlying data and application architecture are still 15 to 20 years old. There is a new generation of Agile software for GRC that elevates the technology's value to the enterprise.

- GRC 5.0 - Cognitive GRC (2021 and beyond):

The influence and impact of cognitive/artificial intelligence technology on GRC may be seen now. Machine learning, natural language processing, and predictive analytics are beginning to take root and propel Agile GRC systems forward. While these capabilities are progressing with particular early adopters, it will be about 2021 before cognitive GRC technologies establish a more robust market foothold and prove themselves with the early adopters.

CHALLENGES OF IMPLEMENTING GRC

Problems with GRC Governance, risk management, and compliance (GRC) implementation can be difficult for multinational corporations. Thorough planning and implementation are essential to ensure that the GRC framework achieves its intended goals.

The challenges of implementing GRC include developing an acceptable plan, ensuring adequate resources are available to support it, managing stakeholder expectations, fostering a culture of accountability throughout the firm, and integrating current systems with new technologies.

The formulation of an appropriate plan is required for the successful deployment of GRC. An effective strategy necessitates articulating clear goals and explaining where and how change is required, as well as how these changes will be realized. This includes determining which processes require monitoring or improvement, as well as which tools or approaches will be used to accomplish this. Furthermore, businesses must examine their current capabilities while designing a strategy to determine what changes may be required to attain their desired goals.

Allocating sufficient resources to GRC implementation is also critical to success. Businesses must allocate enough workers to this effort who understand the need to implement strong controls from both an operational and strategic standpoint. They should also have access to training programs that teach best practices for managing risks associated with various operations tasks, such as financial reporting and data security projects. Furthermore, enterprises should allocate adequate cash for technical expenditures such as automated monitoring solutions that provide real-time visibility into any potential dangers that may arise during operations, allowing them to take rapid corrective action when necessary.

Handling stakeholder expectations is another critical issue associated with the appropriate deployment of GRC frameworks. Shareholders, customers, vendors, and other stakeholders expect firms with whom they do business to adhere to corporate responsibility standards. As part of this expectation, stakeholders usually analyze whether corporations have established comprehensive internal control systems to manage any potential risks linked with activities made by company workers or contractors. Businesses must ensure that they express their commitment to meeting these standards to their stakeholders and that they offer regular updates on their progress in reaching those commitments through various channels, such as public reports and press releases.

Establishing an organizational-wide accountability culture is critical for effective GRC deployments. To build a sense of ownership in employees about risk management policies and practices, leadership teams must promote the principles of integrity, openness, and collaboration while encouraging positive attitudes and rewarding performance. Employees at all organizational levels should take proactive steps to reduce errors or omissions that could lead to noncompliance issues due to poor oversight or other factors.

Such cultures also demand chances for team members to learn and grow in order to achieve higher productivity and efficiency over time, making them more resilient in the face of future uncertainty caused by external forces outside their control.

Decision-makers are challenged to choose the best answer given their position and the context of available resources. To build a powerful, integrated solution that provides maximum value while causing the least amount of disruption to regular course activities, it is vital to develop efficient, trustworthy, and secure connections between various components. Scalability, flexibility, dependability, cost-effectiveness, functionality availability, and the degree of customization required to meet corporate objectives and financial restrictions should all be considered while choosing a platform. Furthermore, it must be capable of interacting with external sources in order for information to flow into data analytics engines and back-end storage systems, which can be a difficult operation.

To summarize, implementing a Governance, Risk Management, and Compliance framework involves careful consideration of several factors in order to overcome the multiple barriers presented at each step. However, successfully implementing it allows enterprises to reap the benefits of having a solid foundation to secure their assets while maintaining high ethical standards and legal requirements to remain competitive in the market.

GRC implementation is a hard task that demands thorough preparation and analysis. We will now examine the possible outcomes of this assessment.

BEST PRACTICES FOR GRC IMPLEMENTATION

Integrating a CRM strategy necessitates careful preparation, devoted resources, and ongoing commitment. The following are some best practices for successful governance, risk management, and compliance:

1. Establishment of a GRC framework adapted to the organization's needs:

Every organization is distinct, with its own set of goals, hazards, and regulatory needs. As a result, implementing a GRC strategy necessitates the creation of a framework based on the organization's specific needs, an understanding of the organization's strategic objectives, and the assessment of potential risks and compliance requirements.

2. Engage stakeholders and foster an accountability and compliance culture:

Governance, risk, and compliance are the responsibilities of everyone in the organization, not just management or a specialized GRC team. As a result, the involvement of all stakeholders in the development process is critical. It is all about conveying the significance of GRC, providing adequate training, and fostering a culture of accountability and compliance.

3. Ensuring that GRC processes are constantly monitored, evaluated, and improved:

The GRC is a continuous process that involves ongoing monitoring, review, and improvement. Organizations should assess their governance, risk, and compliance procedures on a regular basis to ensure that they remain effective and in line with their objectives, risks, and compliance needs. These include monitoring the implementation of governance structures and processes, evaluating risk management measures, and ensuring regulatory and policy compliance.

Adopting GRC in a complex business context is about more than risk management or compliance assurance. It is about getting the organization on the right track. As a result, every firm wishing to flourish in today's dynamic business world and reach new heights of operational excellence should prioritize governance, risk, and compliance.

CHAPTER TWO

UNDERSTANDING GOVERNANCE

GOVERNANCE

Governance in the GRC has no political overtones. Instead, it is concerned with guiding an organization's ship, that is, what its business model should be, how to make critical choices, how departments should communicate, and the company's ultimate aim. It all comes down to building the framework for operations.

Governance is the set of rules, regulations, and processes put in place to provide a standard for corporate or organizational behavior. It is the system through which a corporation runs when taken as a whole.

Good governance is an essential component of any business or institution, regardless of size or industry. It is the process by which decisions are made and implemented. Good governance is critical to maintaining ethical behaviors, accountability, transparency, and strategic decision-making in the context of GRC (Governance, Risk Management, and Compliance). Organizations that lack adequate governance risk financial losses, reputational damage, and noncompliance. This chapter explains the function of good governance and its significance in the context of the GRC.

The governance framework specifies who is authorized to make what decisions and how accountability for outcomes is established. Oversight is provided by governance processes to ensure that risks are effectively addressed. The governance program focuses on establishing and maintaining a framework to provide assurance that information security strategies are aligned with and support business objectives, are in compliance with applicable laws and regulations through adherence to policies and internal controls, and provide accountability, all in order to manage risk.

Understanding the value of effective governance is critical to your organization's long-term performance, whether you are an executive, a board member, or a risk management or compliance specialist. Good governance is essential to the health and long-term viability of any company. This is why:

1. Ethical Practices:

Good governance lays the groundwork for ethical behavior within a company. It provides a code of conduct, encourages honesty, and guarantees that choices are made with all stakeholders in mind.

2. Accountability:

There is a clear accountability structure and a system for holding individuals accountable for their actions and decisions in ineffective governance. This fosters a culture of accountability and helps to connect activities with the organization's goals.

3. Transparency:

Transparent governance procedures encourage openness and honesty in decision-making processes. It gives stakeholders access to information and guarantees that decisions are based on accurate and unbiased facts.

4. Strategic decision-making:

Effective decision-making is facilitated by good governance, which provides a framework for analyzing options, assessing risks, and aligning decisions with strategic objectives. It guarantees that decisions are well-informed, balanced, and in the organization's best interests.

Good governance is especially important in the context of the GRC because it leads to external regulatory compliance, effective risk management, and the attainment of corporate goals. Organizations that lack effective governance may experience legal issues, financial insecurity, and reputational harm. As a result, managers and those responsible for risk management and compliance should prioritize understanding and promoting strong governance processes.

THE RELATIONSHIP BETWEEN EFFECTIVE GOVERNANCE AND CORPORATE SUCCESS

In terms of organizational success, the importance of excellent governance cannot be overstated. A well-managed firm is more likely to achieve its objectives, maintain financial stability, and establish a favorable reputation.

Here are some examples of how excellent governance contributes to corporate success:

1. Effective decision-making:

Good governance includes a structured decision-making process that ensures all options are thoroughly reviewed, and risks are considered. This allows firms to make informed and timely decisions, both of which are critical for success in today's fast-paced business climate.

2. Risk management:

Good governance promotes effective risk management by creating procedures for identifying, evaluating, and reducing risks. Organizations can avoid possible pitfalls and capture opportunities by managing risks proactively, resulting in long-term success and sustainability.

3. Compliance with regulations:

As the number of regulations grows, firms must comply to avoid legal and financial consequences. Good governance assists firms in navigating the complicated environment of compliance regulations, ensuring that all required duties are met.

4. Recruiting and maintaining talent:

Effective governance practices foster a healthy company culture that attracts and keeps top talent. Employees are more likely to be inspired and engaged when they feel their firm works with honesty and transparency, which contributes to higher levels of productivity and success.

In summary, strong governance is required for an organization's success. It establishes the groundwork for ethical behavior, accountability, accounting, and strategic decision-making. Good governance is particularly important in the context of the GRC because it helps firms comply with external requirements, manage risks, and achieve their goals. Organizations can position themselves for long-term success in today's complicated and competitive business market by prioritizing strong governance.

EFFECTIVE COMMUNICATION AND COLLABORATION IN GOVERNANCE

Within the scope of the GRC, effective communication and collaboration are critical foundations of good governance. Organizations must maintain clear and transparent communication with all stakeholders, including employees, management, board members, and external partners, in order to operate effectively and efficiently.

Open and honest communication builds trust and understanding, allowing for improved decision-making and problem-solving. Individuals are better equipped to make educated decisions and take actions that are consistent with the organization's aims and values when information flows freely inside the organization.

Collaboration, on the other hand, fosters a culture of cooperation and shared accountability. Organizations can harness a varied range of perspectives and experiences to handle challenges and grab opportunities by integrating stakeholders from all sectors and organizational levels. Individuals feel invested in the outcomes of their joint efforts, which encourages ownership and responsibility.

Effective communication and teamwork are critical in the context of GRC for compliance and risk management. Organizations can keep employees informed about regulatory changes, rules, and processes, as well as reply to any queries or issues they may have through frequent communication channels. Individuals can comprehend their duties and make appropriate judgments in compliance with legal and ethical norms because of this transparency.

Collaboration also aids in the identification and mitigation of dangers. Organizations can assess risks from diverse perspectives and establish complete risk mitigation strategies by involving stakeholders from several departments. This proactive risk management technique ensures that prospective problems are discovered before they worsen and affect the firm.

Organizations can utilize a range of tools and technology to support effective communication and collaboration. Intranet systems, instant messaging programs, project management software, and video conferencing tools are examples of these. These technologies enable safe and efficient real-time communication, distant collaboration, and the sharing of information and documents.

Finally, effective communication and collaboration are critical components of good governance within the context of the GRC. Organizations may increase transparency, accountability, and risk management by encouraging open and honest communication and collaboration at all levels.

TYPES OF GOVERNANCE IN GRC

1. **Corporate Governance:**

This is the primary sort of governance on which we will concentrate. It is the set of rules, regulations, and procedures that govern how a corporation, organization, or enterprise functions. It covers everything from corporate strategy to compensation, ethics, and management structure, among other things. It essentially describes how an organization operates and gives a road map for assuring the company's success.

2. **Public Governance:**

This is the public counterpart to private corporate governance. It refers to the manner in which governmental entities in the public sector adopt rules and regulations that regulate the populations under their jurisdiction.

Public governance differs significantly from corporate governance in that it dictates how a governing body provides public services, implements public policy, aims for economic progress, and so on. In most cases, there is no profit motivation involved in this style of governance. In a democratic system, it usually incorporates some type of public engagement, such as voting.

3. **Nonprofit Governance:**

This is only a set of standards, policies, and processes for how a non-profit organization operates. The Board of Directors normally confirms management in this arena.

PRINCIPLES OF GOVERNANCE

Organizations, even ones in the same industry and on a comparable scale, can operate in very diverse ways. There is no universally accepted definition of "good" governance. When an organization functions like a well-oiled machine, it's easy to spot, just as weak governance is obvious when a company is struggling.

What works for one company may not work for another. As a result, it is difficult to agree on a precise framework for effective governance. Identifying common ideas that indicate a well-governed organization makes it easier to reach an agreement.

1. **Accountability:**

Once regulations are established, they must be followed. This is dependent on a good organizational structure that defines positions and reporting lines so that expectations may be satisfied. Individual accountability for performance is established by structuring around lines of business.

Personal accountability, like ethics, can be fostered through culture. The culture of a company can define the behaviors of empowerment that manage people by results rather than telling them what to do.

2. Transparency:

Communicating a company's corporate governance is an important aspect of community and investor relations. Board members should establish transparent sets of rules and procedures that harmonize shareholder, director, and officer incentives.

This can go beyond monetary achievement. Good governance also requires ethical business practices and corporate citizenship and ensures that these actions are visible to both the organization and the general public.

3. Consensus-driven:

When it comes to decision-making, those who construct organizational governance must be on the same page. Governance should include a diverse range of opinions in order to achieve a solution that is, at the very least, acceptable to all stakeholders.

Approaching governance in this manner also allows businesses to examine all of a company's stakeholders' requirements and viewpoints, as well as the current and future implications of these decisions.

4. Agility:

In a corporate setting, things can change quickly. Systems and processes must be in place to respond to critical events and convey that response to shareholders.

What is the organization's reaction plan in the event of a crisis, such as an environmental disaster that disrupts operations, and when does public communication begin? How will it be handled if it becomes embroiled in a controversy?

Organizations that are prepared and responsive perform better in these instances because they have thought through the next steps and have the agility to react swiftly.

5. Inclusion, Diversity, and Equity:

Diversity is not just something that every firm should try to enhance in an increasingly complex global economic scene; it can also become a competitive advantage. According to one recent study, organizations with a diverse workforce generate up to 2.5 times more cash flow per employee, and inclusive teams can boost productivity by more than 35%.

Aside from the numbers, there are numerous intangible benefits to attracting and retaining diverse employees, including improved morale, motivation through career advancement, and a more nuanced understanding of multicultural markets.

In terms of governance, inclusion harkens back to consensus-driven decision-making. Employees may feel more dedicated and invested in an organization's mission when their views are heard and their perspectives and unique experiences are taken into account in business policy.

6. Effectiveness and efficiency:

These principles are what create successful company outcomes. When a business develops efficient processes for achieving strategic goals, governance becomes much easier. When called upon, corporate leaders can clearly explain what is happening, when it is happening, and why to the board or shareholders.

The efficient execution of strategic initiatives is the foundation of any successful business. It enables firms to do more with less and removes the uncertainty about what people should be working on. Removing the friction of decision fatigue and cumbersome processes increases focus and frees organizations to accomplish their best work.

ROLE OF GOVERNANCE IN AN ORGANIZATION

Governance is critical to an organization's effective cybersecurity risk management. Governance, when combined with cybersecurity risk management, creates a framework for making informed decisions, allocating resources, and ensuring that cybersecurity measures are well-defined and consistently enforced. Here is how governance helps with cyber security risk management:

1. Alignment with Business Goals:

Effective governance ensures that cybersecurity plans are well connected with the organization's overall business objectives and risk appetite. This alignment guarantees that cybersecurity measures are not only technically effective but also help to achieve business objectives.

2. Risk Assessment and Management:

Risk assessment and management techniques are frequently included in governance frameworks. These procedures aid in the identification, assessment, and prioritization of cybersecurity risks. Organizations may make educated decisions about resource allocation and risk management strategies by incorporating cybersecurity risk assessments into governance policies.

3. Defined Roles and Responsibilities:

Governance establishes IT and cybersecurity roles and responsibilities. This clarity contributes to ensuring that cybersecurity duties are effectively assigned, understood, and followed throughout the business. It reduces the possibility of security coverage gaps.

4. Rules and Procedures:

Governance frameworks define IT and cybersecurity rules and procedures. These rules outline security controls, data protection, access management, incident response, and other topics. They contribute to a consistent and well-defined strategy for cybersecurity risk management.

5. Decision-Making procedures:

Decision-making procedures, such as change management and project approval processes, are defined by governance. These methods, when combined with cybersecurity, ensure that security aspects are taken into account before adopting new technologies or making changes to current systems.

6. Allocation of Resources:

Cybersecurity necessitates the allocation of resources, including financial, human, and technological resources. Governance aids in the appropriate allocation of these resources, ensuring that cybersecurity efforts receive the required support for implementation and continuing monitoring.

7. Measurement and Reporting of IT Performance:

Governance includes procedures for monitoring and reporting IT performance. Organizations can track the performance of their security measures, identify areas for improvement, and report to stakeholders by adding cybersecurity metrics into these methods.

8. Compliance and rules:

Governance frameworks frequently contain compliance controls to ensure conformity with rules and industry standards. Integrating cybersecurity requirements into these controls aids in ensuring that the firm remains in compliance with applicable cybersecurity rules.

9. Continual Improvement:

Governance places a premium on continual improvement. As threats and technologies advance at a rapid pace, this strategy is critical for cybersecurity risk management. Reviewing and updating cybersecurity measures within the governance framework on a regular basis ensures that the firm is resilient to evolving dangers.

10. Board Oversight and Accountability:

Reporting to the board of directors or senior management is a common part of IT governance. Organizations guarantee that cybersecurity risks and strategies receive the appropriate attention at the highest level of the organization by including cybersecurity in these reports.

In essence, governance offers the structure, policies, and oversight required to handle cybersecurity threats successfully. It guarantees that cybersecurity is regarded as an inherent component of the organization's broader risk management strategy rather than as a separate technological issue. Integrating cybersecurity considerations into governance standards results in a comprehensive approach that supports business goals while protecting key assets and information.

ADVANTAGES OF A STRONG GOVERNANCE STRUCTURE

The establishment of a strong governance structure is the foundation of the GRC's effective procedures. A solid governance structure not only outlines the many stakeholders' roles and obligations but also establishes clear lines of authority and responsibility. In this section, we will look at the advantages that businesses can gain from putting in place a solid governance framework.

Improved decision-making is one of the primary benefits of a good governance framework. It is easier to expedite decision-making processes and guarantee that decisions are made by the correct individuals with the necessary information and skills when roles and responsibilities are clearly defined. This reduces the possibility of miscommunication, delays, or competing conclusions.

A well-defined governing system also encourages transparency and accountability. Organizations may hold individuals accountable for their actions and ensure that choices are made in the best interests of the organization by clearly outlining reporting lines and decision-making processes. This level of transparency also contributes to increased trust among internal and external stakeholders.

Another significant benefit of a robust governance system is the capacity to handle risks effectively. Organizations can identify, evaluate, and reduce risks systematically and proactively by using effective risk management frameworks and sharing responsibility. This enables organizations to anticipate future risks and reduce their influence on the organization's goals.

A solid governance system also encourages adherence to regulatory regulations and ethical norms. Organizations may ensure compliance is integrated into all elements of their operations by clearly outlining roles and responsibilities. This reduces legal and reputational concerns while also enhancing the organization's reputation as a responsible and trustworthy institution.

Finally, a robust governance framework allows firms to successfully adapt to and respond to changes in the business environment. Organizations can quickly address growing difficulties and exploit new opportunities by having clear decision-making processes and communication channels. This adaptability is critical in today's dynamic and complex corporate environment.

Finally, for firms to prosper within the GRC, a solid governance framework is required. It enhances decision-making, fosters transparency and accountability, enables effective risk management, assures compliance, and fosters adaptation. We will cover methods that businesses can take to develop a strong governance framework in the following portion of the blog. Stay tuned for practical guidance and ideas for putting in place good governance procedures.

CASE STUDIES THAT DEMONSTRATE THE IMPACT OF GOOD GOVERNANCE

In this section, we'll look at real-world case studies that show how good governance can alter organizations. We may acquire a better grasp of how a robust governance structure might lead to success in the context of GRC by looking at these examples.

Case Study 1: Company X

Global Company X has battled with inefficiencies, communication gaps, and a lack of responsibility due to a weak governance structure. They have, however, built a comprehensive governance structure, recognizing the need for good governance. This has enhanced decision-making processes, reduced duplication, and boosted organizational accountability. As a result, Company X has achieved higher productivity and profitability, as well as improved regulatory compliance.

Case Study 2: Nonprofit Organization Y

The Non-Profit Corporation needed a defined governance structure, which resulted in a lack of transparency and ineffective risk management. They were able to establish clear lines of power and responsibility by developing a strong governance framework, ensuring that choices are made in an ethical and regulatory manner. This not only bolstered their reputation as a responsible organization but also drew in additional donations and supporters, allowing them to have a greater influence on their purpose.

These case studies demonstrate that effective governance only applies to one type of business or industry. Rather, it is a universal principle that, independent of the organizational setting, can produce positive results. Organizations can acquire significant ideas and inspiration for implementing their own governance system by analyzing these examples.

GOVERNANCE'S FUTURE: EMERGING TRENDS AND CHALLENGES

As the corporate landscape evolves, so does the concept of good governance. Let's look at developing trends and problems that businesses must consider in order to stay on top of governance, risk management, and compliance (GRC).

1. Technology-based governance:

As businesses become more reliant on technology, their governance methods must evolve to properly manage digital risks. The rise of artificial intelligence, blockchain, and data analytics necessitates the development of effective safeguards to safeguard sensitive information and assure the ethical use of technology.

2. Cybersecurity and data confidentiality:

To combat the growing threat of cyberattacks and data breaches, a strong governance system centered on cybersecurity and data privacy protection is required. Organizations must prioritize customer data protection, adopt stringent security measures, and adhere to changing data protection rules.

3. Stakeholder involvement:

Modern governance necessitates active engagement with stakeholders, including employees, consumers, investors, and regulators. Transparent and inclusive government fosters trust, accountability, and long-term sustainability.

4. ESG Considerations:

As investors and customers expect greater corporate responsibility, environmental, social, and governance (ESG) factors are becoming increasingly essential. Organizations must incorporate ESG considerations into their governance practices in order to effectively manage environmental and social risks and align with emerging threats.

5. Regulatory complexity:

Firms face compliance issues because the regulatory landscape is always evolving; a proactive and adaptable governance plan is required to keep up with regulatory developments and stay ahead of compliance needs.

Organizations may guarantee that their governance systems remain robust and successful by taking these new trends into account and actively tackling the accompanying difficulties.

CONCLUSION: THE ONGOING SIGNIFICANCE OF GOOD GOVERNANCE IN GRC

Finally, the rising trends and challenges that organizations encounter affect the future of governance. Organizations must adjust their governance processes to successfully manage digital risks as their reliance on technology grows.

In order to preserve sensitive information and comply with data protection rules, cybersecurity and data confidentiality must be essential priorities. The involvement of stakeholders is critical for fostering trust and accountability. The integration of environmental, social, and governance (ESG) factors into governance processes demonstrates corporate responsibility. Furthermore, in order to ensure compliance, firms must continually monitor changes in the regulatory landscape.

Overall, strong governance remains critical in the field of GRC. Organizations may strengthen their governance frameworks and traverse the complex world of GRCs by implementing realistic measures and solutions.

CHAPTER 3
DEMYSTIFYING RISK

Have you ever pondered how firms effectively manage their operations, ensure regulatory compliance, and avoid risks? Let's run it through GRC again: Governance, Risk, and Compliance. This collection of techniques, models, and tools assists firms in navigating the complicated landscapes of governance, risk management, and regulatory compliance.

But why is risk management so important in the context of GRC? Consider a ship navigating through treacherous waters. Without a professional skipper and a vigilant crew recognizing the hazards, disaster would be imminent. Similarly, in the corporate world, risk management functions as a compass and anchor, directing businesses away from potential hazards and ensuring their long-term existence.

In this chapter, we'll look at the importance of risk management in the context of GRC.

RISK MANAGEMENT

Risk is a part of everyday life, and risk in organizations is no different. Almost every facet of business involves risk. Every decision you make is fraught with danger. The key is knowing how to conduct business in a way that protects you and helps you to properly manage business risk.

Any organization's governance and compliance strategy must include risk management. It entails identifying, assessing, and mitigating risks to a company's assets, reputation, operations, financial health, and overall success. Risk management aids businesses in identifying their risk profile, allowing them to make decisions that are in line with their business goals and objectives.

The risk management approach begins with identifying potential risks. This includes reviewing corporate policies as well as industry standards to identify places where compliance or security problems may exist. Organizations must analyze the likelihood of the identified risks occurring and the impact they could have on the organization if they do occur. After examining each identified risk, companies must devise methods to mitigate or lower the likelihood of it occurring in order to defend against potential losses or harm caused by it.

GRC enables firms to remain ahead of the regulatory reporting curve by providing a comprehensive solution for keeping track of regulatory changes and ensuring the timely completion of reports. Software packages also aid in the performance of internal audits that identify flaws in existing controls, allowing firms to make informed decisions when making strategic investments or adopting new technologies/products/services, etc.

Successful risk management necessitates coordination among important stakeholders from various departments within a company. Control frameworks such as a GRC software solution and internal audit processes such as conducting periodic reviews and assessments should be utilized to guarantee that all parties involved have access to the relevant data when making operational activity choices. This also assures compliance with applicable laws and regulations promulgated by regulatory bodies both domestically and globally, allowing firms to thrive even in volatile markets caused by geopolitical events beyond anyone's control.

Risk management is an essential component of any profitable firm, assisting in the assurance that activities are carried out in accordance with standards. Organizations must have effective mechanisms in place to assess their activities for adherence to relevant regulations in order to assure compliance.

You can establish whether your risk management plan is effective in a variety of ways. For example, the consequences of a prospective risk can be weighed against the likelihood that the threat would occur. Another way to accomplish this is to conduct a gap analysis. Your risk management plan may be compared to industry standards to identify any gaps in your system that need to be filled.

COMPONENTS OF RISK MANAGEMENT

Risk management must be methodical, structured, collaborative, and cross-organizational in order to be effective. There are numerous ways to categorize the constituent aspects of an effective risk management process, but at the very least, it should include the risk management components listed below.

1. Identifying Risks:

The process of documenting prospective hazards and then categorizing the actual threats that the firm encounters is known as risk identification. The risk universe is a term that refers to the entirety of possible and existing risks. It is critical to methodically identify all potential risks since it decreases the probability of overlooking potential sources of risk.

When identifying risk, it is critical to consider not just the hazards that the company is currently facing but also those that may emerge in the future. The risk universe changes as technology evolves and firms restructure.

2. Risk Assessment:

After identifying risks, the next stage is to assess their likelihood and potential impact. How vulnerable is the company to a specific risk? What is the possible cost of making a risk a reality? Risks may be classified as "serious, moderate, or minor" or "high, medium, or low" based on their potential for disruption.

The precise technique of categorization is less important than recognizing that some dangers provide a more severe threat than others. Risk analysis assists firms in prioritizing risk mitigation. A danger, for example, may have a potentially serious impact but a very low possibility. When compared to a risk with a high cost and a high probability of occurring, the firm may opt to deprioritize mitigation.

3. Response Strategy:

Response planning provides an answer to the question, "What are we going to do about it?" For example, if you discovered during identification and analysis that the company is vulnerable to phishing assaults because its employees are unaware of email security best practices, your action plan could include security awareness training.

4. Risk Reduction:

Risk mitigation is the execution of your response strategy. It is the action taken by your company and its personnel to reduce exposure. Following on from our previous example, implementation may include security awareness training, the development of onboarding materials to educate staff, and so on. Controls must be designed by the company to limit risk to acceptable levels. These controls must be tested to ensure that they are properly built and function properly.

5. Risk Assessment:

Risks do not remain constant; they evolve throughout time. The potential impact and likelihood of occurrence alter, and what was formerly deemed a minor risk can become a substantial danger to the organization and its revenue. The technique of "keeping an eye" on the situation through regular risk assessments is known as risk monitoring.

It is critical to recognize that risk management is not a one-time event; rather, it is a process that occurs throughout the life of an organization as it attempts to anticipate hazards and deal with them proactively before they have a negative impact.

HOW DOES GRC EVALUATE RISKS?

When developing a GRC risk management plan, a corporation must address several risks, such as data loss, reputational risk, and cyber-attacks. It is critical to understand GRC risk management techniques in order to detect and evaluate these risks.

The following are the three critical stages necessary to develop a good GRC risk assessment framework:

1. Risk evaluation and analysis:

A GRC risk assessment analyzes how vulnerable a firm is to unanticipated risks and cyber threats that could jeopardize its regular business operations, cash, resources, and reputation. It is critical to monitor and evaluate the risk environment on a regular basis in order to detect changes in the organization's attack surface and to keep track of the entire risk management process.

To begin a conventional risk assessment, identify the various information assets that could be impacted by a cyber assault (such as hardware, systems, laptops, customer data, intellectual property, and so on).

2. Risk assessment:

GRC risk evaluation necessitates security specialists reviewing the risk analysis results and comparing them to preset risk criteria in order to find any areas that may require further safeguards and controls.

This can be accomplished by employing a bow-tie methodology. A bow tie is a simple qualitative cause-and-effect diagram that depicts the relationships between the causes and effects of an event or danger. It is concerned with the possibility of an incident, its causes, existing preventative controls, potential mitigating controls, and incident-related effects.

3. Risk reduction:

Risk mitigation is the activity of implementing policies and strategies to mitigate the effects of cyber risk. It includes developing, reviewing, and testing a system recovery plan, automating credential management with a Privileged Access Management (PAM) solution, implementing Event Management (SIEM) solutions, and implementing Endpoint Detection and Response (EDR) solutions.

GRC RISK MANAGEMENT STEPS

GRC risk management strives to improve your risk-based decision-making, detection, continuous risk monitoring, and response capabilities. To accomplish this, you must raise security awareness and implement or change important processes in your organization that affect them.

The following are the steps you must take to develop your GRC risk management policy:

1. Identification and evaluation of risks:

Risk identification and assessment are divided into three key actions. The first phase in the process is to identify the weaknesses in procedures that could be harmful to the organization and its personnel. While identifying risks, it is equally critical to estimate the likelihood of each one occurring and the severity of each one. This might help you prioritize hazards and determine the best line of action to eliminate risk.

2. Establishing roles and responsibilities:

GRC risk management necessitates a methodical approach and accountability at all levels. Every identified risk must be assigned an owner who is responsible for its resolution. A risk management team should include a risk owner who takes action, an analyst who gathers information, and a risk manager who supervises and intervenes when escalations occur.

3. Risk assessment and management:

During risk appraisal, the risk owner and risk manager will rate and prioritize each risk and opportunity based on the likelihood of occurrence and the severity of the impact. This is accomplished through the use of a risk matrix, which details the possibility and impact of various risk kinds, with each block assigned a score.

4. Monitoring of controls:

Control monitoring is the process of determining whether or not controls are in place and whether or not they meet the requirements. This includes implementing methods such as immediate notifications when controls fail, properly routing them to trigger corrective actions, and doing tests to ensure they pass appropriately.

While the purpose of the GRC risk management approach is to reduce the possibility of risks developing (preventive action) and/or the effect of risks through mitigation, it does not guarantee continual compliance. It is critical to check the controls on an ongoing basis for this purpose.

5. Education and awareness:

Employee training ensures that everyone understands their roles and responsibilities in a high-risk workplace. A strong employee is essential for maintaining ethical behavior, minimizing risks, and adhering to regulatory requirements. Training sessions, interactive learning activities, and role-specific training can all be used to deliver GRC risk management training.

ADVANTAGES OF GRC RISK MANAGEMENT

Implementing GRC best practices in your corporate operations can provide numerous benefits. You may efficiently integrate your security posture with various compliance standards and take a practical, organized approach to attain business results by establishing GRC processes.

1. Transparency:

GRC risk management provides firms with a comprehensive perspective of their security posture. It increases openness by giving owners access to and control over how sensitive information is secured. This allows them to better understand the organization's risk profile and run more efficient operations.

2. Cost Savings:

There are numerous financial advantages to incorporating GRC principles into your security operations. GRC assists you in achieving a strong security posture that attracts new clients and promotes consumer trust. It is easier to maintain duplicate controls, tests, problems, solutions, and reporting across several processes with a properly established GRC risk management policy, resulting in cheaper maintenance costs.

Establishing scalability while enabling a flexible and adaptable control mechanism, GRC delivers both short and long-term risk solutions. GRC promotes scalability by efficiently allocating resources, standardizing procedures, integrating data management, and improving organizational communication and collaboration.

3. Optimization:

Non-value-added operations such as duplicate effort, manual tasks, and inconsistent policies are eliminated to save time and minimize unintended consequences. GRC techniques also enable value-added activities such as change management and policy management.

4. Consistency:

In the long run, GRC risk management enhances decision-making and business operations. This is accomplished by aligning risk management objectives with the organization's capabilities to develop data-driven insights and roll out adjustments as needed. As a result, processes are standardized and optimized, resulting in a consistent approach toward a better cybersecurity posture.

TYPES OF RISK MANAGEMENT

If you work in risk management at your company, you will undoubtedly have a great deal of responsibility to guarantee that not just dangers to your company are addressed but that your firm is positioned to fulfill its objectives and make educated decisions. Given the variety of potential hazards that may affect your workplace, we've developed a list of some of the aspects you should consider while developing and implementing your risk management strategy.

1. Health and security concerns:

Risks to general health and security can manifest themselves in a variety of ways, regardless of whether the workplace is an office or a construction site. The key is recognizing the potential dangers, such as physical, ergonomic, chemical, and biological hazards, analyzing the risks, and implementing the necessary control measures to ensure that your staff feels safe and well-cared for, both physically and emotionally. The best workplace health and security standards provide the most protection and dependability.

2. Reputational risk:

All organizations must preserve their reputation with their stakeholders, which include investors, employees, and, of course, customers. Organizational decisions, as well as situations for which they are liable, can generate unfavorable headlines and have a substantial impact on brand perception. Reputational risk has become an even bigger problem for businesses in recent years, thanks in large part to the rise of social media, which allows for practically instant worldwide interactions, making it more difficult for businesses to control how they are regarded. Understanding dangers to your reputation and how to handle them is essential.

3. Operational risk

As day-to-day operations are frequently tried and tested to reduce risks, incidents or unexpected circumstances can still occur, the risk of loss caused by failed internal processes, people, or systems, as well as external events, is referred to as operational risk. Global crises, IT system failure, data breaches, fraud, human loss, and lawsuits are a few examples. Organizations must, therefore, understand the everyday operations, processes, and systems that are vital to the normal operation of their organization and have plans and procedures in place to manage those risks and ensure "business as usual." RiskWare software, for example, can be quite useful in identifying these important functions and enhancing your risk management policies.

4. Strategic risk

While an organization's day-to-day operations are critical, controlling an organization's strategic goals is equally crucial for future success. Strategic risks are external causes or conditions that, if they occur, would be substantial enough to change your company's strategic orientation, affecting its future success or failure. All organizations are vulnerable to strategic opportunities and challenges to differing degrees. Investigating how such changes can affect your organization will aid in mitigating any concerns that may arise.

5. Compliance risk

To ensure ethical corporate activities, government agencies have enacted a slew of industry laws, regulations, policies, and best practices. Noncompliance with these requirements can have serious financial and legal consequences for organizations, putting their goals and operations at risk. However, in today's globalized and fast-paced world, rules and regulations can change quickly, and legal frameworks can be difficult to traverse.

6. Financial risk

The majority of risks have financial effects, such as additional costs or lost revenue. Financial risk, on the other hand, primarily refers to money going in and out of your business and the possibility of unexpected financial loss. If your company extends worldwide, for example, shifting exchange rates constitutes a financial risk that you should consider because they affect the dollar amount your company receives. Finally, no organization's goals can be met without effective financial management, and it is critical to foresee financial risks, assess the implications of those risks, and be prepared to respond to or avert unfavorable events.

PROCESS OF RISK MANAGEMENT

The risk management process serves as a framework for the necessary tasks. Five essential steps are followed to manage risk; these processes are referred to as the risk management process. It starts with identifying hazards, then analyzing them, then prioritizing them, implementing a solution, and finally monitoring them. Each step in a manual system requires extensive documentation and administration.

Here Are the Five Critical Steps in Risk Management:

1. Determine the Risk:

The first stage in risk management is to identify the hazards that the company faces in its operating environment.

There are numerous types of risks:

- Legal dangers
- Environmental dangers
- Market dangers
- Regulatory hazards and so on

It is critical to identify as many risk variables as possible. These risks are manually recorded in a manual environment. If the organization uses a risk management solution, all of this information is directly entered into the system.

The benefit of this strategy is that these risks are now visible to all stakeholders within the company who have access to the system. Instead of being locked away in a report that must be requested via email, anyone interested in seeing which risks have been discovered can view the information in the risk management system.

2. Examine the Risk:

Once a risk has been discovered, it must be investigated. The risk's scope must be determined. It is also critical to comprehend the relationship between the risk and other organizational characteristics. To establish the severity and significance of the risk, consider how many business operations are affected. There are risks that, if realized, can bring the entire firm to a halt, while others will merely cause minor hassles in the analysis.

This analysis must be performed manually in a manual risk management system. One of the most critical basic steps in implementing a risk management solution is mapping risks to various documents, rules, procedures, and business processes. This means that the system will already have a risk management framework in place that will evaluate hazards and inform you of the long-term consequences of each risk.

3. Risk Evaluation or Risk Assessment:

The risks must be ranked and prioritized. Depending on the magnitude of the risk, most risk management solutions categorize risks. Risks that may cause minor discomfort are rated low, whereas risks that may result in catastrophic loss are rated highest. It is critical to rate risks because it allows the organization to acquire a holistic view of the organization's risk exposure. The company may be subject to a number of low-level dangers, but they may not necessitate the intervention of senior management. On the other hand, even one of the highest-rated hazards necessitates rapid action.

Risk assessments are classified into two types: Qualitative risk assessments and Quantitative risk assessments.

- Risk Evaluation in Qualitative Form

Risk assessments are essentially qualitative; while measurements can be derived from hazards, the majority of risks are not measurable. For example, the danger of climate change, which many corporations are now focusing on, cannot be defined in its entirety; only specific components of it can be assessed. There must be a means to conduct qualitative risk assessments while maintaining impartiality and standardization across the company.

- Quantitative Risk Evaluation

Quantitative risk assessments are the best way to estimate financial hazards. Such risk evaluations are so popular in the financial sector because the business largely deals with numbers - whether that number be money, metrics, interest rates, or any other data point that is crucial for financial risk assessments. Quantitative risk evaluations are more objective and easier to automate than qualitative risk assessments.

4. Risk monitoring and evaluation:

Some hazards cannot be eradicated; they are constantly present. Market risks and environmental risks are two types of risks that must be constantly evaluated. Monitoring occurs by dedicated staff in manual processes. These specialists must ensure that all risk factors are closely monitored. The risk management system monitors the organization's whole risk framework in a digital environment. Any change in a factor or risk is immediately obvious to everyone. Computers are also far superior to humans at continuously monitoring dangers. Monitoring hazards also assists your company to maintain continuity.

CHAPTER 4

NAVIGATING COMPLIANCE

Regulatory compliance is critical for organizations across industries in today's business landscape. Adhering to regulatory bodies' laws, regulations, and recommendations is not only a legal duty but also a key strategic concern. It ensures ethical practices, safeguards consumer rights, maintains financial integrity, and promotes environmental sustainability.

Compliance is the act of abiding by laws, rules, and regulations. It pertains to the internal policies of the business as well as the legal and regulatory standards established by trade associations. As part of an organization's overall governance plan, compliance in the context of the GRC refers to the vigilant dedication to abide by regulations, laws, and standards pertinent to a given industry or country, both internal and external.

There are several distinct forms of compliance within the GRC, and each has its own set of guidelines. These might be anything from international standards like ISO 27001 for information security to sector-specific regulations like the Health Insurance Portability and Liability Act (HIPAA) in the healthcare industry or the Sarbanes-Oxley Act (SOX) and Federal Trade Commission (FTC) in the financial industry.

Organizations that establish internal standards and codes of conduct to uphold ethical behavior and protect their values can also be considered compliant; take a financial institution that operates in the US as an example. It must abide by federal financial regulations, including the Dodd-Frank Wall Street Reform and consumer protection laws, in order to remain in compliance with the GRC. In keeping with its goals and principles, the institution could also create internal policies of its own to guarantee responsible lending practices. In this instance, compliance not only shields the company from legal repercussions but also builds stakeholder trust and the organization's reputation.

Compliance protects the integrity of the business by making sure that risk management plans work and that the governance structure is strong. An organization may find itself in a bind if compliance is lacking, leaving it vulnerable to legal action, financial losses, and harm to its brand.

In the corporate world, compliance has two distinct meanings. The Compliance function inside an organization — often denoted by a capital 'C' — oversees all of the actions and processes that keep a company in compliance with numerous laws and regulations. There's also the concept of conformity, which is the ultimate purpose of such actions and processes. A corporation is said to be in compliance with a regulation when it has met all (or almost all) of its set standards and has gotten permission from the governing body that drafted it.

Compliance, however, does not simply refer to external requirements; it also refers to the internal control mechanisms that a corporation imposes on itself. These can include the various business procedures that a company employs to assist it in achieving its goals, such as hiring criteria, R&D, and documentation of best practices.

Compliance is perhaps the easiest of the three entities that comprise GRC for industry novices to grasp. Most individuals are aware that businesses must adhere to various laws and industry standards and that doing so requires some effort and oversight. It's the most straightforward option.

WHAT DOES COMPLIANCE LOOK LIKE IN PRACTICE?

The preceding criteria are arguably so broad as to be meaningless, so let's look at a few examples of compliance in action;

Following the 2008 financial crisis and subsequent economic downturn, the financial services industry was subjected to greater regulatory scrutiny and regulation. The goal of these new regulations was to safeguard investors and provide fair, efficient, and transparent markets, as well as to reduce system risk and financial crime. They were implemented to boost consumer trust in the financial sector, and they cover topics such as advertising, corporate communications, conflicts of interest, and client assets, among others. Financial services firms, in turn, expanded the functions of their compliance departments from consultative to active risk management and monitoring.

Another example is the Sarbanes-Oxley Act of 2002. This rule was passed in the aftermath of several high-profile accounting scandals, including those involving Enron, Worldcom, and Tyco. The act set stricter recordkeeping standards and created strict new procedures for accountants, auditors, and corporate officers in order to safeguard investors against firms knowingly misleading financial reports. The act also imposed new criminal penalties for securities law violations.

The preceding examples are of American financial regulations, but compliance can take many other forms based on criteria such as industry, geography, volume, and company size—and the more elements involved, the more complicated it becomes. Companies must follow distinct local regulations in different states, countries, and even towns, and the laws in an area like healthcare are more severe and particular than in an industry where patient health isn't directly involved. To illustrate, the demands on Amazon's compliance department—which operates on a global scale in industries such as e-commerce, finance, entertainment, cloud computing, and many others—will be far greater than they would be at a small company that only operates in one line of business.

WHAT DOES A COMPLIANCE OFFICER DO?

Every person in a corporation bears primary responsibility for compliance. Few professions do not require some level of ensuring that the company's day-to-day procedures correspond to internal norms, external regulations, or both.

The Chief Compliance Officer of an organization is in charge of identifying rules and implementing compliance processes. They are in charge of monitoring the compliance department and assisting other company departments in meeting their obligations to comply with relevant rules and internal processes. They must also appropriately monitor and manage the company's compliance risks so that they can be avoided or eliminated in the future.

Lastly, but extremely important, is senior company leadership. These people may be less directly active, but it is critical that they are included in all compliance operations so that expectations are well stated. The culture of compliance in the organization begins at the top, as evidenced by their words and actions.

BUSINESS COMPLIANCE

In business, compliance can refer to two things: an "action" and a "standard." To properly comprehend what it is and why it is important in your organization, you must first understand the distinction between these two notions.

Compliance as an action:

Compliance in business or in a firm generally refers to following government laws, health and security standards, or data and security obligations. It is an "action" if the rules and policies are consciously recognized. Compliance becomes a mandatory action when it is deemed vital for the survival of a business or enterprise.

Certain standards set by recognized governing organizations are accompanied by regulatory compliance. To comply in this sense means to meet specific regulations so that your business can operate lawfully and safely.

This also alludes to a company's many duties. Businesses that are in compliance understand that they are accountable to both their staff and their customers. Non-compliance might have catastrophic consequences.

You build a positive business reputation when you clearly meet regulatory obligations. Once you've identified and taken the necessary measures to comply with policies, applicable laws, and regulations, you'll be able to determine which program or framework your organization should run under. This brings us to our next topic of discussion.

Compliance as a standard:

Compliance becomes a norm when you have a well-designed set of rules and regulations in place to help your firm maintain security and stability. These standards are only significant if they are adequately implemented and strictly followed inside the organization. It is not enough to just follow rules and policies to be considered a standard. You must also determine whether following these standards would solve your company's genuine needs.

IMPORTANCE OF COMPLIANCE

The fundamental goal of compliance is straightforward: to discover and avoid potential red flags in your firm. Again, failure to comply seriously may result in future hefty fines or penalties.

Furthermore, corporate compliance promotes responsible behavior among your staff. The greatest corporate compliance program encourages your staff to be respectful of one another at work, to maintain a high degree of professionalism, and to uphold corporate values both within and outside of the office. As a result, it is critical to never take compliance for granted, as it can have a significant influence on your organization both internally and externally.

The following are some of the reasons why your firm should prioritize compliance:

1. To avoid legal ramifications:

No company wants to get involved in large legal battles or face criminal penalties for breaking the law. Legal liabilities can be both a significant blow to your company's reputation and an immediate financial loss. Court hearings and appearances can cause major disruptions to your business operations. To be legally compliant, you must not only learn the important legislation related to your organization, but you must also follow it at all costs.

As a general rule, developing a credible public image is one approach to successfully promote your business. If your company is having problems because of noncompliance, the general public may question your credibility. Remember that your customers' trust and loyalty are vital to your company.

2. To boost your company's productivity:

It was previously highlighted how compliance can help to develop solid corporate standards. This is referred to as internal compliance. It's your company's way of fostering a great work environment and culture. Employees want to work in an environment where they feel safe and well-cared for. This is only possible if the company has a defined model. This model might be a set of principles or policies that assure the fairness and security of employees and clients.

DIFFERENCE BETWEEN INTERNAL AND EXTERNAL COMPLIANCE

Compliance becomes increasingly vital as a company grows and is subjected to new problems and examinations. This, however, is not a justification to disregard established practices. There are various compliance standards in areas such as health, security, data privacy, finance, environmental concerns, and more to avoid any unfair or inadequate corporate operations. Whether your company is huge or small, if you want to expand, you must have a strong balance of both external and internal compliance from the outset.

External compliance:

External compliance, also known as regulatory compliance, refers to adhering to the laws' rules, regulations, and industry standards. These are the rules you must follow if you want to stay in business. For example, registering your company name is an act of external compliance.

You should be aware of the following external compliance requirements:

- Registrations
- ABN (Australian Business Number)
- GST (Goods and Services Tax)
- TFN (Tax File Number)
- Privacy and data security
- The Australian Privacy Principles (APPs) and the Privacy Act (1988)
- The Do Not Call Registry Act of 2006
- Spam Act of 2003
- Quality control
- ISO 9001
- Trading
- Act on Competition and Consumer Protection (2010)
- The Trade Practices Act of 1974
- FTAs (Free Trade Agreements)
- Employment
- Insurance for Workers' Compensation

- WHS stands for Workplace Health and Security.
- Superannuation

Internal Compliance:

Internal compliance, on the other hand, refers to adhering to your company's policies, regulations, and standards of behavior. Having your own compliance program might assist your company in avoiding internal conflicts and maintaining good operating standards. Internal compliance can be demonstrated by implementing a social media policy for your staff.

Other internal compliance guidelines you can implement include:

- Which staff activity can be monitored and how?
- How to handle Discrimination Complaints
- What types of donations can you make on behalf of your company?
- What are the consequences of endangering a company resource or property?
- How to handle staff conflicts of interest.

HOW TO ENSURE COMPLIANCE

Here are ways you can keep your business compliant in the long run:

1. Keep track of new legislation and regulations:

When running a business, it's critical to stay current on new laws, regulations, workplace norms, and industry standards. To avoid unintended violations, obtain legal assistance from a consultant on a regular basis or hire a full-time compliance officer to assist you in developing a compliance program and identifying any regulatory risks. These individuals will be in charge of monitoring and assessing business activities to ensure compliance with applicable laws and internal regulations.

2. Plan regular internal audits:

Regular internal audits allow you to identify areas where you are falling short of compliance requirements and indicate areas where you need to improve. These audits are typically performed by your workers or a compliance officer to ensure that your company closely complies with its internal guidelines and code of conduct. More crucially, they assist your company in preparing for external audits by government or regulatory bodies.

3. Make it mandatory for staff to be compliant:

Employee cooperation is critical for business compliance, so make sure your employees are aware of it. It is your job as an equal-opportunity employer to ensure that your policies are applied properly. Make sure everyone understands your workplace regulations and appropriate norms of conduct, why they are in place, and what the repercussions are if they are not followed. Furthermore, it is crucial that your personnel be well-trained in recording and keeping a record of all critical information and transactions that occur on your behalf.

4. Make use of the appropriate software:

It is no surprise that technology now has a solution for practically every business challenge. By investing in the correct compliance management software, your company can decrease human error and automate the time-consuming effort of recognizing possible red flags before they become a major problem. Before you buy software, be sure it's from a reliable cloud provider and has all of the features required for your industry, as well as the correct integration capabilities to help you get the most out of it.

TYPES OF BUSINESS COMPLIANCE

Just as there are so many parts of a business that must be conducted in the right way and so many types of business, there are different types of compliance in business. Let's take a look at what they are and what they mean.

1. Regulatory adherence:

Regulatory compliance occurs when a company adheres to the local and international laws and regulations that apply to its activities. The regulatory compliance requirements will differ depending on the firm and the industry in which it operates.

If you own a business, you understand how time-consuming it can be to establish trust with your employees, customers, and suppliers. Much of this effort is focused on you and your company doing the right thing, both legally and ethically. Regulatory compliance guarantees that your organization follows the law in order to establish confidence. You may watch your company's reputation increase as it grows.

2. Human resource compliance:

HR compliance encompasses all corporate rules and procedures that ensure your organization is functioning legally and with your employees' welfare at the center of all you do. HR compliance ensures that your company complies with employment legislation and employee-related problems.

HR compliance includes topics such as employee documentation, hiring procedures, when and how to pay overtime, recruiting, and employee perks. When your company follows these HR processes, it is more likely to have a happy and productive workforce and is less likely to suffer HR complaints or legal concerns.

3. Data adherence:

Businesses nowadays acquire and store a large amount of data. Businesses have access to a lot of personal information, whether it's data about their customers or data about their staff. As a result, data compliance is a must.

Data compliance assures that your organization is collecting, organizing, storing, and managing data lawfully and legally. If your company is data compliant, all of its data must be protected from corruption, loss, theft, and misuse.

Data is the fuel of decision-making, continuous improvement, quality, and clinical value demonstration.

Data is to a company what gasoline is to a car. The engine is damaged if the fuel is polluted. If the integrity of the data is jeopardized, it can harm the organization's reputation and even result in a business collapse. Making sure your firm is data-compliant isn't only about safeguarding its reputation; it's also about assuring its success.

4. Health and security compliance:

When most people think of health and security compliance, they think of the healthcare industry. That is understandable. After all, doctors, nurses, and surgeons must follow health and security laws for the protection of their patients as well as the continuous provision of their practice/hospital services.

However, health and security compliance is applicable to all organizations and industries, not only those in the healthcare industry. This is because creating a safe working environment is an important aspect of health and security compliance. This ensures that your staff may work to the best of their skills without putting themselves in danger or risking injury. Failure to comply with health and security requirements can be costly, resulting in serious accidents, illness, and needless workplace events.

UNDERSTANDING REGULATORY COMPLIANCE

The adherence of an organization to laws, regulations, and guidelines created by governments and regulatory agencies that are relevant to its industry and jurisdiction is referred to as regulatory compliance. Specific compliance standards may differ depending on industry, geographical area, and the nature of the organization's operations. Data protection, financial reporting, worker security, environmental sustainability, and consumer protection are all examples of compliance duties.

To achieve their compliance duties, businesses must traverse a complex web of regulations. This includes remaining current on regulatory changes, implementing proper processes and controls, and fostering a compliance culture throughout the firm. Businesses can demonstrate their commitment to ethical practices, defend stakeholders' interests, and reduce legal and reputational risks by doing so.

IMPORTANCE OF REGULATORY COMPLIANCE

Regulatory compliance is critical for various reasons:

1. Legal Obligations and Penalty Avoidance:

Compliance with regulatory standards is a legal requirement that organizations must meet. Inspections, audits, and penalties for noncompliance are all tools used by regulatory authorities to enforce compliance. Regulation violations can result in hefty fines, operational restrictions, and even legal action. Businesses can avoid these penalties and the financial and operational ramifications by ensuring regulatory compliance.

2. Stakeholder Interest Protection:

Regulatory compliance safeguards the interests of a variety of stakeholders, including consumers, employees, investors, and the general public. Compliance requirements frequently address concerns such as data privacy, workplace security, and consumer rights, all of which are vital for protecting the well-being and rights of stakeholders. Businesses that comply with these regulations demonstrate their commitment to responsible and ethical operations, promoting trust and loyalty among stakeholders.

3. Trust and Reputation:

Maintaining regulatory compliance is critical for a company's reputation and creating confidence with customers, partners, and the general public. Breach of compliance can result in unfavorable publicity, harming the company's image, and losing trust. Businesses that prioritize compliance and express their dedication to regulatory norms, on the other hand, can improve their reputation as dependable and trustworthy enterprises. This can result in higher client retention, new company prospects, and a market competitive advantage.

4. Risk Reduction and Operational Effectiveness:

Regulatory compliance assists firms in identifying and mitigating legal and regulatory risks. Organizations can reduce the possibility of non-compliance incidents, such as data breaches, workplace accidents, or environmental infractions, by having comprehensive compliance processes and controls. Compliance also increases operational efficiency by streamlining procedures, assuring consistent quality standards, and lowering the likelihood of disruptions caused by noncompliance events.

5. Profitability in the Long Run:

Long-term profitability can be enhanced by effective regulatory compliance management. Businesses can use compliance techniques to discover and address inefficiencies, increase internal controls, and improve overall operational effectiveness. Furthermore, compliance regulations frequently correspond with industry best practices, allowing firms to remain competitive while meeting customer expectations. Businesses that prioritize compliance can attract and retain customers who value ethical standards and data protection, resulting in revenue growth and long-term profitability.

Regulatory compliance is an essential component of running a profitable and ethical organization. To achieve legal requirements, safeguard stakeholder interests, and limit risks, organizations must prioritize compliance management.

6. Financial Stability:

Any compliance officer will tell you that the first benefit of regulatory compliance is financial security. Noncompliance with regulatory requirements can result in severe fines for the offending entity. This is what happened to Goldman Sachs, Wells Fargo, and JP Morgan Chase in 2020 when they were fined $7.50 billion out of a total of $11.39 billion imposed on all US banks that year.

7. Defense Against Lawsuits:

Compliance with rules and regulations protects organizations from lawsuits, whether initiated by the agency or someone else (e.g., the public), in addition to avoiding financial fines. In 2019, for example, 142 local governments brought lawsuits against firms for noncompliance with the Americans with Disabilities Act (ADA) between 2011 and 2019.

8. Competitiveness and Business Continuity:

Regulatory compliance gives a plethora of guideposts that teach firms what they need to flourish in their industry. Compliance regulations have also evolved to help create market homogeneity and enable businesses to compete fairly, ethically, and on an equal basis. Companies that accomplish regulatory compliance may enjoy a competitive advantage in their industry.

9. Keep a Good Reputation:

An organization that follows regulations and laws provides consumers with a sense of security. In exchange, they place their data, money, and allegiance in such companies.

10. Cybercrime Protection:

Higher-risk businesses, such as healthcare and finance, appreciate the value of the data they collect and recognize that they are attractive targets for bad actors.

Other industries, on the other hand, may believe that they are less likely to be targeted. This erroneous notion frequently results in a lack of regulatory compliance focus and decreased security, increasing the possibility of cyberattacks and data breaches.

Data breaches reduce client retention, which can have disastrous financial consequences for the organization, possibly leading to bankruptcy and closure. Regulatory compliance increases information security by requiring firms to follow laws that protect their assets from threat actors and serves as one of several protections to assure data protection.

CHALLENGES ASSOCIATED WITH REGULATORY COMPLIANCE

Organizations that fail to adhere to mandated regulatory compliance processes risk being obliged to participate in remedial programs that include on-site compliance audits and inspections by the appropriate regulatory agency. Noncompliant organizations are typically subject to monetary fines and penalties. Organizations that commit repeated – or particularly egregious – compliance violations can potentially harm their brand name.

Following compliance regulations can be costly in terms of infrastructure and staff. Companies must invest capital to comply with compliance laws and regulations, but they must also earn a profit to placate stakeholders and maintain business processes. These financial difficulties associated with compliance are especially apparent in highly regulated areas such as finance and healthcare.

Other business strategy problems related to regulatory compliance include the following:

Determining how emerging regulations will impact business direction and existing business models; incorporating and developing a compliance culture and promoting this culture throughout the organization; deciding on and hiring compliance roles and accountabilities, as well as compliance functions required by legal, compliance, audit, and business departments; and anticipating compliance trends and integrating regulatory processes to boost efficiency.

Consumer technologies are always evolving, which complicates compliance for businesses. Employees' usage of personal mobile devices at work, for example, raises compliance risks because these devices store sensitive, compliance-relevant company data. The expansion of the Internet of Things has resulted in a massive increase in the number of endpoints and associated devices, and the absence of security for mobile and IoT devices presents compliance vulnerabilities in enterprises' networks. To be compliant, digitized businesses must keep up with mandatory updates and patch existing software as soon as vulnerabilities are discovered.

Financial Accountability: the foundation of business operations is financial compliance. It assures that financial transactions are accurate, transparent, and legal.

The following are two critical facets of financial compliance:

- Accounting Standards:

Businesses must adhere to accounting standards in order to appropriately disclose their financial situation. Adherence to the Australian Accounting Standards guarantees consistency and comparability in financial statements in Australia, making it easier for investors, creditors, and regulators to evaluate a company's financial health.

- Tax compliance:

Tax compliance is a non-negotiable aspect of business operations. It includes meeting tax requirements such as completing accurate returns, paying taxes on time, and taking advantage of eligible deductions. In Australia, compliance with tax regulations is not only a legal necessity but it is also critical for financial stability and reputation.

COMPLIANCE AND TECHNOLOGY

In a technologically advanced world, the interaction of business compliance and technology is more important than ever. This section delves into the two's symbiotic relationship and how technology is transforming the compliance landscape.

A. Technology's Role in Compliance:

Technology is critical in streamlining and improving compliance operations across sectors. Here's how it's done:

- Data Management and Analysis:

Compliance frequently necessitates the processing of massive amounts of data. Data storage, analysis, and reporting are made easier by technology, making it easier for firms to track and manage compliance-related information.

- Real-Time Monitoring:

Businesses can use technology to establish real-time monitoring systems. This provides for the quick discovery of any compliance violations, allowing for prompt corrective action.

- AI and Machine Learning:

AI and machine learning techniques are increasingly being utilized to detect patterns and abnormalities in data. They can help with risk assessment and compliance monitoring.

- Digital Documentation:

Technology allows for the development and preservation of digital documents, decreasing the necessity for physical documentation. This saves time while also ensuring data security and accessibility.

B. Software Solutions for Compliance:

Compliance-specific software solutions have developed as useful tools for assisting firms in navigating the complex regulatory landscape. It works in the following ways;

- Document Management:

Compliance software streamlines the generation, storage, and retrieval of documents. It guarantees that all required records are easily accessible for audits and reporting.

- Compliance Tracking:

These solutions provide a consolidated platform for tracking compliance requirements, deadlines, and tasks, lowering the risk of missing important deadlines.

- Risk Assessment:

Risk assessment tools are frequently included in compliance software to assist firms in identifying potential compliance issues and making proactive efforts to reduce them.

- Reporting and Analytics:

Dedicated software makes it easier to generate compliance reports. Businesses can use it to develop customized reports for internal and external stakeholders.

C. Compliance Management Automation:

Automation is transforming compliance management by eliminating repetitive procedures and reducing human error. Automation has considerable benefits where compliance rules might be stringent:

- Workflow Automation:

Organizations can automate compliance workflows to ensure that tasks are assigned, done, and tracked in a methodical manner. This minimizes the likelihood of noncompliance.

- Audit Trails:

Automation generates digital audit trails that document every action and change in compliance operations. This transparency is extremely useful for audits and investigations.

- Alerts and notifications:

Automated systems can deliver alerts and notifications about looming compliance deadlines or deviations from established norms, allowing for prompt actions.

- Continuous Monitoring:

Automated solutions can provide continuous monitoring of compliance data, allowing firms to discover and address concerns as they develop.

In today's business context, technology and compliance are inextricably linked, and their synergy is redefining how organizations manage their regulatory requirements. Businesses may enhance productivity, decrease compliance risks, and remain ahead in an environment where compliance standards are always growing by embracing technology.

BUSINESS COMPLIANCE IN THE FUTURE

When we look into the crystal ball of company compliance, we see a landscape that is rapidly evolving and becoming more integrated on a worldwide scale. This section delves into the future of compliance, looking at changing legislation, the influence of globalization, and the opportunities that await.

A. Regulations and Trends in Development:

The integration of technology into company processes is causing significant changes in compliance. Evolving regulations will almost certainly necessitate the adoption of digital compliance solutions, which will make procedures more efficient and transparent.

- Environmental Sustainability:

As the emphasis on sustainability grows, we can anticipate stronger environmental compliance standards. Businesses must adjust by establishing environmentally friendly practices and reporting on their environmental impact.

- Data Privacy:

As data breaches and privacy concerns continue to make headlines, data protection and privacy regulations will become stricter. Compliance with rules such as the GDPR will continue to be a top consideration for overseas enterprises doing business.

- Ethical Business Practices:

Ethical issues will become more important in compliance. Companies will need to integrate their operations with ethical standards, addressing concerns such as CSR and supply chain ethics.

B. The Globalization Effect:

The globalization of the compliance landscape has given both benefits and challenges:

- Regulations that apply across borders:

Businesses that expand globally must manage a complex web of cross-border rules. Foreign law compliance, such as trade, sanctions, and export controls, will become increasingly crucial.

- Complexity of the Supply Chain:

Global supply chains are growing increasingly complex. Compliance throughout the supply chain, including ethical material procurement, will be a top emphasis.

- Cybersecurity:

Organizations must conform to international cybersecurity standards and collaborate across borders to prevent cybercrime because cyber dangers are global in nature,

C. Compliance Predictions and Opportunities

Business compliance's future offers both obstacles and opportunities:

- Compliance as a Competitive Differentiator:

Companies that adopt compliance as a fundamental value proactively will gain a competitive advantage. Customers who value ethical and transparent business operations are more likely to buy from you.

- Compliance Technology:

The advancement of advanced compliance technology, such as AI-powered compliance solutions, will help businesses automate and expedite compliance operations, lowering costs and risks.

- Continual Learning and Adaptation:

To stay up with changing requirements, compliance experts will need to engage in continual learning. This creates an opportunity for compliance education and training providers.

Collaboration and networking will be critical as compliance grows more complex. Collaboration among enterprises, industry groups, and regulatory agencies will be critical as compliance becomes more complex. Businesses can handle the changing market more effectively by networking and exchanging best practices.

A dynamic and linked landscape characterizes the future of business compliance. Evolving regulations, the impact of globalization, and new trends all point to a future in which compliance is more than a legal requirement; it is a strategic imperative. Businesses that embrace these changes and see compliance as a means of growth and sustainability will prosper in this changing environment.

COMPLIANCE FRAMEWORK

Regulatory compliance is a significant barrier for many organizations, but it doesn't mean you should ignore it. On the contrary, mastering compliance is crucial for long-term growth, avoiding data breaches (and the resulting monetary fines from regulators), and keeping a competitive advantage over competitors.

A compliance framework is an important tool for developing your compliance program: it is a guide that can assist your firm in satisfying legal obligations, decreasing compliance risk, and achieving strategic goals.

In this section, we will look at how to properly employ compliance frameworks so that you may achieve and maintain compliance even in today's complicated (and often difficult) business landscape.

A compliance framework is a collection of policies, security management requirements, and recommendations that assist firms in operating within legal and regulatory limitations. Compliance frameworks are intended to assist organizations in establishing a strong security posture while minimizing the possibility of compliance infractions. These security frameworks often comprise a roadmap for establishing security policies, internal controls for incident management, and auditing and compliance requirements.

Compliance frameworks can be industry-specific or general-purpose, and they can be adapted to match the specific demands of various businesses. Organizations can demonstrate their commitment to maintaining a compliant and safe environment by implementing a compliance framework, which can help develop trust with customers, partners, and other stakeholders.

Not every regulation will apply to every firm, but there are some general regulations that cover issues such as employee and consumer personal data. As a result, it's critical to understand which frameworks you should prioritize, what it takes to be compliant, and the potential implications if you don't.

Furthermore, maintaining compliance is more than just avoiding financial fines. In many circumstances, establishing compliance with specific frameworks may be critical in allowing you to do business because if you can't prove compliance with certain standards, you may be denied access to vital services or platforms.

It aids with the following tasks:

- Identifying weaknesses in the security posture to reduce incidents,
- Ensuring business continuity and remaining compliant with applicable compliance frameworks,
- Keep track of new technologies added to the system, system modifications, and issues, and document them,

- Improve efficiency, strategically utilize human and capital resources,
- Increase operational efficiency by combining process, people, and technology in a holistic manner.

COMPONENTS OF COMPLIANCE FRAMEWORK

To achieve the essential standards, key aspects of an effective compliance framework interconnect policies, procedures, people, technologies, resources, and training programs. A compliance framework should not be one-size-fits-all; it should be adjusted to the type of data, industry regulatory needs, budget, and other variables.

Here are some of the main components of a compliance framework:

1. Policy:

It outlines the primary aims, goals, and approach you intend to use to achieve the framework's commitments.

Typically, it should include the following topics:

- Accountability assigned to employees for each activity, along with an expected delivery date,
- The regulation clause or subclause that applies to each activity,
- A process for identifying new compliance needs, implementing applicable technology to meet those obligations, and monitoring the controls that have been implemented,

- Systems, controls, and processes to meet new regulatory requirements, as well as methods for reviewing and testing them.

2. Plan:

The comprehensive compliance policy should also cover the risks associated with each compliance, the frequency of reviewing, and the controls that are in place.

Consider the following when developing your strategy:

- The type, complexity, and objectives of the controls;

How achievable are your control metrics, as well as how well they correspond with policy and processes?

- If the selected controls and framework requirements are clearly aligned;

Using a compliance calendar to ensure timely delivery and visualization of the plan ahead is a smart practice. This assists all parties involved in better understanding their tasks, framework requirements, internal dependencies, and external dependencies.

COMPLIANCE AUTOMATION:

It is difficult to combine spreadsheets, calendars, and task-based accountability, yet it works for some organizations. Most people, however, find it difficult to perform everything flawlessly.

Many people are now considering Governance, Risk, and Compliance (GRC) solutions to manage procedures and reduce manual labor. Management strategy, executory functioning, decision-making, and information management are examples of governance functionalities. Control effectiveness, reporting capabilities, risk profile maps, risk assessment, correcting gaps, and risk analysis are all aspects of risk. Compliance entails identifying requirements, reviewing compliance posture, paperwork, and compliance reports, calculating noncompliance and risks, and managing contacts and policies.

COMMON COMPLIANCE FRAMEWORKS

The following are five of the most common compliance frameworks:

1. The Sarbanes-Oxley Act:

The Sarbanes-Oxley Act (SOX) is a major law in the United States for persons who work with financial data in public companies. It was passed in 2002 in the aftermath of scandals such as Enron, and it is intended to combat fraud by requiring greater transparency and accuracy in how corporations disclose their accounting. In addition to fines for the company, CEOs can be held personally liable for any false financial declarations, with high fines and even imprisonment as enforcement alternatives.

2. National Institute of Standards and Technology (NIST):

The National Institute of Science and Technology (NIST) is not a single set of rules, but rather a collection of guidelines for safeguarding sensitive data. While it is not a legal requirement, being able to demonstrate that you are adhering to NIST standards is critical for any enterprise that handles confidential information, as it demonstrates that you are taking the necessary precautions to protect against the latest cybersecurity threats and have a plan in place to respond in the event of a data breach.

3. Statement on Standards for Attestation Engagements (SSAE-16):

The Statement on Standards for Attestation Engagements No. 16 (SSAE-16) is a financial auditing and reporting standard. It not only outlines a variety of best practices for business operations and internal controls, but it is also a required aspect of the SOX compliance process. This means that specialized stakeholders will have to examine service organization controls (SOC) for any SOX-affected apps and processes, such as financial management systems, in order to identify any compliance issues.

4. Payment Card Industry Data Security Standards (PCI-DSS):

PCI-DSS compliance is essential for every company that accepts debit or credit card payments. These rules define the steps that businesses must take to ensure the security of the cardholder data they collect. They are divided into 12 key requirements that cover everything from network security to encryption and testing processes. Despite the fact that it is an industry-standard rather than a law, firms that fail to comply may face large fines from payment providers and even have their ability to accept or make payments revoked.

5. General Data Protection Regulation (GDPR):

The EU's General Data Protection Regulation (GDPR), one of the most comprehensive compliance regulations introduced in many years, establishes strict regulatory requirements for how businesses handle personal data for both employees and customers. It addresses everything from what companies can do with personal information to individuals' rights to access their own data, as well as stringent reporting requirements for any breaches.

6. Consumer Protection Act of California (CCPA):

The California Consumer Protection Act (CCPA), which is known as California's version of the GDPR, establishes rules for the protection and handling of personal data in the same way that the GDPR does. Whereas the GDPR may not apply to US firms that only operate domestically, the CCPA may be more applicable to many US firms that interact with California residents, even if they are not based in the state. In some ways, the CCPA's rules are even stricter than GDPR, such as when it comes to children's information, so it's critical that businesses, regardless of industry, prioritize this.

7. International Organization for Standardization (ISO):

The International Organization for Standardization (ISO) is a list of internationally recognized frameworks with a variety of subsections addressing numerous industries and criteria rather than a single rule. The ISO 9000 norms, for example, establish quality management standards and will be extremely useful to manufacturers, whereas the ISO 27000 recommendations focus on information security. Being able to demonstrate compliance with the relevant frameworks will be critical for any firm; if you lack certification, you may find it difficult to obtain business.

8. Health Insurance Portability and Accountability Act (HIPAA) of 1996:

The Health Insurance Portability and Accountability Act of 1996 (HIPAA) is one of the most significant standards for healthcare organizations since it oversees the handling of extremely sensitive personal medical information. It applies to hospitals, pharmacies, insurance providers, and any other institution that collects, maintains, or processes this data, and there are severe penalties for noncompliance.

9. Privacy Shield:

Privacy Shield, which replaced the previous EU-US Safe Harbor agreement, which was overturned by a European court in 2015, governs the security of data exchanged between the United States and the EU. It is critical for any company doing international business since demonstrating compliance with its regulatory requirements makes it much easier for US companies to gather personal data from EU citizens while keeping compliant with the relevant local data protection regulations.

10. Federal Risk and Authorization Management Program (FedRAMP):

Cloud services are already a standard means of doing business for many businesses, but there are a number of privacy and cybersecurity dangers that may develop if US government agencies seek to store or process data in the cloud. The Federal Risk and Authorization Management Program (FedRAMP) aims to provide agencies with a safe means to do so by establishing important criteria to help analyze the risks of such services. FedRAMP requirements (such as authorization and continuous monitoring) must be part of your procurement processes if you operate with the federal government/federal agency or help process data for these entities.

11. Center for Internet Security (CIS) Critical Security Controls:

The CIS controls framework is a detailed collection of rules aimed to assist enterprises in improving their cybersecurity initiatives. These best practices are centered on addressing the most crucial security requirements, hence lowering cyber risk. Because they manage sensitive financial data that is a prominent target for cybercriminals, security professionals and finance teams must be aware of the CIS controls architecture. Teams with a solid understanding of these controls can effectively contribute to the creation and execution of robust security management inside their business.

Navigating the complicated world of compliance and regulatory frameworks is a difficult but necessary component of operating a successful business in today's global economy. As previously stated, enterprises must prioritize compliance activities and adopt robust privacy measures to ensure compliance with developing legislation.

Businesses can mitigate compliance risks, defend their brand, and maintain a competitive edge in the market by staying up to date on these policy frameworks and developing a compliance culture within their firm. As compliance evolves, firms must rely on the experience of professionals and stay updated to stay ahead of the curve and protect their long-term success.

COMPLIANCE MANAGEMENT

Every firm, regardless of size or complexity, must follow the regulations. Business requirements, whether government rules, industry standards, or contractual duties, help to ensure quality, privacy, security, and security for customers and businesses.

Compliance, on the other hand, can be difficult. Each industry has its own set of norms, and some have multiple sets, such as the banking sector.

Furthermore, rules and regulations are subject to change. So, staying current can be difficult. The alternative, on the other hand, is even worse. Noncompliance can lead to criminal penalties, heavy fines, the loss of licenses, reputational harm, and even corporate failure.

Businesses provide items and services to alleviate a customer's pain point. However, they must also ensure that their operations, methods, and activities are in accordance with applicable laws, regulations, industry standards, and internal policies. They necessitate compliance management, which is a systematic and deliberate approach to mitigating legal and ethical risks while encouraging openness, accountability, and good governance. Compliance management is critical in many industries, including finance, healthcare, manufacturing, and technology, in order to build brand reputation, prevent legal ramifications, and support long-term success.

Compliance management, at its heart, entails finding applicable rules and regulations that pertain to an organization's operations, such as data protection, environmental regulations, labor laws, and consumer protection, among others. They must create and implement internal rules and processes that are consistent with these external obligations. These rules serve as instructions for employees, laying out the expected behaviors and processes in order to assure compliance.

The practice of monitoring, reviewing, and tracking systems to ensure compliance with applicable industrial, governmental, or regulatory legal requirements is known as compliance management.

As previously stated, compliance generally consists of a sequence of regulations and mandatory requirements. As an example:

- Corporate compliance;

Corporate compliance consists of internal procedures, rules, policies, behavioral norms, and performance requirements that must be followed by all employees in the firm.

- Regulatory compliance;

This comprises laws, regulations, and norms imposed by third-party groups such as employee unions, governments, regulatory bodies, or industry standards. GDPR, FTC, CCPA, HIPAA, CMMC, SOC2, and ISO 27001 are a few examples.

You may be required to comply with more than one rule depending on the sort of service you provide and the industry laws in effect. The examples above are only a few. It is difficult to keep track of several regulations, each with its own set of granular requirements. A compliance management system can help with this.

Organizations can use compliance management systems to track and manage their compliance efforts. These systems aid in the streamlining of procedures, the monitoring of regulatory changes, and the consistency of adherence across departments.

Noncompliance can have serious consequences, including legal penalties, reputational harm, customer loss, and diminished investor trust. Compliance management that is effective reduces these risks and reflects an organization's commitment to ethical behavior and appropriate business practices.

IMPORTANCE OF COMPLIANCE MANAGEMENT

As the world becomes increasingly reliant on technology, industry standards, and legal requirements are becoming more stringent. Compliance management is critical since noncompliance can result in legal and financial penalties, security breaches, and reputational damage to your company. Comprehensive compliance management systems (CMS) ensure that your company's policies are up to date and help to avoid business disruption. Let's look at the top reasons why monitoring and managing compliance within your firm is critical.

1. Avoiding infractions:

Noncompliance can result in significant fines that have a negative impact on the financial health of your company. According to a recent Ponemon and Globalscape study, a firm without a compliance management system pays up to 2.71 times more than an entity that follows compliance rules. Noncompliance costs around $14.82 million per year, compared to $5.47 million to maintain compliance. Following industry and regulatory standards correctly can save your company an average of $9.35 million per year.

2. Assessing security threats:

Effective compliance management systems aid in the assessment and control of security threats. To ensure compliance, these systems require the usage of certain security tools in addition to written records, processes, and functions. Risk assessments assess the level of risk connected with your organization and ensure that you have prioritized compliance and implemented appropriate risk-aversion measures. Furthermore, continuous monitoring technologies can assist in identifying susceptible systems, prioritizing remediation activities, patching noncompliant systems, and validating that changes have been implemented correctly.

3. Protection against data breaches:

Failure to meet compliance rules might lead to a tricky scenario, such as the one confronted by Walmart Photo Center in 2015. The Picture Center data breach allowed hackers to access customers' credit card information as well as other personal information (such as names, emails, and account passwords), costing the corporation 1.3 billion dollars in compensation, legal fees, and account monitoring fees. It was later shown that Walmart was aware of compliance standards but failed to adequately account for them.

CHALLENGES WITH COMPLIANCE MANAGEMENT

While the necessity of compliance management cannot be overstated, the obstacles that many businesses encounter are the root cause of noncompliance. Here are a couple of such examples:

- Constant changes in security and compliance regulations:

Within security and compliance, the only constant is change. New cyber threats and regulations emerge rapidly, necessitating fast action to manage new risks and preserve good standing.

- Large corporations with a high employment rate:

The greater the enterprise's size, the greater the danger of noncompliance. It might be difficult to organize compliance programs and provide training across the entire organization when there are a large number of team members. This increases system complexity and, as a result, the chance of a data breach.

- Distributed working environments:

The shift from on-site to remote work and cloud platforms has made it challenging to obtain an accurate and complete picture of compliance status. As a result, many businesses have found it difficult to manage and monitor risks and vulnerabilities.

INFORMATION TECHNOLOGY COMPLIANCE MANAGEMENT

The fundamental goal of IT compliance management is to ensure that IT operations run smoothly by ensuring that suitable IT governance rules, controls, standards, and risk management frameworks are in place.

This includes data collection and management, audit trails, workflows, database administration, data and security testing, internal and external fraud, supplier management, system availability, and service delivery.

However, achieving this goal will be difficult. Due to the lack of a defined roadmap in the regulations, various industry-specific suggestions and best practices are released to provide clarity and support.

Other concerns include:

- Poor employee training
- Individual mobile devices that bypass corporate IT infrastructure are examples of shadow IT difficulties
- Applications that have not been approved
- Problems with service providers (cloud computing and data centers)
- The Application of Social Media
- The amount of current regulations, changes, and new laws
- Components of an Effective Compliance Management Program

According to the international consulting firm Deloitte, compliance management programs should do the following:

Determine the applicable laws, rules, norms, and standards in your operational area. Do you take credit card payments at your business? Then, you must comply with PCI DSS. Are you a medical professional? If so, HIPAA compliance is required. And so forth.

Incorporate compliance requirements into daily activities and procedures. Starting at the top, a "culture of compliance" is required for successful, ongoing regulatory compliance. Thomson Reuters Legal suggests the following six criteria for creating and maintaining a compliance culture:

- Awareness
- Education in Communication
- Incentives for effective technology
- Case management and incident reporting
- Controls for compliance should be monitored.
- Conduct regular compliance audits and internal compliance reporting.
- Train employees to understand and follow the regulations.
- Corrective action, including internal controls, should be taken in response to failures.
- Create and maintain ties with regulators.

WHICH ACTIVITIES ARE INCLUDED IN COMPLIANCE MANAGEMENT?

A successful compliance management program includes a large number of individuals, corporate divisions and operations, and activities that all collaborate throughout the year.

Among the compliance management activities are:

- Policy and procedure development to achieve compliance
- Company-wide compliance training
- Internal examinations
- Audits by third parties to check that vendors and contractors are also in compliance.
- Procedures and controls for security
- Reporting on compliance
- Tracking and monitoring of compliance
- External audits, when necessary
- Corrective measures
- Response to consumer complaints

BEST APPROACHES TO COMPLIANCE MANAGEMENT

The strongest compliance management strategies are built on a solid foundation of forethought and strategy. When it comes to compliance management, implementing a thorough, enterprise-wide, risk-based approach helps secure your company's success.

1. Determine your end goals early on:

Knowing where you're headed allows you to create your compliance program in a more direct and effective manner. The Commodities and Futures Trading Commission (CFTC), for example, applies to InfoSec and privacy in the financial sector but also to any industry. Do the following to prevent fraud, errors, breaches, and other dangers from occurring;

- Policies and procedures in writing
- Employee education
- Existing problem resolution
- Dedication of the resources (money, personnel, and skill) required for success.
- The compliance function's structure, oversight, and reporting

2. Understand your industry's rules:

The regulations, legislation, and standards that your firm should (or must) follow may be relatively simple--PCI DSS if you are a retail shop that accepts credit card payments but does not have an internet store. It could also be exceedingly complex, as in the case of financial institutions, healthcare, and manufacturing. Knowing which applies to you and selecting the appropriate frameworks to assist you in complying with them is an important first step in creating your compliance management program.

3. Create solid, well-defined internal policies and processes:

Your employees, contractors, senior management, and board members must all understand which regulations to follow and how to follow them.

4. Impose accountability:

Build in Controls and balances, and hold people accountable for their mistakes or malfeasance.

5. Train your employees:

Many noncompliance issues develop as a result of errors that may be easily prevented with comprehensive, engaging, interactive training. As a result, conduct your study to ensure that the compliance training you deliver is effective.

6. Examine yourself:

A strong foundation is required for a robust program, and a baseline is required to establish where to focus your compliance efforts and avoid duplication. Because many compliance frameworks overlap, achieving the requirements of one regulation, statute, or standard will almost certainly bring you in conformity with others. Knowing your controls and weaknesses from the outset will allow you to design your compliance management program more swiftly and effectively.

7. Manage compliance for risk, not only for compliance:

Checking items off a list of compliance criteria to satisfy regulators or auditors may appear to be the simplest solution, but it may short-change your organization.

Instead, assume you're going to invest time and money in obtaining qualifications. Why not go the additional mile and attempt to reduce and mitigate your organization's risks? Your ultimate goal should be to protect your organization, systems, data, and customers.

8. Keep an audit trail:

A "paper" trail documenting all of your compliance actions will be invaluable not only if you need audits but may also assist you in escaping harsh fines if a breach or other non-compliance issue occurs. Collect and store all evidence in one location so that it can be quickly retrieved when needed, or use quality GRC software to handle this for you.

ADVANTAGES OF COMPLIANCE MANAGEMENT

Taking compliance management seriously has numerous advantages. Here are a few examples:

1. It reduces legal risks and saves money in the long run:

Compliance will help your company avoid legal liabilities. Settlements and litigation can cost you tens of millions of dollars. Fines and other reparation fees may also accumulate.

Even if you are able to meet these costs, your sales may drop dramatically. If you protect your client's credit card information and prevent fraudulent purchases, you will most likely retain customers who have lost faith in your company.

It could take years to restore your company's reputation. It's difficult to say how much financial damage it can cause. It is best to use strong data protection and avoid making any compromises at all.

2. It increases the customer base's trust:

Compliance with government regulations shows your customers that you care about their security. While lawsuits or penalties will tarnish your reputation, a track record of compliance will show that you run a trustworthy company.

3. Engage your staff:

Employees can be a major headache when it comes to compliance management. A breach can occur, for example, when an employee opens an email that they should have deleted. Furthermore, they may be careless with passwords and other sensitive information.

Mobile devices have the potential to undermine your security measures. Your corporate network, for example, may be completely secure, but a breach is possible if your employees enter sensitive information on their mobile phones and laptop computers.

Bring your employees into the process of improving your cyber security. Inform them that they are critical to your company and its data. Use the opportunity to teach them how to protect company data and consider rewarding those who do so.

   4. Create an amazing story to share with your customers:

A reliable and secure business reputation is a significant source of positive public relations. The most effective public relations strategies Avoid negative press and generate positive stories about your company.

Inform your customers if you've improved data security, It will make them feel more at ease providing credit card information if they know their accounts are safe.

STEPS TO MANAGING COMPLIANCE

A proactive and systematic approach to compliance management is required. While the devil is in the details, many steps are universal.

Here are five steps for managing compliance:

   1. Determine the applicable laws and regulations:

The first step to compliance management is identifying the laws and regulations that apply to the organization. For example, enterprises that process personal data on behalf of their clients must comply with data protection rules, such as the General Data Protection Regulation (GDPR) in Europe or the California Consumer Privacy Act (CCPA) in the United States.

   2. Perform risk analysis:

Once you have found the applicable rules and regulations, undertake a risk assessment. Pinpoint areas for improvement and determine which systems and processes represent non-compliance risks. For An organization, this generally involves completing a complete evaluation of data processing procedures, identifying potential security threats, evaluating the effectiveness of existing policies, and then prioritizing the cure according to criticality.

3. Create compliance rules and regulations:

The next stage is to design comprehensive compliance management guidelines and procedures to address the identified risks and meet the requirements of relevant laws and regulations. Furthermore, corporations must adopt rules and procedures to assure actual compliance. An example of regulatory compliance management is data protection.

For example, an organization must develop policies controlling how the organization securely keeps, processes, and transfers personal data as per data protection laws.

A code of conduct, on the other hand, would be a business compliance guideline. The policy would outline how workers should handle business assets, gifts, conflicts of interest, donations, and so on.

4. Employees should receive compliance training:

More than merely creating a compliance guideline is required. Organizations must foster a compliance culture in order to achieve consistent execution. To that end, staff training on policies and procedures is critical, as it helps them comply with compliance requirements and understand their role in ensuring compliance. Establishing a compliance team to monitor and enforce compliance is also part of managing compliance.

5. Regularly review and update policies:

The final step in properly managing compliance over time is continuous monitoring and assessment. Conduct internal audits, review rules and processes, and evaluate the efficacy of the compliance management system. Furthermore, update the system as needed to ensure compliance with new legislation affecting the industries.

COMPLIANCE MANAGEMENT CHALLENGES

There are also other elements that complicate compliance management. According to Accenture, environmental, social, and governance (ESG) issues, shifting business models, and overworked compliance professionals all have the potential to wreak untold harm by preventing adherence to the letter of the law.

The following are some compliance management challenges:

1. Scarcity of resources:

The establishment of well-defined policies and safeguards is at the heart of compliance management. Creating protocols is one thing; executing and adhering to them is another. Then there's the issue of business scale; the larger the company, the more difficult it is to detect abnormalities and non-compliant operations.

And this is where most businesses fail. They frequently lack the necessary human resources, time, and technology to effectively manage compliance. As a result, they are forced to rely on fragmented channels such as emails, spreadsheets, and an asynchronous data system, resulting in unpredictable compliance.

2. Maintaining compliance with ever-changing requirements:

Another compliance management difficulty is keeping up with the regulatory environment's lightning-fast changes. It is constantly evolving, becoming more complex with each passing year as a result of external influences such as fast technological usage.

This puts a lot of strain and hurdles on businesses to stay compliant. The epidemic, for example, increased the amount of personal data processed and handled by organizations. As a result, the European Data Protection Board (EDPB) provided mandatory recommendations for healthcare organizations.

To make matters more complicated, each country and industry has its own set of regulators, making compliance more difficult for organizations that operate in various industries. As a result, compliance management can become fairly chaotic.

3. Misunderstanding regulations:

Many regulations, standards, and specifications are complex by default. It often gives a lot of opportunity for interpretation, which leads to misunderstanding and inadvertent noncompliance.

GDPR, for example, requires enterprises to seek individuals' explicit and specific consent before using personal data. The regulation, however, does not clarify what constitutes legitimate consent.

APPROACHES TO COMPLIANCE MANAGEMENT

Given the importance of compliance management and its complications, various approaches to compliance management have emerged. In general, there are three approaches to compliance management;

1. Authority and command:

This strategy, often known as stringent compliance management, entails strict regulation enforcement. Employees must follow the defined protocols and procedures in compliance programs, which are highly structured. There is no room for negotiation or flexibility, with a few exceptions, and breaking the rules might find you in hot water.

Command and control are utilized in highly regulated areas such as healthcare and banking, where regulators scrutinize every move. This method is used by organizations that are concerned with adhering to specific rules, regulations, and standards.

A command and control example;

A FinTech company that uses a strict compliance management approach to ensure compliance with banking requirements such as the Bank Secrecy Act (BSA) or the Anti-Money Laundering (AML). It would have strict regulations and processes in place to undertake client due diligence, keep records, and report questionable activities. The top management would make certain that they were followed throughout the organization.

2. Hands-off and flexible:

The second method of compliance management allows for more flexibility. In this situation, corporations establish a compliance framework in which standards can be reduced if they boost production while not compromising legal or ethical principles.

This method is also:

- More responsive to changing laws, regulations, and company requirements,
- Identifies essential legal and regulatory requirements relevant to the business and develops rules that allow users to make judgments on any specific law, policy, or regulation,
- Measures are put in place to reduce the dangers associated with noncompliance,

- This adaptability is critical for firms that adhere to standards that overlap or may conflict.

Hands-off and adaptable example;

To satisfy each country's differing data protection regulations, a worldwide company operating in four countries would benefit from a flexible compliance management approach.

They would determine the basic needs and develop policies and processes in that country to achieve them while allowing for flexibility to respond to any changes.

3. Partnership:

To manage compliance, the third option requires internal collaboration between departments and stakeholders. Organizations that use this strategy foster a culture of compliance as a shared responsibility. Employees are provided training and resources to help them do so because everyone is a participant in enforcing the laws and regulations,

Example of Partnership;

Assume an organization employs the partnership model to manage compliance with the US Foreign Corrupt Practices Act (FCPA). It would form cross-functional teams to create and implement anti-bribery and anti-corruption policies.

The optimum method of compliance management for a company is determined by criteria such as the type of business, the regulatory environment, and the level of risk.

Regardless of the approach chosen, a thorough compliance system is required to ensure compliance with applicable laws, rules, and standards.

Chapter 5

THE CYBER SECURITY TRIAD

The CIA Triad, or Confidentiality, Integrity, and Accessibility, is one of the first ideas you will learn when studying cybersecurity. The three primary pillars that support information and data security are as follows. The idea of the CIA trio is not exclusive to any one individual or geographic location, in contrast to the majority of the main cybersecurity pillars. The idea of triad confidentiality was initially put forth in a 1976 study conducted by the U.S. Air Force, although availability wasn't widely accepted until 1988.

The three ideas came together as the cohesive trio we know today in 1998, according to the cybersecurity community. The CIA Triad, which stands for Confidentiality, Integrity, and Availability, is a paradigm designed to help organizations establish information security policy. To distinguish it from the Central Intelligence Agency of the United States, it is also known as the CIA Triad.

According to this concept, "Confidentiality" refers to the safeguards put in place to make sure that specific individuals inside a corporation can access certain data or information. "Integrity" is the assurance that the data is trustworthy, accurate, and unchangeable by outside parties. "Availability" refers to the ability of authorized individuals to access information continuously and as needed. The CIA Triad is comprised of these three principles.

THE HISTORY OF THE CIA TRIAD

The CIA Triad's History dates back to 1977 publication by the National Institute of Standards and Technology (NIST). The definition of I.T. security provided by NIST in post-processing audit tools and techniques is: "the protection of data and system resources against accidental and deliberate threats to confidentiality, integrity, and availability."

The ideas themselves, though, go much farther. One of the oldest examples of data encryption for confidentiality that we know is from Mesopotamia, circa 1500 BC. A craftsman employed this method to conceal the formula for a certain type of ceramic ice that is in great demand. Since it appears improbable that people divulged their secrets on every occasion prior to that period, we may presume that the practice of maintaining some confidential information dates considerably earlier than that. Encryption was utilized to protect military and other confidential secrets throughout Julius Caesar's lifetime. It even has a number called after him, the Caesar number, which is a straightforward replacement number that encrypts a message by shifting each letter a predetermined amount to the left or right. The methods used to protect personal data have advanced throughout time. The twentieth century saw a significant advancement thanks to the widespread usage of devices like the Enigma during World War II. As computer technology became more widely used in the second half of the century, the concepts around privacy started to be defined and researched more thoroughly. A 1976 study written for the U.S. Air Force is among the first records of confidentiality in the world of computer technology. Privacy in the digital realm is becoming more and more important as computers get quicker and more and more daily functions are being done digitally. In the decades that followed, encryption techniques advanced significantly since earlier approaches could no longer protect data from adversaries with the necessary tools. Information integrity protocols date back much further than any of our records. "A Comparison of Commercial and Military Computer Security Policies" was one of the first studies published in 1987 that emphasized the significance of integrity in the computer environment.

More advanced approaches for verifying data integrity, such as digital signatures, were introduced in the late 1970s but gained widespread acceptance in the 1980s and later.

The availability history is more difficult to determine. When data existed solely in a more physical form, you could access it if you had the original or a carbon copy. According to Ben Miller of cybersecurity firm Dragos, the debut of the Morris Worm was a watershed point in the way we think about availability in the digital world.

Morris Worm quickly swept throughout the Internet in 1988, killing a substantial number of Internet devices. Although it is thought that the worm only took between two and ten thousand computers, this was at a period when the Internet was much smaller than it is today.

The Morris Worm may have inspired a lot of discussion in the industry about the mechanisms they could use to make data access more resilient and ensure availability, as one of the first major incidents that impacted a substantial part of the Internet and made large amounts of data inaccessible.

CONFIDENTIALITY

Information confidentiality is a pretty straightforward concept. It is the property to limit access to data and resources to those who are authorized to use them and to keep them secret from all other parties.

This means that, in order for the information to be really confidential, no one should be able to look at it or hold it, not even determined hackers or the nauseating old lady down the street. Confidential data must be kept confidential at all times, which means we must devise methods to keep unauthorized parties from accessing it when it is stored, in transit, and even during processing.

Attackers have a variety of strategies at their disposal to gain access to data and violate their privacy. Among these include, but are not limited to:

- Taking possession of an unprotected hard drive or laptop
- Malware installation on a device
- Take control of an account by exchanging SIM cards.
- Social engineering attacks like phishing
- Port scanning
- Capturing network traffic

- Password and other identity information theft
- Shoulder surfing

With so many unscrupulous persons on the Internet and a plethora of diverse tactics for violating data privacy, we must pay close attention to the security procedures we employ to prevent unwanted access.

But we must be concerned about more than just the assaults. Accidents, spying, and other forms of negligence can all result in unauthorized invasions of privacy. Individually, this can involve things like leaving important documents in the printer drawer or forgetting to encrypt a communication. Faults that compromise privacy at a higher level may include misconfiguration of security mechanisms or other administrative faults.

Even if these activities are not intentional, the penalties for persons affected by the violation and the accountable organization can be severe. An unintended offense may expose the individuals involved to harmful activities such as fraud, while the guilty organization may face legal consequences as well as a variety of additional costs.

Following adequate security procedures can assist in lowering the risks of accident and assault threats, as well as the chance of data privacy violations.

HOW TO KEEP DATA CONFIDENTIAL

If you have secret intentions to take over the world and want to keep them secret, you may keep them confined in a room. You can presume that your secret plans will remain secret as long as you are the only one with a key and no one attempts to break in.

One method for keeping data confidential is to restrict physical access, as seen in the preceding example. In the digital world, we commonly utilize encryption methods such as AES and RSA, as well as a variety of different numbers.

At this point, attackers cannot break these algorithms since they function so well. However, safe algorithms such as AES and RSA must still be properly implemented in order to be secure. Another important consideration is that techniques such as AES and RSA can only ensure confidentiality, provided the keys used to encrypt the data are not compromised. If an unauthorized entity obtains the keys, these encryption techniques will no longer be able to keep the data private.

Measures such as sufficient personnel training, access control mechanisms, authentication systems, and data classification are typically used in conjunction with encryption techniques.

INTEGRITY

Now that we've covered confidentiality let's move on to the I in the acronym: Integrity. When we talk about integrity, we mean the safeguarding of data accuracy and veracity. We must have safeguards in place to ensure that data is not tampered with, altered, or corrupted.

Of course, this does not preclude us from modifying our data ourselves; purposeful and permitted changes are not deemed a breach of integrity. We are primarily concerned with preventing, identifying, and correcting unauthorized or unintentional data integrity breaches.

Attackers can compromise data integrity by launching viruses, breaching and manipulating security mechanisms, or even attempting to transmit false data as original data.

Authorized user errors, such as unintentional file deletion or alteration, the execution of incorrect scripts, and the submission of inaccurate data, can also result in a breach of data integrity. Administrators may also misconfigure systems, resulting in larger-scale information integrity issues. Data can also be corrupted during transmission or over lengthy periods of storage; thus, we must detect and repair these integrity violations as well.

Does encryption provide integrity?

In some circumstances, encryption can aid in the preservation of a message's integrity. After all, it is more difficult to modify simple-text data if an attacker cannot access it.

However, preserving data integrity is different from what encryption is intended to do, and it should never be relied on as the sole technique to ensure data integrity.

This is due to two factors. One issue is that some flow numbers are changeable, which means an attacker might manipulate the data without knowing the encryption key.

This allows an attacker to violate the data's integrity while maintaining its confidentiality.

An attacker can also compromise communication integrity by exchanging an encrypted message for a previously seen encryption message.

As an example, suppose an attacker intercepts and transfers messages between two parties, Alice and Bob. To make the situation more understandable, let's say Alice and Bob encrypt using Caesar encryption. The plain content of the encrypted communication could look like this:

Sophia: Do you believe Nathan is a nasty person?

John: Yes

Sophia: Should I give Nathan another $100?

John: No.

If we use a Caesar number to move each letter and character one space to the right (such that A becomes B, B becomes C, C becomes D, and so on), each letter and character becomes a different letter and character. Please keep in mind that the exclamation sign is a character on the right of the space in the ASCII encoding (from which exclamations are derived). The encrypted version of the chat would be as follows:

Sophia: Ep!zpv!uijol!Tufqibojf!jt!cbe@

John: Zft

Sohia: Tipvme!J!tujmm!hjwf!Tufqibojf!%211@

John: Op/

Even if the attacker is unable to decrypt and read the messages, they can still compromise the conversation's integrity by sending the first response again and ignoring the second message. If they did, the conversation would go something like this:

Sophia: Ep!zpv!uijol!Tufqibojf!jt!cbe@

John: Zft Tipvme,

Sohia: !J!Hé!Tufqibojf!%211

John: Zft

This means that the recipient will have witnessed the following exchange when the final message is decrypted:

Sophia: Do you believe Nathan is a nasty person?

John: Yes

Sophia: Should I give Nathan another $100?

John: No.

As you can see, even if the attacker had no idea what they were doing, they managed to compromise the conversation's integrity and may have gotten the recipient to do something he shouldn't have done. Another critical reason why we cannot rely on encryption to ensure data integrity

MECHANISMS FOR ENSURING DATA INTEGRITY

Data requires protection procedures to preserve its integrity in the face of dangers such as those listed above. A variety of measures can help ensure data integrity inside a given security system.

These techniques, like encryption, can help safeguard other security qualities, but their primary goal is to act as a confidentiality mechanism. The various security controls must cooperate to ensure integrity. In isolation, there may be ways for attackers to get around them or for errors to arise.

Measures that can help protect data integrity are;

- Electronic signatures

- Cryptographic hash functions, Controlsums, and message authentication codes

- Encryption

- Access controls like Identification, authentication, authorization, and accountability

- Intrusion detection systems

- Employee training

AVAILABILITY

Finally, we arrive at the letter A, availability. Confidentiality and integrity are self-evident; we need procedures in place to keep hackers out of our data and prevent them from making unauthorized changes. The significance of availability may be less obvious, but we can clarify it through analogies.

An example of availability:

Assume you don't trust banks and want to keep all of your money for yourself. You could put it in a box, take it into the woods, and bury it 10 feet underground. Your money should be safe as long as no one follows you and you do not leave the terrain plainly disturbed. Because no one else is likely to uncover it, its location, like the amount of money you placed in the box, is private. If money is locked in a box alone, far underground, it should retain its integrity. Unless you truly want to use your money to buy stuff, this money-saving method can be beneficial. Walking through the forest, excavating 10 feet, and then walking back is hardly the most convenient way to get bread.

While your money is kept private and secure, it is not easily accessible. While it may be an effective method for hackers to bury their riches until the next time they browse, it is just not a practical way to store money that we must utilize on a daily basis.

The same is true for data. If we need to use data on a regular basis, it must also be readily available. You could secure your data with an encryption method so powerful that decrypting every machine on the planet would take 10 billion years. This ensures an incredibly comfortable security margin.

However, if the encryption technique is too complex, it can take a long time to decrypt, which means that your information is not easily available when you need it. These are data that are similar to being buried in the woods; while confidentiality and integrity can be ensured, the approach could be more practical.

If your security procedures make it too difficult for authorized staff to access data, the system as a whole may be rendered ineffective. This is related to the compromise and priority of security attributes discussed earlier in the text.

ATTRIBUTE OF AVAILABILITY

In more technical words, when we talk about the availability attribute, we want authorized users to be able to access data when they need it, on time, and without interruption.

This is critical for job performance; how can we get anything done if the data is not consistently available when needed? How could someone trust a company's service if they had yet to learn if it would operate or not?

To continue with our strong encryption scheme example, in order for the data to be considered suitably available, we require sufficient processing power to access the data in an acceptable and consistent timeframe. We would have to rethink our entire security approach if we needed the requisite I.T. resources to protect data while providing the availability we require adequately.

Many factors can influence availability, including:

- DoS or DDoS assaults:

An attacker can use Denial of Service or Distributed Denial of Service attacks to take control of a server, preventing valid traffic from passing.

- Server Failure:

Some servers may fail as a result of issues such as a missing disk or being overcrowded.

- Large-scale failures:

Power outages, catastrophic weather catastrophes, and other major disasters can cause entire server farms to fail.

- Data loss, theft, or failure of a hard drive:

If data is stored on a single disk and no backup is available, data may be lost.

- Ransomware:

Hackers can get access to an organization's networks and encrypt critical data, keeping it as a ransom until the company pays them. When hackers get payment, they frequently do not deliver the decryption key to the company, which implies that the data may become permanently unavailable if it is not saved.

- Network Issues:

If communication between different sections of the network is disrupted, data and services may become inaccessible.

- Software Failure:

Errors in the code may result in data loss. Attackers can also use bugs to turn off systems and data.

- Accidental Modification or Deletion:

Files and folders can be edited or destroyed by mistake, rendering the original version unavailable.

- Incorrect object categorization:

If data or other items are classified wrongly, they may be difficult to retrieve when needed, rendering them unavailable.

HOW TO MAKE DATA AVAILABLE

As previously demonstrated, numerous issues can result in data unavailability, either by mistake or on purpose.

Because there are so many things that may go wrong, we must carefully design our systems with a range of various methods to guarantee that the data is as accessible as possible.

We cannot, however, promise that the data will always be available. Even Internet behemoths with unlimited resources, such as Facebook and Amazon, face downtime from time to time.

We need to design resilient systems in order for our data to be as trustworthy as possible. These should include the following:

- Infrastructures that are capable of handling high tensions and demand,

- System design that prevents single points of failure,

- Redundancies for all important systems and they should be tested on a regular basis,

- Business continuity plan in case of a crisis,

- Backups for all important data: there should be many versions of everything, including at least one on a different site.

- Access controls such as authentication, authorization, and accountability

- Monitoring tools for network traffic and performance,

- Denial-of-service attack protection mechanisms.

CIA TRIAD EXAMPLES

Consider a bank ATM, which can provide users with access to bank balances and other information, to demonstrate how the CIA trinity works in practice. An A.T.M. is equipped with tools that address the three triad principles:

It protects data by demanding two-factor authentication (a physical card and a P.I.N. number) before granting access.

By ensuring that all transfers or withdrawals performed through the machine are recorded in the accounting of the user's bank account, the A.T.M. and banking software assure data integrity. Because it is in a public setting, the machine is available even when the bank branch is closed.

However, there is more to the three principles than just what's on the surface. Here are some instances of how they function in real-world computer environments.

CIA triad confidentiality examples

Much of what laypeople think of as the term "cyber security"—essentially, anything that restricts data access—falls under the category of confidentiality.

This encompasses the two primary dimensions of information security:
Authentication refers to the mechanisms that allow systems to determine whether a user is who they say they are. Passwords and the other ways available to establish identification include biometrics, security tokens, cryptographic keys, and so on.

Authorization, which determines who has access to the data; because a system recognizes you, it does not necessarily open all of its data for your review! One of the most significant approaches to protecting privacy is to build know-how mechanisms for data access. This way, users whose accounts have been hacked or who have become fraudsters cannot compromise crucial data. In this regard, most operating systems provide privacy by making many files available only to their creators or an administrator, for example.

Public-key cryptography is a widely used architecture that follows two principles: You establish your permission to participate in the encrypted discussion by authenticating that you are who you claim to be using cryptographic keys.

Non-technical measures can also be used to enforce confidentiality. Keeping hardcopy data, for example, behind a lock and key, can keep it confidential, as can computer air-gapping and countering social engineering attempts. When someone who shouldn't have seen the data reads it, there is a breach of confidentiality. Large data breaches, such as the Marriott hacking, are great examples of privacy violations.

CIA triad integrity examples

Data integrity techniques can be applied to what many would consider separate professions. Many privacy policies, for example, include data integrity; after all, you cannot maliciously edit data that you do not have access to. We also noted the data access rules used by most operating systems: in some circumstances, files can be viewed but not edited by specific users, which can help protect data integrity and availability.

However, data integrity can be compromised in ways other than by malevolent intruders attempting to destroy or modify it. For example, corruption penetrates data in standard RAM far more frequently than you believe, owing to interactions with cosmic rays. This is at the end of the spectrum, but any approach designed to safeguard the physical integrity of a storage medium can likewise protect its virtual integrity.

Many methods of defending against integrity violations are aimed at assisting you in detecting when data has changed, such as data summaries, or restoring it to a known state, such as performing frequent and meticulous backups. Integrity violations are less common or obvious than the other two principles, but they can include, for example, modifying business data to influence decision-making or hacking into a financial system to temporarily inflate the value of a stock exchange or bank account and then removing the surplus. A failure attack is a simpler—and more prevalent—version of a data integrity attack in which hackers change the HTML of a website to vandalize it for amusement or ideological purposes.

CIA triad availability examples

Maintaining availability frequently falls on services that are not closely related to cybersecurity. The best method to ensure that your data is accessible is to keep all of your systems operational and ensure that they can handle the expected network demands. This includes maintaining current hardware, monitoring bandwidth usage, and providing failure and disaster recovery capability in the event that systems fail.

Other strategies related to this idea involve establishing how to balance availability against the triad's other two considerations. Returning to the file permissions contained in each operating system, the concept of a file that can be read but not edited by some users is a way of balancing competing needs: that data be accessible to a large number of users while also protecting its integrity.

A denial-of-service attack is a classic example of a bad actor's loss of availability. In some ways, it's the most heinous cyberattack: you don't change your victim's data or look at things you shouldn't; you simply crush them with traffic so they can't maintain their website. However, DoS assaults are extremely damaging, which demonstrates why availability is part of the triad.

CHALLENGES FACED BY THE CIA TRIAD

1. Internet of Things (IoT) Security:

This is a significant difficulty because the number of Internet-compatible gadgets on the market grows at an increasing rate each year. The Internet of Things (IoT) allows actual items or "objects" to collect and transmit data but also poses security problems. Many of these gadgets have easily hacked software and very weak security passwords. Although some of these gadgets do not communicate important information, a hacker can obtain sufficient information. As a result, IoT devices provide a potential entry point for these hackers to carry out their operations. In the absence of sufficient security controls, an IoT could be utilized as a separate attack vector or as part of a thingbot.

2. Internet of Things (IoT) Privacy

Almost any physical entity or object that can be assigned a unique identification and interact autonomously via the Internet or a local network is vulnerable to attacks that could expose private information. IoT devices are often equipped with low-power and low-memory CPUs, limiting their ability to process information at high speeds and complicating efforts to guarantee confidentiality and integrity in IoT systems. Digital signatures via public key infrastructure can aid in the mitigation of these dangers in IoT systems.

3. Big Data:

Because of the ever-increasing volume of data that must be secured, big data poses a significant challenge to the CIA paradigm. As technology progresses, more devices are added to the expanding stream of data in various formats. Furthermore, because the primary goal of big data processing is often to collect and understand information, appropriate data monitoring needs to be improved. This subject was asked in a public arena when whistleblower Edward Snowden revealed information concerning the National Security Agency's acquisition of vast amounts of personal data from U.S. people.

BEST PRACTICES FOR IMPLEMENTING THE CIA TRIAD

1. The CIA Triad in Cybersecurity:

The Internet network is the primary source of computer hazards and dangers. Potential malware and social engineering programs can infiltrate incoming traffic, whereas unchecked outgoing traffic can encourage users to create hazardous websites and expose an organization to hostile attacks.

Protecting an organization's network and all linked devices with modern network security solutions is a required action for the CIA Triad in an organization.

Individuals in a company can stay secure online no matter what they do when accessing the Internet, thanks to integrated surveillance software and hardware firewalls. Continuous monitoring, testing, and reporting in a single network protection system is critical for ensuring data integrity as well as overall company security.

2. The CIA Triad in ISO 27001:

ISO 27001 is a framework for information security that assists enterprises in protecting their information assets. The CIA Triad is an ISO 27001 guiding principle. Other security frameworks, such as SOC 2 and PCI DSS, are based on CIA concepts. ISO 27001 contains a risk assessment method, organizational structure, access control mechanisms, information security policies and procedures, monitoring and reporting requirements, and a risk assessment process.

Organizations use risk assessments and access control methods to examine the risks, threats, and vulnerabilities that may jeopardize the confidentiality, integrity, and availability of their systems and data. They meet one or more of the CIA Triad Principles by establishing security procedures to limit these risks.

When establishing a security program, the CIA Triad might be a useful tool to justify the necessity of considering security measures. All security actions will invariably result in one or more of the three principles. The development of appropriate methods and processes that emphasize the security of customer information is one of the strategic implications of managing the use of the CIA Triad. The application of the CIA Triad in business also necessitates constant monitoring and updating of critical information systems in order to reduce security risks and maximize the capabilities that enable the CIA.

PROTECTION AGAINST LOSS OF CONFIDENTIALITY

Organizations use access controls and encryption to protect against privacy loss. Users, for example, must first authenticate before access is provided based on their established identity. In summary, users are granted access to data via permissions. Access is forbidden to users who do not have permission.

However, there are numerous more scenarios in which someone can access the data without proving their identity. A sniffer, for example, can capture any data flowing over a cable. Furthermore, any data that is at rest, such as on a hard drive or a portable USB device, can be stolen and easily accessed. Encryption can safeguard this data from loss of privacy.

Encryption transforms plaintext data into encrypted data. If unauthorized individuals acquire or intercept encrypted data, it cannot be read (at least not readily). It is anticipated that an attacker will need hundreds of years to crack several of today's sophisticated encryption systems. In contrast, with the correct software, poor encryption algorithms (such as WEP used with earlier wireless networks) can be cracked in seconds.

Today, several different types of encryption algorithms are in use. The Advanced Encryption Standard (A.E.S.) is a quick and efficient technique for encrypting data at rest. TPM modules, which can encrypt entire hard drives, are useful for laptops. Emails are encrypted (and digitally signed) using S/MIME. Many more protocols, including SSL, T.L.S., IPsec, and others, encrypt data transferred via cable over the Internet or internal networks.

PROTECTION AGAINST LOSS OF INTEGRITY

Hashing is one of the most prevalent methods for ensuring integrity. Simply put, a hash is a number that may be calculated using a hashing algorithm for a file or string of data. The hash will remain the same as long as the data does not change (and the same hash technique is utilized). Today, the two most common hash algorithms are Message Digest 5 (MD5) and Secure Hashing Algorithm 1 (SHA-1).

For example, using the MD5 hash technique, the hash of the word "I Love Security" remains E7F8B292F4F5C2F98E5DF1435EB73D1B. The hash is 2F088A01343CFD65B7BC4EB050503CB7 if the text is slightly edited to "ILiveSecurity" (the "o" is changed to "i"). When you compare the two hashes and observe that they differ, you know that the original data generated by each of the hashes differs.

One application of hashes is in detecting systems that calculate the hashes of crucial files. Then, detection systems check these files to see if the hash is the same. If the hash is altered, the file loses its integrity and is regarded as suspicious. Users can also transmit communications with a digital signature. The hash is computed before the message is sent, and it is sent together with the message. When the message is received, the hash is recalculated and compared to the original hash. If the hashes disagree, the message's integrity has been compromised. Even if a digital signature's primary function is to offer authentication and non-repudiation, it nonetheless safeguards against loss of integrity.

PROTECTION AGAINST LOSS OF AVAILABILITY

Enterprises primarily use backups, redundancy, and defect-tolerant systems to protect against availability loss. Defect tolerance means that a system can fail but tolerate it and continue to function. This is frequently accomplished with redundant systems, such as duplicate disks or redundant servers. Backups ensure that critical data is safeguarded and can be restored if the original data becomes corrupted.

Several levels of defect tolerance and redundancy can be introduced. RAID-1, for example, is a two-disk mirror; if one disk fails, the other disk keeps all of the data. In the event of a disk loss, the RAID-5 (trailer with parity) uses three or more disks plus parity to reconstruct data. The RAID-10 matrix combines the characteristics of a RAID-1 and a RAID-0 matrix.

By configuring servers in a chess group, you can provide redundancy. Failure clusters are made up of two or more nodes (servers inside the cluster), and if one node fails, the remaining nodes can take over. This occurs automatically and has little influence on end users.

If a disaster destroys an entire location, alternative sites can be used. A hot site is up and operating, complete with all of the equipment and data required to take control in an emergency.

A cold site is an empty structure with electricity and running water that must be moved to an alternate location before it can be used. Hot sites are expensive, while cold sites might take a long time to get up and running. A hot site is a cross between a cold site and a hot site.

THE IMPORTANCE OF THE CIA TRIAD

The CIA Triad is the guiding principle for the development of security systems in organizations. The CIA Triad plays a crucial role in keeping information secure against cyber threats and risks. When theft of information or a security breach occurs, it often implies that an organization has failed to implement one or more of these principles in the CIA Triad. It is harmful to an organization when the GDPR (General Data Protection Regulation) is violated.

However, depending on the organization's security priorities, the industry's regulatory requirements, or even the nature of the business the organization is engaged in, one of these principles may prevail over the others.

The availability of information is essential in the e-commerce and health sectors. However, there can be a compromise by giving priority to one of the principles over the others. But overall, organizations need to use the security mentioned above Controls to improve their cybersecurity position.

CHAPTER 6

GRC AND RMF FRAMEWORKS

AN OVERVIEW OF GRC FRAMEWORKS

Global organizations must establish Governance, Risk Management, and Compliance (GRC) frameworks to achieve regulatory compliance. GRC frameworks provide a systematic approach to identifying, controlling, and mitigating operational risks. They assist businesses in generating successful business strategies that adhere to applicable laws and regulations while achieving their goals. GRC frameworks guarantee that businesses follow a variety of standards and regulations, such as SOC2, CMMC, ISO, HIPPA, PCI, and GDPR.

GRC strategies help firms protect themselves against potential losses caused by noncompliance or mismanagement of resources by providing visibility into organizational risk exposure across departments. The ability to track performance indicators in real time enables a more efficient approach to tracking progress toward framework-defined goals. GRC solutions enable executives to make informed decisions about how to best allocate resources for the greatest return. Furthermore, GRC systems allow businesses to anticipate changes in industry trends by enabling proactive monitoring of their environment for any new threats or opportunities that may arise from external sources, such as market shifts or competitor moves.

Organizations must have effective governance structures in place to ensure that their operations function smoothly and without delays owing to insufficient monitoring or control over specific business sectors. Governance defines roles and responsibilities across the organization so that each level understands who is responsible for what task; this enables proper delegation of authority, which eliminates potential conflicts between stakeholders and improves staff cooperation for successful project completion within budgeted and stipulated timeframes.

Risk Management Frameworks provide guidance on how to detect potential risks before they become costly delays, financial losses, a tarnished brand, dissatisfied consumers, and legal ramifications. These frameworks also clarify the procedures for adopting preventative measures to lessen the likelihood of such situations occurring in the first place. This includes, among other things, developing strong internal controls, policies, protocols, and standards to limit the effects of any unforeseen incident.

Compliance Frameworks ensure that government regulations, industry standards, corporate policies, security requirements, and data privacy legislation are followed. Businesses must understand the rules in order to remain compliant; failure to do so may result in penalties, suspensions, or revocations if prompt action is not taken.

Firms may ensure that their regulatory reporting is up to date and in accordance with applicable standards by understanding the value of a governance framework. Transition Sentence for the Following Heading: To achieve this goal, it is critical to understand how multinational corporations build and maintain GRC systems.

GOVERNANCE FRAMEWORKS

Governance frameworks are the rules that govern a corporation's operations. They define how a company is managed, how decisions are made, and how resources are allocated. Governance frameworks guarantee that firms function efficiently and in accordance with applicable rules and regulations. Governance frameworks define the roles, responsibilities, and expectations of all organizational stakeholders.

Governance frameworks increase accountability for decision-making processes by providing clear lines of authority across different levels of management. These frameworks provide visibility into organizational operations, enabling the early discovery of any faults or inconsistencies. Furthermore, these frameworks provide monitoring of financial processes like as budgeting and audits in order to prevent fraud and other unethical behavior.

Existing business governance framework models include ERM, CSR, CAS, ICS, and PMS, each with its own set of goals ranging from cost reduction to service development, ethical behavior promotion, and fraud detection. Each model has its own set of objectives, which may include lowering operating costs, improving customer service standards, encouraging ethical behavior among employees, and preventing fraud within the organization.

ERM, for example, focuses on recognizing risks associated with various aspects of business operations, such as finance or IT security, whereas CAS is in charge of regulatory compliance issues, such as data protection requirements and anti-corruption efforts. Similarly, ICS aims to enhance internal controls over finances through monitoring methods such as segregation of duties, whereas PMS assesses departmental performance using key metrics such as return on investment (ROI) ratios or customer satisfaction scores.

Finally, while making strategic decisions, CSR considers both economic and social ramifications. These may include environmental sustainability projects as well as community outreach programs. All of these models combine to form an effective governance framework for firms looking to comply with industry regulations while boosting profits in an ethical manner.

Frameworks provide businesses with a framework for ensuring legislative and policy compliance, as well as an overview of risk management. To improve the organization's overall risk posture, it is critical to understand how to use various risk management frameworks.

RISK MANAGEMENT FRAMEWORKS

Global organizations require risk management frameworks to discover, assess, and respond to possible threats. A risk management framework is a set of procedures that allows a company to identify, assess, monitor, and minimize operational risks. The framework provides ideas on how to manage risk within the firm's broader governance structure.

The importance of risk management frameworks cannot be overstated since they provide clarity and direction for controlling organizational dangers. These frameworks assist CFOs and other finance leaders in making educated decisions about how to effectively shield their organizations from losses or harm caused by unplanned events by providing a comprehensive method to examining potential risks and their associated ramifications.

Identifying, evaluating, responding to, and minimizing potential risks are the fundamental components of a risk management system. CFOs and other financial professionals must take the lead in implementing a risk management framework, proactively identifying threats, developing mitigation strategies, tracking changes in severity or probability over time, and reporting findings related to mitigation initiatives. They can limit the costs or harm caused by unanticipated events by taking a proactive approach to evaluating the likelihood of specific threats and applying countermeasures. Furthermore, monitoring changes in severity or probability over time is required for evaluating the efficacy of mitigation operations and reporting findings related to those efforts. This thorough plan enables businesses to be more prepared for any situation.

Today, risk management frameworks include qualitative methods such as scenario analysis or Monte Carlo simulations, as well as quantitative methods such as Value at Risk (VaR) assessments, which estimate financial exposure under various scenarios. Other prominent strategies include enterprise-wide models, such as ISO 31000, which is used by many multinational corporations, and industry-specific models, such as Basel III, which was created specifically for financial institutions around the world.

Another popular model is ISO 31000, which outlines how organizations can implement policies that govern their internal procedures for recognizing and assessing risks and vulnerabilities. It then takes the appropriate steps to reduce any identified negative impacts while also boosting positive outcomes whenever possible.

A well-defined risk management system enables risk identification, evaluation, and control. To ensure compliance inside a firm, it is vital to understand the application of several compliance frameworks.

COMPLIANCE FRAMEWORKS

Compliance frameworks are required by global enterprises to ensure that regulatory rules and industry standards are met. A compliance framework outlines the rules, regulations, policies, and procedures that a corporation must follow in order to comply with applicable laws and regulations, as well as evaluate risk management processes and internal controls. It's also used to assess risk management strategies and internal controls.

The importance of compliance frameworks cannot be overstated. Compliance frameworks protect firms against legal responsibility by ensuring that they follow applicable rules and regulations while maintaining their reputation as ethical businesses that follow generally recognized norms of behavior. Compliance frameworks can help businesses manage the risks associated with noncompliance with legal requirements or unethical acts by guiding them on how to address these risks effectively.

Various sorts of compliance frameworks are available depending on the company or sector in which a firm operates. Depending on the industry, there are many regimes, such as FSR, BR, HCR, ER, and DPL. Each category has its own set of regulations that must be followed in order for an organization to remain compliant.

The Data Protection Law is critical; it governs the protection of personal data collected by consumers or clients and stored electronically or otherwise. The recent passage of Europe's General Data Protection Regulation (GDPR) has set a precedent for harsh fines for any breach, even if it is unintentional. Enterprises must have their finger on the pulse of private information protection and data security practices in order to remain competitive and in compliance with regulations.

Compliance frameworks provide businesses with a consistent approach to assuring compliance and managing risk. Firms can develop a compliant, efficient, and operations-optimized system by adopting GRC frameworks.

INTEGRATION OF GRC FRAMEWORKS

Firms can gain various advantages by combining Governance, Risk, and Compliance (GRC) frameworks into a unified system. When GRC frameworks are properly integrated, they create a risk management strategy that protects the company from financial losses and legal issues. Companies can better anticipate potential threats to their operations and take preventative action by leveraging the strengths and weaknesses of each framework.

Integrating GRC frameworks gives firms a more comprehensive view of their operations. It helps users quickly study how various business components interact with one another and how their performance affects one another. Firms can gain insight into potential improvement areas to satisfy regulatory standards or save operating expenses by combining governance procedures with compliance requirements or risk assessments, for example. Furthermore, implementing GRC standards allows executives to easily track the development of crucial activities across multiple organizational areas.

Organizations must consider the appropriate integration of existing systems before installing new GRC solutions. This necessitates the complete replacement of existing systems in some cases, while in others, it necessitates the implementation of adjustments to ensure that all components work together without disrupting current operations or incurring additional maintenance or training costs. Businesses should also verify that any new solutions adhere to industry-standard security standards to guarantee that data remains secure throughout the IT infrastructure's life cycle.

Microsoft Dynamics 365 Compliance Accelerator's integrated GRC architecture integrates Office 365 technologies such as SharePoint Online and Exchange Online with Azure Security Center's enhanced security monitoring capabilities into a holistic package. This solution gives management control over business data privacy laws such as HIPAA/HITECH Act and GDPR/CCPA, among others, for a variety of industries, including healthcare and financial services. Analytics reports provide users with real-time insight into the personal information that is being obtained, saved, shared, or accessed, allowing them to make informed decisions on risk mitigation techniques moving forward without requiring technical skills or programming experience. Governance; Risk Management; Compliance Frameworks; Real-Time Analytics Reporting; Integrated GRC Framework

Integrating all aspects of governance, risk management, and compliance inside a business encourages uniform policy, process, and control implementation and enforcement across all divisions, departments, functions, and roles. Its dedication to transparency, accountability, integrity, dependability, and sustainability results in greater organizational efficiency, profitability, liability reduction, and stronger customer relationships.

GRC frameworks must be integrated into an organization's activities to ensure regulatory compliance and a secure environment. Organizations must be aware of the many issues that may arise while implementing GRC frameworks.

THE DIFFICULTIES OF IMPLEMENTING GRC FRAMEWORKS

For global organizations, implementing a GRC framework can be a hard and time-consuming process. It advocates for the consolidation of various governance, risk management, and compliance systems into a single system. This can provide a number of challenges for CFOs and other finance executives tasked with overseeing GRC projects.

Choosing whether to incorporate old frameworks into the new GRC system is a key challenge. To make an informed decision about which frameworks best fulfill their specific requirements, executives must examine each framework's scope, relevance to their organization's objectives, complexity, costs associated with adoption and maintenance, and so on.

Another challenge is ensuring that all GRC system components are properly linked to the existing IT infrastructure. Organizations must ensure that data flows smoothly across diverse platforms in order to reduce anomalies or errors in the reporting of due diligence requirements. Firms must carefully evaluate the cost and usefulness of various technology solutions before deciding on the best one for their GRC system.

Employees must be trained on how to use GRC systems, including topics such as risk assessment methodology, regulatory changes, proper documentation procedures, data security protocols, audit preparation processes, incident response plans, and so on so that they understand how these tasks relate to the organization's governance, risk management, and compliance objectives. Employers should provide their employees with a wealth of knowledge and crucial skills that will allow them to stay ahead of the curve in order to achieve this goal.

Regardless of the challenges, businesses should consider building GRC frameworks to ensure compliance with global laws and reduce risk. To summarize, knowing the stages required to install a solid GRC system is critical for maximizing its benefits for a business.

GRC ROLES AND RESPONSIBILITIES

A successful GRC program incorporates organizational culture, ethics, and principles. Compliance is about more than simply regulations; it is also about behavior. Professionals at various levels of the firm, such as the chief risk and compliance officer, have become an essential nexus of GRC insight throughout the organization. Let us have a look at a few executive jobs that are commonly regarded by organizations in order to take on the challenge of maintaining world-class GRC programs across the organization:

1. Director of Finance:

Financial reporting, performance management, budgeting, and other financial processes give the CFO a complete understanding of the operations of nearly every business, division, and department inside the organization. Furthermore, because the benefits and possible hazards of managing financial processes and enterprise compliance are relatively comparable, the CFO might give leadership in the areas of company-wide financial compliance and SOX certification.

2. Director of Compliance:

Compliance Managers are responsible for ensuring that the organization has the systems and controls in place to meet the needs of governmental agencies, regulators, and industry mandates such as Anti-Money Laundering, Foreign Corrupt Practices Act, GMP, GLBA, or internal rules. However, as multiple compliance initiatives become more intertwined from both a regulatory and organizational standpoint, Chief Compliance Officers are focusing on effective control rationalization to provide a clear, unambiguous process for compliance management and to provide a single point of reference for the organization.

3. Chief Risk Officer:

The work of risk managers has shifted from controlling a preset set of risk exposures to identifying essential business areas where the company should be willing to retain risks in order to grasp growth opportunities and generate returns for investors. This connects risk management to business performance and shifts risk management from a centralized function to a federated, top-down approach that is centrally aligned with business objectives, with reporting and assessments distributed to lines of business for ownership, execution, and accountability. Chief Risk Officers now manage organizational behavior by controlling risk appetite and risk response.

4. Director of Internal Audit:

Audit Managers are responsible for monitoring risks and ensuring compliance across organizational silos, and the role is expanding into a standalone, horizontal function. This necessitates the development of a unified framework for all sorts of audits - financial, risk, operations, internal, suppliers, and compliance - so that auditing priorities are defined by an enterprise-level risk-based approach rather than departmental and tactical imperatives.

5. Quality Assurance Officer:

Product proliferation, outsourced manufacturing operations, a tough regulatory environment, and stringent customer requirements are driving Quality Managers to manage their quality processes proactively. Quality managers are implementing best practices that need integrated procedures to ensure compliance with internal quality standards and regulations, as well as industry mandates such as TS 16949, ISO 13485, ISO 22000, Six Sigma, and TQM.

6. Director of Information Technology:

With the IT governance and compliance process involving multiple internal and external stakeholders, organizations are increasingly implementing an integrated IT governance framework to ensure information and system integrity, data security and privacy, and compliance with quality mandates such as COBIT, ISO 17799/27002, ITIL, SAS 70, and others.

7. Director of Legal Affairs:

Cultivating a compliance culture and sustaining a high level of integrity among employees are becoming increasingly difficult as a result of increased regulatory supervision and investor activism. Legal counsels assist employees in implementing rules and procedures, adhering to the code of ethics, and adhering to corporate governance principles.

8. Chief Human Resources Officer:

To ensure the effective execution of governance programs, guidelines, monitoring mechanisms, and constant access to information, as well as rigorous training and awareness campaigns on compliance and ethics, are required. Most human resource managers offer an integrated training platform to assure compliance with HR policies and procedures, legislative health and security requirements, and compliance training and certification.

9. Chief Sustainability Officer:

Top sustainability executives are in charge of an organization's environmental, social, and governance components. This includes, among other things, supporting green practices, monitoring environmental impact, and fostering diversity, equity, and inclusion in the workplace. With an increased regulatory focus on ESG, sustainability officers must now remain on top of regulations, assess and report ESG posture using multiple ESG frameworks such as GRI, SASB, and TCFD, and verify compliance.

10. Chief Sourcing Officer:

Third-party risk prediction and prevention is crucial for today's dynamic enterprises that rely heavily on their supplier ecosystem for mission-critical operations. Chief sourcing officers are responsible for monitoring and mitigating new and current supplier risks, as well as controlling costs and accelerating company performance.

EXAMPLES OF GRC FRAMEWORKS

The GRC framework is a collection of tools that assist firms in implementing policies, assessing risks, eliminating silos, and becoming compliant. You can accomplish these goals by utilizing the following basic frameworks:

1. GRC solution:

GRC software is a single integrated program that incorporates essential business operations, risk management, auditing needs, and internal controls. It assists enterprises in methodically managing and implementing GRC-centered functions to unify multiple business operations.

2. User management:

Stakeholders, workers, consultants, and other company colleagues require access to specific tools and files to complete their jobs. These functions require privileged or role-based access control to certain systems. User management aids in the management, control, and monitoring of access authorization in order to keep everyone from accessing more than they need.

3. Virtual CISO Services:

A virtual or vCISO provides remote services on a wide range of security-related duties. It does risk assessments, enhances overall security posture, strategizes policies, and implements controls, among other things. vCISOs collaborate with IT administrators and top management to secure people, data, and the overall infrastructure.

4. Auditing system:

When implementing a GRC framework, it is critical to measure its effectiveness in order to ease compliance evaluation. Audit management tools assist you in mapping usage, monitoring controls, and collecting data. It can be used to determine whether your performance is in line with your objectives.

5. SIEM tools:

SIEM (Security Information and Event Management) tools aid in gaining a full understanding of the information security ecosystem. It gives real-time visibility into breach attempts, generates a log of system events combined from several sources, aids in breach investigation, and warns in the event of an incident. Some SIEM technologies can augment the system's intelligence by drawing correlations between events using historical data.

This discussion on the importance of governance, risk management, and compliance frameworks for multinational organizations concludes that these are critical components for ensuring regulatory compliance. Organizations can ensure that their operations continue to comply with applicable rules by incorporating GRC frameworks into their procedures. Although developing GRC frameworks is critical, understanding the challenges associated with putting them into practice is essential for optimal results.

GRC frameworks necessitate major financial and time investments. They must be tailored to the individual needs of each company and reviewed on a regular basis as regulations change or new threats develop. Furthermore, a lack of understanding among those responsible for implementing GRC rules may result in costly errors or omissions when seeking to comply with regulatory standards.

CFOs and other financial professionals must grasp GRC principles thoroughly in order to properly oversee the execution process and identify areas where further monitoring may be required. Companies will be able to not only comply with current regulations but also predict future changes, helping them stay ahead of the curve in terms of regulatory reporting solutions for international enterprises.

NATIONAL INSTITUTE OF STANDARDS AND TECHNOLOGY (NIST)

The National Institute of Standards and Technology, usually known as the NIST, is a government laboratory in the United States that works to create, test, and promote best practices for federal agencies and other businesses in areas such as online security. The NIST develops metrics, benchmarks, and rules, such as the Federal Information Protection Standard, to assist in increasing the reliability and security of emerging technology. When dealing with confidential government data, all federal institutions are obligated to meet NIST standards in their specialized field. The NIST's standards and regulations are worldwide recognized, which means that any organization that follows the NIST's standards for its business sector can be trusted to adopt the best practices in technology. NIST has developed standards and regulations for a wide range of Science, Technology, Engineering, and Mathematics (STEM) sectors, from astrophysics to cybersecurity.

The NIST cybersecurity framework is a valuable resource for organizing and improving your cybersecurity program. It is a set of standards and best practices designed to assist organizations in developing and improving their cybersecurity posture. The framework proposes a series of suggestions and standards to help companies better prepare for identifying and detecting cyber-attacks, as well as rules for responding to, preventing, and recovering from cyber disasters.

This framework, developed by the National Institute of Standards and Technology (NIST), tackles the absence of standards in cybersecurity by providing a consistent set of rules, guidelines, and standards for enterprises to apply across industries. The National Institute of Standards and Technology (NIST) Cybersecurity Framework (NIST CSF) is widely regarded as the gold standard for developing a cybersecurity program. Whether you're just starting with a cybersecurity program or you already have one in place, the framework may provide value by serving as a top-level security management tool that helps assess cybersecurity risk across the enterprise.

All cybersecurity capabilities, projects, processes, and daily activities are classified into these five fundamental functions by the framework:

1. NIST CSF: Identify

The first function of the framework, NIST, defines the Identify function as the need to "develop the organizational understanding to manage cybersecurity risk to systems, assets, data, and capabilities." The focus is on the business and how it relates to cybersecurity risk, especially taking into account the resources available:

- Asset Management
- Business Environment
- Governance
- Risk Assessment
- Risk Management Strategy

The NIST Identify function establishes the framework for your organization's future cybersecurity operations, determining what exists, what risks are connected with those settings, and how they relate to your business goals.

The successful implementation of the Identify function leads organizations to grasp all assets and environments within the enterprise, define the current and desired states of controls to protect those assets and develop a plan to transition from the current to desired states of security. The result is a clearly defined state of an organization's cybersecurity posture articulated to both technical and business-side stakeholders.

2. NIST CSF: Safeguard

According to NIST, the Framework's key functions are to help an organization express its cybersecurity risk management by organizing information, sharing sensitive information, enabling cybersecurity risk management decisions, addressing threats, and improving by learning from previous activities.

The Framework Core's Protect function is vital since its mission is to define and apply necessary protections to assure critical infrastructure service delivery. The Protect Function assists in limiting or containing the impact of a potential cybersecurity event. Identity Management and Access Control, Awareness and Training, Data Security, Information Security Protection Processes and Procedures, Maintenance, and Protective Technology are examples of result Categories within this Function, according to NIST.

Whereas Identify is mainly concerned with baseline and monitoring, Protect is when the Framework becomes more proactive. The Protect function includes categories including access control, awareness, and training. Two- and multi-factor authentication techniques to manage access to assets and environments, as well as employee training to reduce the risk of accidents and socially engineered breaches, are manifestations of these categories and the Protect function as a whole.

With breaches becoming more regular, implementing correct protocols and policies to decrease the risk of a breach is becoming increasingly important. The framework's Protect function serves as a guide, dictating the outcomes required to achieve that purpose.

3. NIST CSF: Detect

The Detect function necessitates the creation and implementation of the necessary operations to detect the occurrence of a cybersecurity incident.

The Detect function enables the timely discovery of cybersecurity events. Examples of outcome Categories within this Function include Anomalies and Events, Security Continuous Monitoring, and Detection Processes.

Aligning with the framework entails listing all of your actions and labeling them with one of the five function designations. The Identify label, for example, will be for tools that help your inventory assets. However, depending on their capabilities, they would be placed in Detect alongside your IDS and SIEM. Respond contains your issue response tools and playbooks. Recover includes backup and recovery tools.

HISTORY OF THE NIST CYBERSECURITY FRAMEWORK

On February 12, 2013, Executive Order (EO) 13636 — "Improving Critical Infrastructure Cybersecurity" — was issued. This marked the start of NIST's partnership with the private sector in the United States to "identify existing voluntary consensus standards and industry best practices in order to build them into a Cybersecurity Framework." The result of this collaboration was the NIST Cybersecurity Framework Version 1.0.

The 2014 Cybersecurity Enhancement Act (CEA) expanded NIST's efforts to build the Cybersecurity Framework. The NIST CSF is still one of the most extensively used security frameworks across all businesses in the United States today.

NIST FRAMEWORK IMPLEMENTATION TIERS

The framework proposes four implementation tiers to assist private sector firms in measuring their progress toward implementing the NIST Cybersecurity Framework:

> Tier 1 - Partial:

The organization is familiar with the NIST CSF and may have implemented certain controls in certain areas of the infrastructure. The implementation of cybersecurity activities and protocols has been reactive rather than proactive. The organization has a low level of knowledge of cybersecurity issues and does not have the processes or resources in place to enable information security.

> Tier 2 - Risk Informed:

The organization is more aware of cybersecurity concerns and informally exchanges information. It lacks an organization-wide cybersecurity risk management process that is planned, repeatable, and proactive.

> Tier 3 - Replicable:

The firm and its top leaders are aware of cybersecurity threats. They have built a scalable, enterprise-wide cybersecurity risk management strategy. The cybersecurity team has developed an action plan to monitor and respond to intrusions efficiently.

> Tier 4 - Adaptive:

The organization has become cyber resilient, relying on lessons learned and predictive indicators to avert cyberattacks. The cybersecurity team is constantly improving and advancing the organization's cybersecurity technology and procedures, as well as rapidly and efficiently adapting to changes in threats. Risk-informed decision-making, policies, procedures, and processes are used across the enterprise to manage information security risks. Cybersecurity risk management is integrated into budget decisions and organizational culture in adaptive enterprises.

EXAMPLES OF NIST FUNCTIONS AND CATEGORIES INCLUDE THE FOLLOWING:

1. Identify:

In order to protect against cyberattacks, the cybersecurity team must have a complete awareness of the organization's most significant assets and resources. Asset management, business environment, governance, risk assessment, risk management strategy, and supply chain risk management are all categories under the identified function.

2. Protect:

The protect function is responsible for establishing and executing suitable safeguards and protecting vital infrastructure. Identity management and access control, awareness and training, data security, information protection processes and procedures, maintenance, and protective technology are the categories.

3. Detection:

The detect function implements steps that warn a company of a cyberattack. Anomalies and events, continuous security monitoring, and detection processes are among the detection categories.

4. Respond:

The response function categories ensure that cyberattacks and other cybersecurity situations are dealt with appropriately. Response planning, communications, analysis, mitigation, and enhancements are some of the specific areas.

5. Recover:

Recovery actions put cyber resilience strategies into action and provide business continuity in the case of a cyberattack, security breach, or other cybersecurity incident. Recovery functions include recovery planning enhancements and communications.

The NIST CSF's instructive references draw a direct correlation between the functions, categories, and subcategories of other frameworks' specific security measures. These frameworks include the Center for Internet Security (CIS) Controls, COBIT 5, the International Society of Automation (ISA) 62443-2-1:2009, the International Organization for Standardization and the International

Electrotechnical Commission 27001:2013, and the National Institute of Standards and Technology SP 800-53 Rev. 4.

The NIST CSF does not specify how to inventory physical devices and systems or software platforms and applications; instead, it gives a checklist of tasks to be done. An organization can adopt its own way of doing inventory. If a company requires additional assistance, it might look to the instructive references to similar controls in other complementary standards. The CSF allows for a great deal of flexibility in selecting the solutions that best meet an organization's cybersecurity risk management needs.

ESTABLISHING A NIST FRAMEWORK CYBERSECURITY RISK MANAGEMENT PROGRAM

The NIST Cybersecurity Framework provides a step-by-step roadmap for developing or improving an information security risk management program:

1. Prioritize and scope:

Develop a clear picture of the project's scope and priorities. Establish high-level business or mission objectives, business demands, and the organization's risk tolerance.

2. Orient:

Inventory the organization's assets and systems, as well as identify applicable legislation, risk management strategies, and risks to which the firm may be exposed.

3. Create a current profile:

A current profile is a snapshot of how the organization is currently managing risk, as described by the CSF's categories and subcategories.

4. Conduct a risk assessment:

Assess the operational environment, emerging hazards, and cybersecurity threat information to estimate the likelihood and severity of a cybersecurity event affecting the firm.

5. Create a target profile:

A target profile describes the information security team's risk management goal.

6. Determine, assess, and prioritize gaps:

By identifying the gaps between the current and target profiles, the information security team can develop an action plan that includes measurable milestones as well as the resources (people, funding, and time) needed to address these gaps.

INTERNATIONAL ORGANIZATION FOR STANDARDIZATION (ISO)

In today's hyperconnected, data-driven world, cybersecurity is a top priority for individuals, businesses, and governments alike. The International Organization for Standardization (ISO) has established a portfolio of cybersecurity standards to provide enterprises with a methodical approach to protecting sensitive data and establishing digital resilience in response to the ever-changing dangers in cyberspace. This extensive article delves into the realm of ISO standards for cybersecurity, providing a thorough explanation of its significance, major standards, and role in protecting information in the digital age.

What is ISO (International Organization for Standardization)?

The International Organization for Standardization (ISO) is a non-governmental organization that develops and publishes a wide range of proprietary, industrial, and commercial standards. It is made up of representatives from various national standardization organizations.

The organization's abbreviated name, ISO, is not an acronym; it is derived from the ancient Greek word isos, which means equal or equivalent; because the organization will have multiple acronyms in different languages, the founders chose the abbreviation ISO.

UNDERSTANDING THE INTERNATIONAL ORGANIZATION FOR STANDARDIZATION (ISO)

The International Organization for Standardization was established in 1947 and is based in Geneva, Switzerland. The International Federation of National Standardization Associations (ISA) was founded in the 1920s. Following the suspension of the International Organization for

Standardization (ISO) during World War II, the United Nations Committee for the Coordination of Standards (UNCCC) recommended a new global standardization agency, and the International Organization for Standardization was founded.

ISO is present in 167 countries. The organization's members are the primary standardization organizations in their respective countries; each country has only one member. While individuals cannot become ISO members, industry professionals can engage with ISO in a variety of ways. The ISO General Assembly is held once a year to debate the organization's strategic aims. There is also a 20-person board of directors with rotating members that provide counsel and governance for the company.

THE HISTORICAL DEVELOPMENT OF ISO

Following WWII, worldwide standards were required to be established to ensure that products and services were safe, reliable, and of high quality across national borders. This is why, in 1946, ISA and the United Nations Coordinating Committee on Standards (UNCEN) joined forces to explore mutual goals, and the first standard was released in 1951 (ISO/RA:1951).

Since then, the ISO has produced an increasing number of standards, and there are now over 22,000 in total. They include all elements of business and technology, and for many in the B2B industry, they serve as a guideline for selecting suppliers and business partners. ISO is a powerful player with a substantial influence on standardization and quality assurance in several industries after more than 75 years.

WHAT IS THE SIGNIFICANCE OF ISO STANDARDS?

An organization must specify the objectives, needs, and processes connected to its operations in order to establish an effective and quality-oriented management system. International standards aid in the definition of product, service, and continuing maintenance specifications. However, in addition to assisting in the management of this activity, ISO standards can contribute to a number of other areas that offer value to your firm.

1. Establish a structure for compliance work:

Some ISO standards serve as milestones, while others serve as completion directions. As a result, don't expect ISO standards to provide specific requirements or extensive descriptions of how your business should use a standard from A to Z. ISO standards, on the other hand, can help establish the framework for an organization's activities, making it easier to develop a targeted plan.

2. Reduce risks:

Working more effectively with hazards is another underlying benefit of standardizing your procedures. When you have complete control over your operations and understand all of the risks, your firm will be able to effectively manage them and implement mitigation plans. When issues develop, your organization will be better prepared to meet and overcome all challenges.

3. Encourage a compliance culture:

Implementing an ISO standard can improve the quality of your organization's operations and foster an internal compliance culture that will benefit your staff and their everyday jobs. Setting goals and procedures allows management and employees to better focus and keep an eye on what is important. It is easy to lose concentration during a hectic day of work and multitasking.
Increase your profits.

4. Increase your profitability:

An ISO certification can also boost an organization's profit potential. Both in the form of advertising and, for example, in the framework of public sector tenders. ISO accreditation is frequently required in this industry. Many larger firms seek quality certification from their vendors. So, if you want to increase your market share, you should research what standards are in demand in your business. Certification is particularly advantageous if your company plans to enter new markets in other countries since it ensures the interoperability of goods and services across national borders.

5. Strengthen the reputation of your organization:

ISO standards can help your organization improve the efficiency of your organization's operations while enhancing the credibility of your products and services, as they will continuously meet your customers' expectations. This will strengthen your customers' loyalty and help build a strong long-term reputation.

WHAT ARE THE RELEVANT ISO STANDARDS FOR GRC?

Various ISO standards address governance risk and compliance (GRC). Some of the ISO standards that provide guidance and guidance for the GRC include:

- ISO 20000 (Service Management)

- ISO 22301 (Business Continuity)

- ISO 27001 (Information Security)

- ISO 27005 (Information Risk Management)

- ISO 31000 (Risk Management)

- ISO 31700-1:2023 (Privacy by Design for consumer goods and services)

> ISO 38500 (Corporate Governance of Information Technology)

Companies can use a hybrid management system, where they combine several standards and frameworks to create a solution that meets the requirements of organizational stakeholders.

TYPES OF ISO STANDARDS

Each ISO standard can be classified into the following categories:

1. ISO 9000-Quality Management:

The ISO 9000 standard is internationally recognized as the best practice for quality management. It defines the criteria for a quality management system to help companies improve quality and customer relationships. A standard is a set of tools and practices that companies can use to identify areas of improvement.

2. ISO/IEC 27000 Information Security Management Systems:

ISO/IEC 27000 sets standards to protect information assets. Companies that manage customer personal, financial, intellectual property, or sensitive data can use these standards to ensure that their information is protected at all times.

3. ISO 31000-Risk Management:

Every business decision involves a certain risk. ISO 31000 provides a framework for managing these risks by applying best practices to identify risks and manage their consequences.

WHAT ARE THE MOST USEFUL ISO STANDARDS?

The most popular ISO standards are listed below;

- ISO 9001:

As mentioned above, it is a standard for the establishment, implementation, and maintenance of a quality management system (QMS) for any enterprise, regardless of its business sector, capital, or size.

- ISO 14001:

This ISO standard provides guidelines on the implementation of an environmental management system (EMS). The requirements of ISO 14001 provide you with a framework and guidelines for creating EMS for any organization.

- ISO 27001:

This ISO standard is intended for information security. Organizations that meet these requirements can be certified by an accredited certification body after successfully being audited.

- ISO 22000:

This standard details the requirements of a food security management system (FSMS). Compliance with this standard enables an organization in the food services industry (directly or directly) to demonstrate that it follows best practices in security and hygiene.

- ISO 50001:

ISO 50001 is a voluntary standard that provides organizations with a framework for managing and improving their energy performance. It deals with the measurement, documentation, and reporting of energy use and consumption. In addition, ISO 50001 includes best practices for designing and purchasing energy-intensive equipment as well as other factors affecting energy performance that organizations can monitor and influence.

- ISO 31000:

It is a risk management standard that contains principles for safe risk management. Implementation of ISO 31000 facilitates safe business operations and helps organizations reach their goals, identify opportunities and threats, and allocate resources for risk management.

- ISO 26000:

A relatively new standard, ISO 26000 emphasizes social responsibility. It provides companies with guidance on how to work socially competently by explaining their social duty. It also provides advice on how to pursue the activities identified with the objectives of corporate social responsibility.

- ISO 31700-1:2023:

This is the most recent ISO standard, which was published in January 2023. It prioritizes privacy in consumer goods and service design, establishing high-level requirements to protect consumer privacy throughout their interactions with your product.

RELATIONSHIP BETWEEN GRC AND ISO 27001

GRC and ISO 27001 certification have a synergistic and aligned relationship because the two frameworks share common goals:

- Risk Assessment and Management:

Both the GRC and ISO 27001 stress the necessity of risk assessment and management. The GRC risk management component can assist enterprises in identifying information security risks, which is required for ISO 27001 compliance.

- Compliance:

ISO 27001 is a widely recognized standard for ensuring information security compliance. By incorporating ISO 27001 into a CRM framework, an organization's information security procedures are aligned with compliance requirements, lowering the risk of noncompliance.

- Governance:

The GRC encourages good governance practices, which are critical for the success of ISO 27001 implementation. To manage information security, clear roles and responsibilities, documented policies, and effective decision-making frameworks are required.

- Documentation and Reporting:

GRC and ISO 27001 place a strong emphasis on documentation and reporting. GRC technologies can aid in the automation of the documentation and reporting processes required for

- ISO 27001 certification:

Continuous monitoring and improvement: ISO 27001's emphasis on continuous improvement aligns with the CRR framework, which promotes continual evaluation and adjustment of risk management and compliance efforts.

ADVANTAGES OF ISO STANDARDS FOR CYBERSECURITY

In today's digital environment, organizations must prioritize cybersecurity to secure the security of their data and, ultimately, their business. However, laws and compliance may be burdensome for businesses of all sizes. The International Organization for Standardization (ISO) provides a framework that can aid in ISO 27001 cybersecurity compliance. In this blog, we will discuss the key benefits of ISO 27001:2022 and why it should be the cybersecurity standard you use.

1. Risk administration:

The necessity of risk management is emphasized in ISO 27001:2022. It assists companies in identifying, evaluating, and managing risks through the implementation of security measures that can reduce or eliminate possible threats, thereby minimizing vulnerabilities. Companies can build a thorough security strategy that describes the procedures and steps they must follow to protect their data using the principles of ISO 27001:2022.

2. Increased credibility:

The ISO 27001:2022 accreditation demonstrates your organization's dedication to cybersecurity. You can apply for certification from an appropriate certification authority once your processes have been aligned with ISO 27001:2022. Certification can help you strengthen your reputation with consumers, regulators, partners, investors, and internal stakeholders by instilling trust in your business.

3. Financial savings:

Cybersecurity threats are on the rise. Companies that have been the victims of a cyberattack risk losing revenue as well as the trust of their clients and customers. Companies can lower the likelihood of a security event by using the practices defined in ISO 27001:2022. As a result, they save money on downtime, computer repairs, cybersecurity experts, and reputation damage.

4. Compliance with Regulations:

Another significant benefit of ISO 27001:2022 is its interoperability with various rules and standards. Companies that utilize this standard match their cybersecurity processes with the standard, making it easier to comply with other requirements like the GDPR or NIST Cybersecurity. ISO 27001:2022 also contributes to ensuring compliance in highly regulated industries such as finance and healthcare.

5. Enhancement of overall security posture:

The final and most critical benefit of ISO 27001:2022 is improved security posture. Companies that comply with this worldwide standard will be better able to identify threats, strengthen security, and manage risks. They will also be able to respond to cyber incidents with confidence, safeguarding their reputation and financial situation.

CHALLENGES AND CONSIDERATIONS

A. Implementation Difficulties:

Adoption of ISO standards may present problems in terms of resource allocation, training, and organizational culture shifts.

B. Ongoing Maintenance:

ISO standards necessitate continuing monitoring, assessment, and improvement. Maintaining compliance can be time-consuming and expensive.

C. Evolving Threat Landscape:

Cyber risks and legislation are always changing. To keep up with emerging risks and requirements, organizations must remain adaptable.

ISO STANDARDS AND CYBERSECURITY

Cybersecurity is booming nowadays because of the increasing number of security events and attacks on information and IT systems that organizations are experiencing; the necessity for controls to ensure the security of devices, communication networks, and information assets is unquestionable. The concept of cybersecurity sprang from this requirement.

The goal of these attacks is to gain access to, alter, or delete sensitive information belonging to organizations.

Implementing effective cybersecurity measures is difficult because cybercriminals continuously find new ways to carry out their assaults due to the large number of equipment and technology used. However, there is a method of applying data and information security measures that makes the process of implementing these IT security measures more straightforward and natural.

These are the ISO cybersecurity and information security standards and regulations. The International Standards

Organization (ISO) creates and publishes ISO standards. ISO and the IEC (International Electrotechnical Commission) are the world's foremost standards experts. They develop worldwide standards to standardize specific processes in areas such as information security through technical committees comprised of ISO and IEC member organizations.

Today, these standards are an essential component of organizations' compliance processes, providing them with a reputation and international recognition. The added value that ISO standards implementation provides organizations over their competitors is due to the fact that these certified standards are reviewed and audited on a regular basis to ensure compliance, which significantly improves the organization's standing in the eyes of stakeholders such as clients and shareholders.

ISO standards are sequentially numbered according to the area they handle and are classified into families, which combine those that deal with comparable concerns together. The goal of these standards and regulations is to specify procedures, policies, guidelines, skill development, and so on in relation to the subject matter (security, continuity, and quality, for example).

ADVANTAGES OF ISO CERTIFICATION

According to The ISO Survey of Management System Standard Certifications, the total number of valid ISO certificates worldwide in 2022 will be 71,549, indicating global acceptance of its significance.

The following are the primary advantages of ISO certification:

ISO certifications provide professionals with a thorough understanding of security principles, risk management, and compliance. As a result, individuals can deal with various challenges more successfully.

- Career Advancement:

Obtaining ISO certification improves a professional's marketability and career prospects greatly. It distinguishes them as information security professionals, distinguishing them from their colleagues. This qualification allows you to advance to higher-level positions, take on leadership roles, and pursue exciting career prospects.

- Higher Earning Potential:

In the information security sector, certified experts frequently attract higher compensation. Employers strongly value the particular knowledge and abilities earned through this qualification. Organizations understand the value brought by trained individuals and are prepared to invest in their skills.

- Global Recognition:

Because ISO certification is globally recognized, individuals can collaborate on a variety of projects with firms all over the world. It broadens their professional experience by exposing them to new cultures, business methods, and cybersecurity issues, making their jobs more dynamic and global in nature.

- Demonstrated Commitment to Security:

ISO certification demonstrates a professional's commitment to information security. It displays their dedication to maintaining the highest levels of data security and confidentiality. This commitment is highly valued by firms wanting to improve their security posture and safeguard critical data.

- Improved Problem-Solving Skills:

Real-world scenarios and case studies are frequently used in the certification process. Such methods assist professionals in learning to successfully assess and solve complex security problems, as well as developing abilities that will be important in future leadership positions.

- Expansion of Network:

Pursuing ISO certification exposes professionals to a network of like-minded individuals and subject matter experts. This network can be a useful resource for exchanging expertise, collaborating, and staying up to date on industry trends and best practices.

In a competitive work environment, ISO certification distinguishes professionals from non-certified individuals. It is a reliable sign of their knowledge and commitment to information security.

SERVICE ORGANIZATION CONTROL 2 (SOC 2)

SOC 2 is an abbreviation for a number of things, including a report that can be provided to third parties to demonstrate a sound control environment, an audit performed by a third-party auditor to provide this report, and the controls and "framework" of controls that allow an organization to obtain a SOC 2 report.

According to the AICPA, SOC 2 is a "report on the controls of a service organization regarding security, availability, integrity of processing, confidentiality, or privacy." The American Institute of Certified Public Accountants (AICPA) created the SOC 2 Framework, which is the most extensively utilized voluntary cybersecurity certification by service firms with clients, partners, and other stakeholders, primarily in the United States.

To obtain a SOC 2 report, an organization must be audited by a third of its system and organizational Controls, providing these auditors with evidence and documentation to demonstrate that internal auditors are adequately represented by management, which is a long way of saying that third-party auditors ensure that companies seeking a SOC2 certification are discussing their security Controls. To prepare for a SOC 2 audit, a business must implement policies, procedures, and controls that meet the SOC 2 standards. Although the American Institute of CPAs (AICPA) does not perform SOC 2 audits, they do provide advice on the criteria that a corporation must meet in order to meet SOC 2 regulations. To prepare for an external audit, an organization may need to establish and implement access controls, data protection controls, and internal audits during the implementation process.

The benefits of an unqualified SOC 2 report are numerous, depending on the type of SOC2 report (there are two versions), and include:

Justifying diligence or security questionnaire efforts:

Many clients, partners, and stakeholders would rather read a SOC 2 report than provide customized responses to diligence or security questionnaires.

Increase consumer, partner, and stakeholder trust.

Certification of sound internal control design and/or operational performance:

ISO 27001, which has significant overlap with the SOC 2 criteria, is widely used globally and was developed by the International Organization for Standardization (ISO) to address a comparable need.

SOC 2 FRAMEWORK

The SOC 2 framework is intended for use by all sorts of service organizations and is particularly popular among SaaS firms. As a result, the criteria provide flexibility in how they might be applied and hence confirmed. Unlike more stringent cybersecurity frameworks, SOC 2 allows the service organization to determine how its cyber-security measures are implemented, as long as they match the desired requirements and are suitably risk-focused.

SOC 2 is closely linked with the 17 COSO framework principles issued in 2013. It bases several common trust services criteria on these concepts, which are discussed in the next section.

In the United States, SOC 2 has become the de facto norm for service organizations that certify the quality of their service controls. Service firms who want to do business with customers in the United States understand that obtaining the SOC 2 certification is now required in order to get new business and/or preserve a current business.

WHAT ARE THE SOC 2 PREREQUISITES?

SOC 2 has five trust service characteristics:

- Security (common criteria)
- Availability
- Processing integrity
- Confidentiality
- Privacy

Each SOC 2 report begins with the Security Trust Services Criteria, which means that each SOC 2 will have common criteria in the security category. Depending on its business nature, organizational objectives, or the needs of its clients or partners, each organization can then opt to add one of the four remaining Trust Services (TSC) criteria: availability, confidentiality, integrity of processing, and/or privacy.

Each of the five categories has a distinct emphasis:

1. Security (common criteria):

Information and systems are protected from unauthorized access, unauthorized disclosure of information, and system damage that could jeopardize the availability, integrity, confidentiality, and privacy of information or systems and impair the entity's ability to achieve its goals. Security is the foundation of every SOC 2 report and will be covered in all SOC 2 reports. Organizations can opt to have only security Controls reviewed. The Security TSI would cover controls such as firewall and configuration management, supplier management, identity, access, and authentication management, and, if applicable, data security and data center control.

2. Availability:

Information and systems are available to operate and be used to achieve the entity's goals. Recovery Controls, service level agreements, and capacity planning are prioritized in reviews that contain availability requirements.

The processing integrity: the system's processing is complete, valid, accurate, timely, and approved in relation to the entity's objectives. The processing integrity requirements concentrate on data inputs and outputs, data quality, data processing schedule, and reporting.

3. Confidentiality:

Information labeled as confidential is safeguarded for the entity's objectives. Confidentiality is the SCT inspecting and erasing confidential information by a firm. A corporation can classify several sorts of data as confidential, including customer data, sensitive data, intellectual property, and contracts, among others.

Personal information is gathered, utilized, kept, disclosed, and deleted in accordance with the entity's purposes. Confidentiality expressly refers to personal information, i.e., interactions with real people and their identities. Personal information might include HIPAA-protected data, personally identifiable information (PII), and other sorts of sensitive data about a person. These criteria, which heavily overlap with HIPAA and other privacy-related frameworks and principles, can assist firms in demonstrating their commitment to privacy. The confidentiality criteria, in essence, need controls surrounding data breaches and incident notification.

PRINCIPLES OF SOC 2

Unlike other compliance frameworks, which have a set of predefined conditions for all enterprises, SOC 2 requirements are different for each organization. Depending on their own operating patterns, each organization must formulate its own security controls in order to comply with the Five Trust Principles.

- Security:

In general, the principle of security applies to the protection of data and systems against unauthorized access. For this purpose, you may need to implement some form of access control, for example, access control lists or identity management systems.

You may also need to strengthen your firewalls by introducing stricter rules for outputs and inputs, introducing intrusion detection and retrieval systems, and applying multi-factor authentication.

- Confidentiality:

Data is considered confidential if only a specific group of people has access to it. This can include the application's source code, usernames and passwords, credit card information, business plans, etc.

To comply with this principle, confidential data must be encrypted, both at rest and during transit. In addition, while providing access to confidential data, adhere to the least privileged principle, i.e., grant the minimum permissions and rights that people need to do their work.

- Availability:

Systems must always comply with availability SLAs. This requires building systems that are inherent in defect tolerance and that do not collapse under a high load. It also requires organizations to invest in network monitoring systems and implement disaster recovery plans.

- Privacy:

The collection, storage, processing, and disclosure of any personally identifiable information (PII) must comply with the organization's data use and privacy policy, as well as the terms set out by the AICPA in the Generally Accepted Principles of Privacy (GAPP).

PII is any information that can be used to identify only an individual, e.g., name, age, telephone number, credit card information, social security numbers, etc. An organization must implement strict controls to protect personal data from unauthorized access.

- Processing Integrity:

All systems must always operate according to their design, free of delays, vulnerabilities, errors, or bugs. Quality assurance and performance monitoring applications and procedures are essential to achieving adherence to this principle.

SOC RISK ASSESSMENT STEPS

Understanding SOC 2 risk assessment in five critical steps is essential to an organization's risk management plan. The first step in the SOC 2 risk assessment process is to identify potential risks that may lead to data breaches or fraud.

1. Determine your business goals:

Establishing your business goals is a crucial step in the SOC 2 risk assessment process. Understanding and communicating your business goals ensures that your risk management efforts align with your company's priorities and future direction. An effective audit process begins with the identification of these business objectives.

An essential part of the audit process is to assess how these objectives influence decision-making within your organization. This is important when considering the risks inherent in the processing of sensitive information. The I.S. Partners team supports companies in discovering the potential risks associated with achieving their business goals.

Identifying your team's involvement in risk management is also part of the process. The involvement of a team is critical because it allows the team to fully comprehend business objectives and potential dangers. Additional research on these roles aids in the successful implementation of SOC 2 controls. This procedure ensures that the overall security of your company's information is not jeopardized while pursuing strategic objectives.

2. Identify important systems:

It is critical to identify the important systems that support your business goals while managing the SOC 2 risk assessment. These systems frequently comprise hardware, software, networks, and other technological components that are critical to your operations.

Determining where your company's vulnerabilities are or whether your current controls are robust enough to withstand possible attacks requires a thorough grasp of your systems. This is equally important when dealing with an audit. Identifying and protecting essential systems from hazards aids in the smooth running of audits and strengthens your overall security framework.

A thorough audit identifies areas where existing control mechanisms must be tweaked for optimal system operation. Remember that system control is a continuous endeavor to ensure that your organization's security systems are robust, efficient, and adaptable to ever-changing cyber threats.

3. Conduct a risk assessment:

A thorough risk analysis is required as part of the SOC 2 risk assessment procedure, It helps uncover potential threats that may harm your essential systems. Conducting a complete risk analysis frequently necessitates the acquisition of specialized skills in order to assess, appraise, and manage risks appropriately. Critical information such as the nature of the risk, its influence on your business goals, and the best mitigation solutions for each identified risk are often evaluated throughout the risk analysis.

An audit can provide a more sophisticated framework for this investigation. Auditing is a continual process of risk assessment and proactive management, not a one-time event. The audit results provide information on areas that require improvement. They also aid in determining the effectiveness of risk management measures. As a result, risk analysis, backed up by extensive audits, should be a critical component of your entire SOC 2 risk assessment plan.

4. Document Risk Responses:

In the field of cybersecurity, risk response documentation is critical for SOC 2 risk assessment and is a critical component of achieving security compliance after completing a risk analysis and finding vulnerabilities in your important systems. This entails devising a strategy for dealing with each potential hazard and documenting it in a complete report.

This approach strives to identify and apply effective controls that reduce the identified risks to a tolerable level based on your organization's management and stakeholders' risk appetite. The complete report ensures that responsibilities and actions are clearly communicated, which contributes to good risk management.

This documentation will then be an essential component of the audit process since it will assist external auditors in determining the efficacy of security measures in meeting your business objectives. Proper documentation of risk responses is crucial for providing information and establishing a solid framework for future threat management and mitigation.

5. Keep consistency:

The fifth and final element of this SOC 2 risk assessment process is consistent maintenance. It is critical to regularly assess and manage the risks that may alter your system's needs and impact compliance. Consistency necessitates a commitment to regular audits, process monitoring, and policy reviews.

In the middle of the scaling image of information dangers, this keeps relevant and effective controls. The frequency of audits should be determined by the level of risk and the type of systems involved. Less evident but vital feedback from these audits must be included in the processes to ensure the program's effectiveness. Participation in regular audits also aids in the early detection and control of potential risk factors.

A risk assessment method that is aligned with an effective risk management system will boost your organization's resilience to threats and SOC 2 compliance.

IMPORTANCE OF SOC 2 FRAMEWORK FOR ORGANIZATIONS

The following are the advantages of implementing the SOC 2 framework:

- Security:

SOC 2 provides a rigorous and established methodology for validating an organization's security controls and processes against industry best practices.

- Trust:

SOC 2 certification has a high degree of credibility in the industry because it establishes a high-quality requirement. SOC 2 accreditation helps boost the trust of all stakeholders and regulators involved in an organization's security and privacy procedures.

- Compliance:

Complex compliance and the frequent updating of legislation are corporations' greatest fears. The SOC 2 framework comes to the rescue because it already complies with the E.U. General Data Protection Regulation (GDPR), the California Consumer Privacy Act (CCPA), ISO 27001, HIPAA, and a slew of other regulations. Indeed, SOC 2 establishes the gold standard for compliance.

- Risk management:

The AICPA SOC 2 framework assists enterprises in identifying, mitigating, and improving their overall security vision.

- Continuous enhancement:

It encourages firms to continuously enhance and upgrade their security and privacy procedures in order to fulfill industry regulations and standards.

WHAT DOES THE SOC 2 FRAMEWORK ENTAIL?

The SOC 2 framework incorporates five trust principles: security, availability, processing integrity, confidentiality, and privacy. Each of these criteria focuses on a different aspect of information security that your program should support.

Each item defines a set of compliance objectives that your firm must achieve through its own controls in order to comply with the SOC 2 framework.

1. Security:

The SOC 2 framework is based on the security principle, which mandates companies to create effective controls to safeguard their systems and data from unauthorized access, use, disclosure, modification, or destruction. The security concept encompasses a wide range of security issues, including access controls, network security, data encryption, and incident response.

2. Access controls:

Access controls are implemented to ensure that only authorized users have access to systems and data in order to conduct the necessary actions. This includes implementing role-based access limits, multi-factor authentication, and password resets on a regular basis. Access restrictions can also be used to track and audit user activities as well as detect potential security incidents.

3. Network security:

Network security is one of the most essential components in the SOC2 framework. To prevent security breaches, firms must secure their networks from unwanted access, attacks, and data theft by using firewalls, intrusion detection systems, and network segmentation.

4. Data encryption:

According to a report on global encryption trends, the majority of survey participants (corporate organizations) ranked customer data as the top priority for encrypting. In 2021, however, only 42% of respondents employed data encryption to protect client data.

To secure sensitive data from unwanted access and theft, organizations must encrypt it both at rest and in transit.

Implementing encrypting methods such as the Advanced Encryption Standard (AES) to discard sensitive information is a good example of data encryption procedures.

5. Incident response:

Unexpected events can completely devastate a company. Having a plan in place to respond promptly to security incidents and mitigate damage, if required, can save a company millions of dollars in the event of a disaster. It is made up of the following parts:

- Regular mock drills and testing,
- Well-defined incident response plan, and
- Having the right tools and processes to detect and respond to security incidents and breaches.

6. Availability:

The SOC 2 framework's availability principle demands companies ensure that their systems and data are available to authorized users when they need them.

In today's fast-paced environment, unavailability concerns like service outages, data loss, and poor system performance can undo years of hard work. Disaster recovery and business continuity plans can reduce the effect of outages and ensure availability in all circumstances.

7. Disaster relief:

Disaster recovery strategies are critical for ensuring system and data availability in the case of an accident or natural disaster. Identify important systems and data to recover in the case of a disaster and design a plan to restore them.

8. Business continuity:

SOC 2 requires the identification of alternate data sources and systems, as well as the establishment of protocols for their use in the case of failure.

9. Processing integrity:

Processing integrity is a major element of the SOC 2 framework, which requires enterprises to verify that their systems properly process and maintain data in compliance with the SOC 2 processing rules.

Having controls in place improves data processing accuracy and integrity. Implementing data validation and reconciliation mechanisms and performing routine data quality checks are two ways to achieve process integrity.

Procedures for data verification and reconciliation

Consider the following to evaluate the accuracy of the data entered into the systems:

- Integrate data validation standards,

- Conduct data quality Controls and reconcile data with external data sources like spreadsheets.

- Data quality evaluations

Data quality assessments include:

- Performing data audits,

- Evaluating data completeness and accuracy, and

- Conducting data profiling and trend analysis.

10. Confidentiality:

According to the SOC 2 AICPA framework's privacy principle, companies must have rules and processes in place, such as adopting data access controls, data encryption, and data categorization policies, to ensure that confidential information is not divulged to unauthorized persons.

Data access controls to ensure data confidentiality include:

- Role-based access controls are being implemented,

- Multi-factor authentication

Encryption of data:

To maintain the security of encrypted data in compliance with the AICPA SOC 2 framework, encryption measures include the use of encryption algorithms such as the Advanced Encrypting Standard (AES) and key secure management techniques.

Data categorization:

Organizations should categorize their data based on its sensitivity and implement appropriate level controls, which include:

- Data retention policies must be implemented

- Procedures for data backup and disaster recovery, and

- Policies for data destruction

11. Privacy:

Organizations must acquire, use, and disclose personal information in line with their privacy policies and applicable laws and regulations under the concept of secrecy.

Simply put, to maintain the confidentiality of personal information by completing risk assessments and privacy impact assessments on a regular basis,

12. Regular risk assessments:

Regular risk assessments are an integral component of the SOC 2 framework to preserve the confidentiality of personal information. To avoid unforeseen occurrences, organizations must regularly assess the risks connected with their privacy procedures and find areas for improvement.

13. Privacy impact assessments:

The AICPA SOC 2 standard requires firms to conduct frequent privacy impact assessments to identify any threats or weaknesses.

HOW DOES A COMPANY DEMONSTRATE ONGOING COMPLIANCE WITH THE SOC 2 FRAMEWORK?

1. SOC 2 audit scope and goal determination:

The scope and objectives of the SOC 2 audit framework are defined as the first step in its preparation. SOC 2 audit reports consider the SOC's infrastructure, data, people, risk management policies, and technologies, to mention a few. In each of these categories, you must decide who and what should be audited.

Furthermore, selecting your scope necessitates a choice between type 1 and type 2 SOC ratios. Switch to Type 1 if you are more concerned with well-designed controls and wish to save resources.

Choose Type 2 if the quality of your real-world Controls is more important to you. Furthermore, clients frequently prefer type 2 reports due to their stricter harshness.

2. Select your reliable service criteria:

SOC 2 audits assess your Controls against the five trust service criteria outlined in the SOC 2 compliance requirements:

Security: You must safeguard information and systems against unauthorized access or data misuse.

Availability: Your systems and data must always be available.

Process Integrity: Your systems must perform functions accurately in order to meet the aims of your organization.

Confidentiality: Take the utmost caution while dealing with non-personally identifiable information and data.

Privacy: Make certain that sensitive information, such as personally identifiable information (PII), is kept secure.

3. Conduct a preliminary preparation assessment:

A preparation assessment is similar to a practical version of the present SOC 2 framework audit. If you know how, you can do it yourself, but hiring an auditor is usually the best option for getting an unbiased point of view.

The CFA or auditor examines all systems, processes, and controls, documents all important processes, and then writes a management letter outlining any flaws or shortfalls discovered, as well as recommendations.

The initial evaluation of the SOC 2 preparation will assist you in identifying areas for improvement and will give you an indication of the overall audit.

4. Conduct a gap analysis and close each one:

Before the actual audit, you should do an in-depth gap analysis to analyze your existing situation and then resolve concerns that meet SOC 2 compliance guidelines.

It may take several months to analyze and repair the flaws. Among the actions you may identify as important in your gap analysis are:

- Implement controls
- Interviewing employees
- Training employees on Controls
- Create and update control documentation
- Modify workflows

You can even outsource your gap analysis, as with your preparedness assessment, to another organization that specializes in the SOC 2 audit process. It may be costly, but it can save you time and give you specialist support.

5. Conduct a final preparedness evaluation:

Consider doing a final availability assessment to detect and address risks after closing the gaps between your organization's present status and SOC 2 compliance.

After you've addressed all of the issues in your trust services criterion, opt for a formal SOC 2 examination.

IMPORTANCE OF SOC 2 COMPLIANCE

Outsourcing, and thus third-party and fourth-party risk, has never been more prevalent. Every company outsources elements of its business frequently to many vendors. These suppliers then subcontract a portion of their business to other vendors.

This is why SOC 2, third-party risk management, vendor risk management, and robust security policies in general are so vital. Vendor risk must be carefully handled through vendor surveys, security evaluations, and industry benchmarking.

The most crucial thing to grasp is that customers don't care if data breaches and leaks are the result of your mishandling of their data or the mismanagement of your provider. They are concerned that their information was disclosed or sold on the dark web. Consider incorporating SOC 2 compliance into your information security policy and risk assessment process.

One technique to assess whether your vendors are using safe data protection and data processing protocols is to meet SOC 2 compliance criteria. Consider investing in a platform that can automatically monitor your vendors' security performance and automate security questionnaires in addition to looking for SOC 2 compliance. Better yet, look for a CVE-compliant tool. Also, seek shared evaluations that allow your business to acquire a thorough report on your service provider's controls and validate the facts in the report.

Digital forensics will not always provide meaningful information, and even if it does, policing cyber intrusions can be difficult due to their scattered nature. It is considerably preferable to avoid a data breach than to attempt to clean it up after it has occurred. Many firms have discovered that once data is exposed, it can be impossible to recover.

CMMC (CYBERSECURITY MATURITY MODEL CERTIFICATION)

The Department of Defense's (DoD) most recent verification approach is the Cybersecurity Maturity Model Certification (CMMC). This certification is the Department's first attempt to establish explicit cybersecurity criteria for contractors. The CMMC's ultimate purpose is to deploy an acceptable level of cybersecurity across the military-industrial base's (DIB) supply chain. The DIB supply chain involves over 300,000 companies, all of which are required by the CMMC to secure unclassified information (CUI).

The US Department of Defense (DoD) regards information security as a fundamental requirement for the Defense Industrial Base (DIB) supply chain. As a result, commencing in late 2021, the US DoD is committed to developing and requiring a consolidated Cybersecurity standard to specify required security practices and controls within the DoD Acquisition process. The Cybersecurity Maturity Model Certification standard was implemented to strengthen security measures against malicious cyberactivity and to avoid the theft of Controlled Unclassified Information (CUI).

CMMC will specify three degrees of cybersecurity readiness, which will be invoked on the DIB supply chain by all US DoD contracts. Over 300,000 DIB contractors are expected to be affected over the course of the 5+ year deployment, with the majority requiring a Level 1 through Level 3 certification. These requirements will enable DIB contractors to establish appropriate cybersecurity protocols that are as effective and dependable as possible. The standards also set parameters for Relying Party (RP) and Recovery Point Objective (RPO) to construct acceptable information security procedures.

CMMC FRAMEWORK

The CMMC framework contains a "comprehensive and scalable certification element to verify the implementation of processes and practices associated with the achievement of a cybersecurity maturity level.

The framework is meant to ensure that defense contractors can adequately protect sensitive unclassified information, accounting for information flow down to subcontractors in a multi-tier supply chain. The key to the CMMC is in the name, in that it follows a maturity model. The idea behind it is the embodiment of security, as opposed to just kind of checking off a list of things that you make sure you do, like changing your password and that sort of thing.

The framework aligns a set of processes and practices with the type and sensitivity of the information to be protected and the associated range of threats. The model incorporates maturity processes and cybersecurity best practices from multiple cybersecurity standards and frameworks.

Ultimately, according to the Department of Defense, the CMMC "adds a certification element to verify the implementation of processes and practices associated with the achievement of a cybersecurity maturity level."

What are the five levels of the CMMC?

In contrast to NIST 800-171, the CMMC model comprises five levels. "The model is cumulative whereby each level consists of practices and processes as well as those specified in the lower levels," according to the Department of Defense.

Each level is comprised of a set of processes and practices ranging from "basic cyber hygiene" at level 1 to advanced or progressive cybersecurity at level 3. The processes are classified as "performed" at level 1 and "optimizing" at level 3.

Essentially, each level higher suggests a higher level of protection for sensitive data. To achieve a given CMMC level, a company must demonstrate achievement of all preceding lower levels. Furthermore, companies must demonstrate to assessors that they have institutionalized both processes and practices and if an organization displays differing degrees for one or the other, the organization will be certified at the lower of the two levels.

CMMC levels are classified as follows:

CMMC level 1: Protect government contract information

CMMC level 2: Serve as a transition stage in the advancement of cybersecurity maturity to secure controlled unclassified information.

CMMC level 3: CUI protection.

According to Bai, just a small percentage of the DIB will require a level 3 certification, and this will most likely apply mainly to enterprises dealing with data that foreign nation-states are targeting.

Level 1 only includes measures that meet the fundamental safeguarding standards for federal contracting information.

According to the DOD, Level 2 requires businesses to create and document the procedures and policies that will drive their CMMC implementation efforts.

Level 3 security requirements include the 110 security requirements specified in NIST 800-171, as well as safeguards outlined in other standards such as NIST 800-53, the Aerospace Industries Association National Aerospace Standard 9933: Critical Security Controls for Effective Capability in Cyber Defense, and the Computer Emergency Response Team Resilience Management Model. Organizations must design, maintain, and provide resources to support a strategy to demonstrate management's ability to meet these standards at Level 3. According to the DOD, the plan may include information on missions, goals, projects, plans, resourcing, training, and the involvement of important stakeholders.

With level 3, firms must have all of the security and technical infrastructure to not only host that CUI data but also the government wants to ensure that you can still provide service.

Organizations desire to be able to show the DOD that they have the "security, infrastructure, and operational status" to carry out a DOD contract for the duration of its term.

"You've got more policies and procedures, and you have to show that you're executing them," he said. "So, you have artifacts associated with that."

CMMC COMPLIANCE: HOW TO OBTAIN AND MAINTAIN CERTIFICATION

According to the DOD, authorized and accredited C3PAOs are responsible for conducting CMMC assessments of contractors' unclassified networks and granting appropriate CMMC certificates, depending on the results of the assessments.

However, obtaining certification through CMMC is expected to be a time-consuming procedure, at least until the CMMC-AB certifies additional C3PAO firms. There are now just two certified C3PAOs capable of assessing the cybersecurity credentials of over 300,000 businesses in the defense industrial sector. So that makes it very, very difficult.

Cardaci advises contractors to become acquainted with the CMMC requirements, beginning with level 1 and working their way up. He underlines that enterprises should not consider the CMMC as a one-time check because, in order to remain compliant, firms must consider cybersecurity "as part of your operational function going forward."

A CMMC certification will be valid for three years, according to the DOD.

Compliance isn't security, but compliance is a way to document what you've done to secure things.

If key workers depart a company without documentation of institutional cybersecurity expertise, security can erode, and complacency can creep in. Documentation might give justification for specific security practices in place.

THE BENEFITS OF CMMC

While some may see cybersecurity compliance standards as a restriction, there are numerous official and informal benefits to your firm obtaining CMMC compliance in addition to standard corporate IT services and security.

- Opportunity for Defense Contracting:

Of course, one of the primary benefits of obtaining CMMC is that it allows your organization to work on DoD contracts. CMMC is increasingly becoming a required requirement for any DoD activity involving sensitive information. If your organization is participating in a defense contract, you will be required to have this type of certificate.

Given that military contracts account for around $3.4 trillion in government spending per decade, your company cannot afford to miss out on these types of contracts.

- Long-Term Security:

Another benefit of CMMC is that it aids in long-term corporate security. By implementing a consistent security system, you ensure that your company's security is not dependent on a single individual. Assume you have someone working for your internal local IT support services who is in charge of your company's security systems.

If the person bases his work on CMMC standards, you can easily replace him with another worker who has been trained in the same standards.

- Using Widely Accepted Standards:

While it may appear that CMMC is solely applicable to military projects, the certification has a far broader scope. The certification was based on widely accepted National Institute of Criteria and Technology cybersecurity criteria.

This means that by adhering to DoD standards, your organization may also become compliant with a variety of non-military cybersecurity regulations. In some cases, you may be able to work on both civilian and military projects while using the same set of CMMC standards.

On both civilian and military projects, using only one set of CMMC standards.

- Reduced Assessment Costs:

The high assessment fees are a significant disadvantage of many cybersecurity certification standards. The good news is that CMMC has the ability to considerably cut those expenditures. Companies operating at level one (and a subset of companies operating at level two) can verify compliance by self-assessment under the CMMC 2.0 framework. This not only helps your firm save money but also minimizes your company's reliance on external actors.

- Flexibility and Speed When You Need It:

Finally, CMMC can provide your firm with flexibility and quickness when it is most needed. If you find that compliance is difficult or impossible, you may be able to contact the government and request that some of the CMMC requirements be waived. While this is only applicable in a few cases, this feature of CMMC may be useful in preventing your project from going off the tracks.

- Meet the requirements for DoD contract eligibility:

On US DoD contracts, CMMC Levels will be stated; contracting firms must hold the applicable CMMC certification prior to contract award. Organizations that do not have CMMC certification may be barred from bidding on contracts that require certified suppliers.

- Meet Flow-down Requirements:

All DIB contractors throughout the supply chain will be subject to CMMC regulations. Prime contractors will be expected to follow the CMMC cybersecurity criteria. Depending on the type and quality of information passed down from the prime, most DIB subcontractors will need to earn Level 1 or Level 3 certification.

- Improve Security Posture:

The cybersecurity standards described within CMMC were carefully chosen from globally known best practices in both the corporate and public sectors. In summary, the succinct and well-defined requirements will provide clarity on how enterprises of all sizes and shapes can strengthen their cybersecurity posture.

- Allowable Costs:

Under the FAR regulations, CMMC certification costs have been declared permissible and reimbursable as reasonable and allocable to the necessary contract. As a result, enterprises may be able to incorporate certification expenses into their overall security posture improvements.

- Confidence in a "Trust, But Verify" Methodology:

Unlike current NIST compliance, CMMC will demand third-party verification of controls, giving an organization's customers peace of mind and adding value throughout the supply chain. As CMMC moves down the supply chain, all partners will have a shared knowledge and confidence of where businesses stand in terms of information (and consequently supply chain) security.

CIS (CENTER FOR INTERNET SECURITY)

The Center for Internet Security (CIS) is a non-profit organization focused on strengthening cybersecurity preparedness and response in the public and business sectors. CIS promotes Internet security around the world through four program divisions:

The division of the Integrated Intelligence Centre is responsible for developing and disseminating comprehensive and coordinated security information. It fosters partnerships between government and private sector institutions in order to ensure the security of public and private Internet-based services and transactions.

The division of the Multi-State Information Sharing and Analysis Center aims to improve overall cybersecurity for state, local, territorial, and tribal governments. It focuses on collaboration and information sharing among members, private-sector partners, and the United States Department of Homeland Security.

The Security Benchmarks division is in charge of developing and promoting consensus-based good practice standards to improve the security and privacy of Internet-connected systems. Its goal is to safeguard the integrity of public and private Internet-based operations and transactions.

The Trusted Purchasing Alliance was created to assist the public and private sectors in acquiring cybersecurity technologies and policies at a low cost. It strives to ensure that the public and private sectors obtain the cybersecurity safeguards required to protect their data and systems.

The CIS is committed to providing the essential tools, resources, and guidance to the public and private sectors to ensure their cybersecurity preparedness and response. It aims to create and disseminate complete and coordinated security information, as well as to promote the application of consensus-based good practice standards. The CIS also works to improve the overall cybersecurity of state governments and local, territorial, and tribal communities, as well as to assist the public and private sectors in acquiring cost-effective cybersecurity tools and policies.

The Centre for Internet Security is a priceless resource for both the public and corporate sectors. It is devoted to delivering the tools, resources, and guidance needed to ensure cybersecurity readiness and response. CIS seeks to improve worldwide Internet security and ensure that the public and private sectors acquire the appropriate cybersecurity safeguards to protect their data and systems through its four program divisions.

TYPES OF CIS SECURITY CONTROLS

The CIS has a total of 20 important security controls, with the first six being prioritized as "basic" controls that all businesses should execute for cyber security preparation. The scope of all 20 CIS key security Controls is broad in terms of what is required for robust cybersecurity protection. The recommendations of the CIS address not only data, software, and infrastructure but also people and processes.

CIS essential security Controls are intended to assist businesses in protecting their networks and data, as well as ensuring that users only have access to the resources required to complete their duties. The controls are classified into three types:

- Basic controls:

They are the most critical and should be put in place early. They address fundamental security concepts like access control, asset management, and vulnerability management.

- Foundational Controls:

These controls build on basic controls by providing more specific guidance on data, network, and application security.

- Organizational controls:

These provide suggestions on how to handle security throughout the organization, such as adopting rules and procedures and implementing security awareness training.

CIS critical security controls are intended to be applied iteratively, with each check building on the prior one. This enables organizations to begin with the fundamentals and subsequently add more advanced controls as their security posture evolves. The controls are also intended to be adaptable, allowing them to be adjusted to the specific demands of an organization.

Critical CIS security checks are not a one-size-fits-all solution. They are intended to work in tandem with other security measures, such as firewalls and antivirus software, to provide full protection. To further reinforce their security stance, organizations can consider adding extra measures such as encryption and multi-factor authentication.

In conclusion, the CIS critical security controls offer a comprehensive set of security controls divided into three areas. They are intended to be applied iteratively, with each control building on the previous one, and are adaptable enough to be adjusted to the specific demands of an organization. To further enhance their security stance, organizations might consider adding extra security measures.

ESSENTIAL CIS SECURITY CONTROLS

The Center for Internet Security (CIS) has put together a list of 20 important security Controls that businesses may apply to strengthen their cybersecurity posture. These measures are intended to assist organizations in protecting their systems and data against cyber threats such as hackers, malware, and other types of cyber attacks.

The Top 20 CIS Nations A priority set of steps that firms can do to strengthen their cybersecurity stance is critical security checks. They are intended to be practical and successful and are based on real-world cyber threat experiences and observations.

The first six Controls on the list are regarded as the most important and are sometimes referred to as "basic Controls." The following are the basic controls:

- Inventory and Control of Hardware Assets

- Inventory and Control of Software Assets

- Continuous Vulnerability Management

- Controlled Use of Administrative Privileges

- Secure Configuration for Hardware and Software on Mobile Devices, Laptops, Workstations and Servers

- Maintenance, Monitoring, and Analysis of Audit Logs

All businesses, regardless of size or field of activity, should implement these six basic controls.

They are regarded as the core of a strong cybersecurity program and may greatly lower the risk of cyber assaults in enterprises.

The next 14 controls are similarly critical, but they are considered more complex and may necessitate additional money and experience to execute. Among these controls are:

- Email and Web Browser Protections
- Malware Defenses
- Limitation and Control of Network Ports, Protocols and Services
- Data Recovery Capability
- Secure Configuration for Network Devices, such as Firewalls, Routers, and Switches
- Boundary Defense
- Data Protection
- Controlled Access Based on the Need to Know
- Wireless Access Control
- Account Monitoring and Control
- Security Skills Assessment and Appropriate Training to Fill Gaps
- Application Software Security
- Incident Response and Management
- Penetration Tests and Red Team Exercises

Each of these controls is intended to target a distinct area of cybersecurity risk and can assist firms in improving their overall cybersecurity position. Organizations can dramatically minimize their risk of cyber attacks and secure their systems and data by implementing all 20 controls.

CIS Controls are not a one-size-fits-all solution, and businesses may need to tailor them to their individual needs and situations.

Furthermore, CIS controls are not intended to replace other cybersecurity frameworks or standards but rather to supplement them in order to offer a comprehensive cybersecurity program.

Who are the CIS critical security Controls intended for?

The CIS Critical Security Controls (CSCs) apply to every company that keeps, processes, or transmits sensitive data, which includes the vast majority of modern-day organizations. Organizations of all sizes, from tiny to large, as well as governmental institutions and non-profit organizations, are included.

CSCs are intended to provide a comprehensive set of security measures that can be adjusted to the specific requirements of any enterprise, regardless of size or industry. CSCs are built on a set of fundamental principles and best practices that apply to every company that deals with sensitive data. These are the fundamental principles:

- Identification of Threats
- Implementing proper controls to counteract these threats
- Monitoring of these controls to ensure their continued effectiveness

The CSCs are meant to provide a jumping-off point for enterprises to establish their security policies and procedures. The CSC advises on the types of controls that must be adopted to protect an organization's sensitive data's confidentiality, integrity, and availability. It is, however, the responsibility of each organization to establish what controls are necessary for its specific environment and to develop protocols for the implementation, monitoring, and application of such controls.

IMPORTANCE OF CIS CONTROLS

The Center for Internet Security (CIS) has produced a collection of security guidelines to assist enterprises in protecting their IT assets against cyber threats. They are critical for enterprises of all sizes to stay secure from cyber threats.

There are three tiers of CIS controls:

Level 1: Emphasizes fundamental cybersecurity principles like patch management, secure configuration, and user education.

Level 2: Concentrate on advanced cybersecurity procedures like monitoring, incident response, and repair.

Level 3: Concentrate on cutting-edge cybersecurity tactics, including threat intelligence and sophisticated analysis.

CIS Controls offer enterprises a complete set of security rules based on real-world cyber risks that are frequently updated to stay up with the evolving threat landscape. Organizations can ensure that their IT assets are safeguarded against the most recent threats by adhering to the CIS controls.

The following are the reasons why CIS controls are important:

They make it simple for enterprises to assess their security posture and identify areas where they are vulnerable.

They enable firms to teach their personnel on fundamental cybersecurity best practices. This ensures that employees are aware of the security risks associated with their jobs and that they can take precautions to protect themselves and their organizations from cyber threats.

In summary, CIS Controls are a critical set of security standards that can assist enterprises in protecting their IT assets from cyber threats. By adhering to the CIS regulations, organizations may ensure that their IT assets are protected from the most recent threats, analyze their security posture, identify areas for improvement, and train their workers on basic cybersecurity best practices.

STANDARDS OF CIS

The Center for Internet Security (CIS) benchmarks are a set of security standards developed by the CIS to assist enterprises in improving their security posture.

The benchmarks are used for the following purposes:

- Examine the security settings
- Determine any probable flaws.
- Provide guidance on how to secure systems and applications

There are two types of CIS benchmarks:

Level 1: Intended to assist companies in reducing their vulnerability to surface attacks. These benchmarks concentrate on the fundamentals of security, such as password policies, patch management, and antivirus software.

Level 2: More extensive benchmarks with detailed guidance on how to secure basic cyber security. This encompasses network security, authentication, and encryption.

The following organizations utilize the CIS benchmarks:

Organizations of all sizes to ensure system and application security

Government agencies, such as the Department of Defense, must ensure system security

Auditors and security experts to analyze an organization's security posture CIS benchmarks are a valuable tool for firms trying to improve their security posture:

The benchmarks include extensive instructions for securing systems and applications, as well as identifying potential vulnerabilities.

The benchmarks are updated on a regular basis to ensure that they stay current and effective.

The CIS benchmarks can assist organizations of all sizes in securing their systems and applications.

CIS FRAMEWORK

The CIS Framework (Center for Internet Security) is a collection of best practices and standards aimed to assist enterprises in improving their cybersecurity attitudes and protecting themselves from cyber threats. It provides a comprehensive and adaptable approach to cybersecurity, encompassing network devices, mobile devices, operating systems, and end-user devices. Government agencies, security professionals, and enterprises of all sizes all around the world recognize and employ the CIS framework. It establishes a minimal level of security Controls and assists companies in identifying and mitigating security flaws and vulnerabilities. Organizations can strengthen their security defenses, minimize the risk of security events, and align themselves with regulatory frameworks and cybersecurity standards by applying the CIS framework. It also emphasizes security hygiene, secure settings, patch management, access control, and user accounts.

Furthermore, the CIS framework encourages the development of a strong cybersecurity program and a proactive approach to cyber threat identification and response.

IMPORTANCE OF CIS FRAMEWORK

The CIS framework is critical for improving cybersecurity procedures, raising compliance standards, and adopting effective risk management techniques. The CIS framework assists companies in strengthening their security posture and mitigating cyber threats by providing a complete set of recommendations and best practices.

The ability of the CIS framework to build extensive regulatory frameworks is one of its key features. It assists companies in understanding the various security controls required to secure network devices, operating systems, and end-user devices. This enables them to assess their security posture and implement secure configurations to protect themselves against common attacks and security flaws.

Furthermore, the CIS framework encourages computer hygiene practices by emphasizing the significance of continually improving and updating systems, maintaining user accounts and privileges, and conducting penetration tests. Organizations can strengthen their security awareness program, reduce the danger of unwanted access, and ensure that authorized and safe software is utilized by following these suggestions.

The CIS framework not only assists firms in developing a mature cybersecurity program but also assures compliance with industry norms and standards. It assists firms in aligning their security policies and procedures with recognized cybersecurity frameworks, such as the NIST CSF, and meeting government agency and regulatory requirements.

ADVANTAGES OF CIS FRAMEWORK

The CIS (Centre for Internet Security) architecture provides numerous advantages to enterprises looking to strengthen their cybersecurity posture. It assists enterprises in understanding the security controls required to safeguard their network devices, operating systems, and end-user devices by offering complete regulatory frameworks. This enables a thorough assessment of security levels as well as the creation of secure configurations to prevent common attacks and weaknesses. Furthermore, the CIS framework encourages computer hygiene activities such as frequent system patching, user account and privilege control, and penetration testing. Following these principles aids in the improvement of security awareness programs and reduces the risk of unauthorized access and the usage of unauthorized software.

Furthermore, implementing the CIS architecture assists firms in developing a mature cybersecurity program that ensures compliance with industry norms and standards. It integrates security policies and procedures with recognized cybersecurity frameworks, such as the NIST CSF, and meets government agency and regulator criteria. Overall, the CIS architecture provides a solid foundation for enterprises to improve their security posture, manage risks, and remain compliant with regulations.

1. Enhanced Security Posture:

The CIS framework is critical for enterprises looking to strengthen their security posture. Organizations can improve their ability to prevent and guard against common and complex cyber attacks by implementing basic and advanced security Controls.

The framework contains a comprehensive set of controls that cover a wide range of cybersecurity topics, including network devices, mobile devices, operating systems, user accounts, access control management, patch management, and more. These rules are specifically developed to solve the most prevalent security flaws and vulnerabilities.

Implementing the policies defined in the CIS assists companies in establishing a solid security foundation by assuring secure configurations, reducing the risk of unwanted access, and simplifying effective patch management. It encourages IT hygiene and assists firms in establishing a strong security life cycle, which includes everything from security awareness initiatives to penetration testing and incident response.

Organizations that join the CIS framework can achieve a greater degree of security by proactively identifying and mitigating cyber risks. They can also connect company security policies with industry standards and regulatory frameworks, assuring compliance and lowering the risk of penalties for security breaches.

Finally, the CIS framework is a helpful resource for organizations looking to strengthen their security posture, protect against cyber threats, and implement a robust cyber security program.

2. Increased compliance standards:

Implementing the CIS framework is critical for firms looking to fulfill the heightened compliance demands imposed by key data security and privacy frameworks, including NIST CSF, HIPAA, and PCI DSS. The framework's CIS criteria offer firms with a road map for aligning their security procedures with various regulatory frameworks.

The CIS benchmarks are precise rules and best practices for secure system and application configuration. Organizations can verify that their setups fulfill industry standards and regulatory requirements by following these benchmarks. As a result, noncompliance and associated financial challenges caused by non-conforming security setups are reduced.

Organizations that process healthcare information, for example, must follow HIPAA laws. Organizations can develop safe settings for their network devices, mobile devices, and operating systems by implementing the CIS HIPAA standards, ensuring that the appropriate security controls are in place to protect sensitive patient data.

Similarly, firms that process cardholder data must follow PCI DSS guidelines. Organizations can retain their security position and decrease the danger of unauthorized access to cardholder data by adhering to the CIS PCI DSS criteria, which can result in costly infractions and legal penalties.

3. Enhanced cyber hygiene practices:

In today's digital landscape, where cyber threats are evolving and becoming more complex, improved computer hygiene measures are critical. The CIS framework is critical in developing and implementing these practices, which provide businesses with robust security against possible attacks.

Antivirus software is critical in ensuring an organization's cybersecurity. Organizations may defend their systems against developing threats and vulnerabilities by frequently upgrading antivirus software with the most recent virus definitions. Automatic updates and scans are critical components of computer hygiene because they ensure that antivirus software is up-to-date and capable of identifying and mitigating the most recent threats.

One of the primary benefits of centralized antivirus software management is excellent monitoring and detection. Central administration enables security personnel to see the status of antivirus software on all devices and systems in real-time. It enables them to immediately detect and respond to any antivirus software that is out of current or has issues, lowering the risk of potential intrusions.

Furthermore, activating measures that protect against software vulnerabilities improves an organization's cybersecurity posture. Real-time scanning of potential vulnerabilities in operating systems and apps is one of these aspects. Organizations decrease the area of attack and effectively mitigate the risk of exploitation by discovering and addressing vulnerabilities in a timely way.

4. Effective risk management strategy:

In today's fast-evolving cybersecurity market, having an effective risk management strategy is critical for enterprises. Organizations may detect, assess, and proactively mitigate possible threats and weaknesses with a thorough risk management plan. Organizations may strengthen their security posture and mitigate the effect of any security incident by employing a risk management approach.

An effective risk management approach includes a risk assessment procedure. This process entails assessing the organization's assets, identifying potential threats and vulnerabilities, and analyzing the likelihood and effect of these risks. The risk assessment method becomes even more successful in identifying system weaknesses and formulating strategic responses for improved security when undertaken within a cybersecurity framework such as the CIS framework.

Organizations can acquire a full understanding of their risk profile by following the risk assessment process in a cybersecurity framework. This includes detecting and removing dangerous software and hardware, detecting emerging threats, and upgrading cybersecurity policies. Risk assessment assists companies in prioritizing resources and allocating them to where they are most required. It also aids decision-making by giving useful information about the organization's security posture and risk landscape.

5. Comprehensive regulatory frameworks:

Comprehensive regulatory frameworks, such as the NIST CSF, HIPAA, and PCI DSS, are critical in guaranteeing compliance by firms in regulated industries. These frameworks are compatible with the CIS framework and aid in the prevention of noncompliance caused by poorly designed IT systems.

The National Institute of Standards and Technology Cybersecurity Framework (NIST CSF) is a voluntary set of rules, standards, and best practices for enterprises to manage and reduce cybersecurity threats. It assists organizations in identifying, protecting, detecting, responding to, and recovering from cybersecurity problems. Compliance with the NIST CSF guarantees that firms have a strong cybersecurity program in place to secure their data and systems.

The Health Insurance Portability and Accountability Act (HIPAA) is a regulatory framework that was created expressly for the healthcare industry. It safeguards sensitive patient data by creating standards for health information security and confidentiality. HIPAA compliance necessitates the implementation of administrative, physical, and technical protections to protect electronically protected health information. (ePHI).

PCI DSS (Payment Card Industry Data Security Standard) is a collection of guidelines for businesses that handle credit card transactions. PCI DSS compliance is critical for preventing data breaches and securing cardholder information. It involves requirements such as designing safe network setups, establishing strong access control methods, regularly monitoring and testing networks, and developing information security policies.

These comprehensive regulatory frameworks provide firms with a road map for maintaining a secure and compliant cybersecurity posture. They specify critical elements such as risk assessment, vulnerability management, incident response, access control, and security awareness programs. Organizations can limit risks, prevent noncompliance, and protect sensitive data and systems by adhering to these principles.

ELEMENTS OF THE CIS FRAMEWORK

The CIS Framework (Center for Internet Security) is a comprehensive set of principles and best practices aimed at assisting enterprises in improving their cybersecurity posture. It offers a structured approach to IT risk management and mitigation, as well as a road map for enterprises to improve their overall security stance. CIS controls, CIS benchmarks, and essential security control measures are all part of the CIS framework. These components assist organizations in evaluating, monitoring, and implementing security measures to safeguard their networks, systems, and data from cyber threats. Organizations that adhere to the CIS architecture can lay a solid foundation for their cybersecurity program, ensuring effective security controls are applied and vulnerabilities are mitigated. The CIS framework is widely considered an industry standard, and it is utilized by security experts, government agencies, and other organizations all over the world to strengthen their security defenses and protect themselves against cyber attacks.

IMPORTANT SECURITY CONTROLS

The CIS framework (Center for Internet Security) offers enterprises with a comprehensive set of critical security tests to defend their systems and networks from common cyber threats. These procedures are intended to address the most prevalent and successful attack vectors and improve an organization's security posture.

Patch management, user access control, and secure configuration are some of the essential security controls incorporated in the CIS framework. Patch management ensures that systems and software are constantly updated with the most recent security patches, reducing the chance of known vulnerabilities being exploited. By adopting stringent authentication and permission standards, user access control helps prevent unauthorized access to critical data and systems. Secure configuration guarantees that systems and devices are correctly configured, reducing the possibility of incorrect setups resulting in security flaws.

Implementing proactive and preventive steps in these controls plays a critical role in averting cyberattacks. Patching on a regular basis helps to prevent vulnerabilities that may be exploited by malware and other harmful actors. User access control guarantees that only those who are permitted have access to vital resources, lowering the risk of illegal access and data breaches. Secure setup guarantees that systems are correctly designed to withstand common attack approaches and decreases security risk exposure.

Implementing the critical security Controls outlined in the CIS framework improves an organization's security posture and lowers the likelihood of successful cyber assaults. These tests lay the groundwork for a comprehensive cybersecurity policy and assist firms in protecting their data and sensitive systems from emerging cyber threats.

CIS CERTIFICATION

A CIS certification validates that a corporation has met the CIS control standards and can function in a hardened CIS environment. The Center gives it to Internet Security (CIS), a non-profit organization dedicated to improving the security of customers by developing secure setups and best practices.

The CIS benchmarks are a set of security standards and guidelines that businesses can use to help them design safe systems and networks. Companies that have gained CIS accreditation have demonstrated a high level of security and the ability to operate in a safe and harsh environment.

Obtaining CIS certification entails a thorough study and evaluation of the company's security posture. A third-party auditor conducts this evaluation, which is based on a number of criteria, including:

- The security controls and processes in place

- The security architecture
- The security policies and procedures

The auditor will also examine the company's systems and networks to ensure they fulfill CIS standards. Following the completion of the audit, the auditor will provide the company with a report highlighting areas of noncompliance and making recommendations for improvement. In order to achieve CIS certification, the company must adopt the auditor's proposed adjustments.

Any organization can benefit from CIS certification because it:

- Show that the organization has taken the required precautions to secure its systems and networks.
- Provides clients and partners with trust that the organization is committed to security and can provide a secure environment for their data and transactions.

CIS certification is a critical step for any organization that wants:

- The provision of CIS benchmarks as a service
- Customer and partner service provision
- The organization exhibits a commitment to security and a high degree of security assurance by acquiring CIS accreditation.

CIS CONTROL FRAMEWORK IMPLEMENTATION

The Internet Security Control Centre (CIS), originally known as the CIS Critical Security Control Framework, is a strong but adaptable set of protocols designed to defend businesses of all sizes and in all industries from a wide range of attacks. Their implementation necessitates:

- Choosing the extent of your implementation, including mapping and monitoring
- Installing safeguards in accordance with the requirements of your chosen implementation group
- Evaluate your implementation and provide continuous long-term monitoring and maintenance.

Working with a security program adviser or a virtual information security manager (vCISO) to optimize every step of the process is one of the finest ways to deploy CIS measures efficiently.

   1. Determine the scope of your project:

The first stage in any CIS Controls implementation is to determine which controls must be installed. Each control contains a number of safeguards that are organized into three implementation groups (IG). Determining the scope entails selecting an IG and the associated assurances.

However, it may also include establishing how to overlay your current cybersecurity controls on them.

Many other legal frameworks, such as the Payment Card Industry Data Security Standard (PCI), the overall Data Protection Regulation (GDPR), and the Health Insurance Portability and Liability Act (HIPAA), have a similar overall structure. If you already meet one of these criteria or are moving toward it, mapping is the most successful deployment method.

2. Install Safeguards for Your Implementation Group:

The CIS control framework as a whole has 153 cybersecurity safeguards. However, businesses are only required to execute some of them at the same time. Instead, organizations should select the implementation group appropriate to their needs.

Implementation Group 1 is intended for smaller and younger enterprises. It incorporates at least one protection from practically every CIS control, which all work together to establish a security foundation known as "essential cyber hygiene." This is the foundation for all CIS restrictions.

Implementation Group 2 is intended for medium- to large-sized organizations with heterogeneous IT systems. If your company groups sectors with sensitive data, IG could be a good fit.

Implementation Group 3 is for the most mature and big enterprises. Its security builds on IG 1 and IG 2 to give the most advanced protection against sophisticated and persistent threats. At this level, security competes with the majority of other regulatory frameworks.

3. Examine the effectiveness of your CIS controls:

After you have installed the CIS framework controls on your target IG, you must ensure that they are functioning properly. CIS evaluations using the CIS Control Self-Evaluation Tool (CSAT) allow you to validate your installation and ensure your stakeholders' security.

The CSAT, which is available through the CIS by subscription, allows enterprises to report on their security. It also includes capabilities to mitigate difficulties and manage assessments at multiple levels (i.e., lower or greater IG standards) for different roles or segments inside your organization - or third parties.

While it is intended to help with self-assessment, working with a compliance expert maximizes the benefits of CSAT. CSAT simplifies compliance reporting for other laws, but certification requires collaboration with certified vendors.

CHALLENGES OF IMPLEMENTING CIS CONTROLS

While implementing CIS standards can be difficult, it has become a critical requirement for many organizations. It's because the CIS framework promises to create proper cybersecurity structure and security measures in small and large organizations and prevent a large number of data security and protection issues in the industry.

One big challenge related to deploying CIS standards in a company is the increasing number of cyberattacks and new techniques hackers use to penetrate IT systems. These new techniques can pose new challenges, especially when you work with an inexperienced cybersecurity team.

A professional and up-to-date cybersecurity team is equipped with the latest technologies and practices, and they know and understand which tools and security plans work best for your specific industry.

One notable challenge is the limited budget many organizations specify for their cybersecurity when there are more expenses than the budget. Implementing CIS standards and requirements in a medium or large organization necessitates developing a detailed plan, which your security team will make real in several parts. It provides you with a reliable security posture, but implementing CIS controls without any issues needs spending.

A remarkable challenge all industries face today is that there is a lack of professional cybersecurity experts to work on their projects. CIS controls require your organization to work with a certified security service provider that ensures all the requirements will be implemented in your company.

PAYMENT CARD INDUSTRY DATA SECURITY STANDARD (PCI DSS)

The Payment Card Industry Data Security Standard (PCI DSS) is a set of security standards formed in 2004 by Visa, MasterCard, Discover Financial Services, JCB International, and American Express. Governed by the Payment Card Industry Security Standards Council (PCI SSC), the compliance scheme aims to secure credit and debit card transactions against data theft and fraud.

While the PCI SSC has no legal authority to compel compliance, it is a requirement for any business that processes credit or debit card transactions. PCI certification is also considered the best way to safeguard sensitive data and information, thereby helping businesses build long-lasting and trusting relationships with their customers.

PCI DSS CERTIFICATION

PCI certification ensures the security of card data at your business through a set of requirements established by the PCI SSC. These include a number of commonly known best practices, such as:

- Installation of firewalls
- Encryption of data transmissions
- Use of anti-virus software

In addition, businesses must restrict access to cardholder data and monitor access to network resources.

PCI-compliant security provides a valuable asset that informs customers that your business is safe to transact with. Conversely, the cost of noncompliance, both in monetary and reputational terms, should be enough to convince any business owner to take data security seriously.

A data breach that reveals sensitive customer information is likely to have severe repercussions on an enterprise. A breach may result in fines from payment card issuers, lawsuits, diminished sales, and a severely damaged reputation.

After experiencing a breach, a business may have to cease accepting credit card transactions or be forced to pay higher subsequent charges than the initial cost of security compliance. The investment in PCI security procedures goes a long way toward ensuring that other aspects of your commerce are safe from malicious online actors.

PCI DSS COMPLIANCE LEVELS

PCI compliance is divided into four levels based on the annual number of credit or debit card transactions a business processes. The classification level determines what an enterprise needs to do to remain compliant.

Level 1 Applies to merchants processing more than six million real-world credit or debit card transactions annually. Conducted by an authorized PCI auditor, they must undergo an internal audit once a year. In addition, once a quarter, they must submit to a PCI scan by an Approved Scanning Vendor (ASV).

Level 2 Applies to merchants processing between one and six million real-world credit or debit card transactions annually. They're required to complete an assessment once a year using a Self-Assessment Questionnaire (SAQ). Additionally, a quarterly PCI scan may be required.

Level 3 Applies to merchants processing between 20,000 and one million e-commerce transactions annually. They must complete a yearly assessment using the relevant SAQ. A quarterly PCI scan may also be required.

Level 4: This applies to merchants processing fewer than 20,000 e-commerce transactions annually or those that process up to one million real-world transactions. A yearly assessment using the relevant SAQ must be completed, and a quarterly PCI scan may be required.

PCI DSS REQUIREMENTS

The PCI SSC has outlined 12 requirements for handling cardholder data and maintaining a secure network. Distributed between six broader goals, all are necessary for an enterprise to become compliant.

Secure network:

1. A firewall configuration must be installed and maintained

2. System passwords must be original (not vendor-supplied)

Secure cardholder data:

3. Stored cardholder data must be protected

4. Transmissions of cardholder data across public networks must be encrypted

Vulnerability management:

5. Anti-virus software must be used and regularly updated

6. Secure systems and applications must be developed and maintained

Access control:

7. Cardholder data access must be restricted to a business need-to-know basis

8. Every person with computer access must be assigned a unique ID

9. Physical access to cardholder data must be restricted

Network monitoring and testing:

10. Access to cardholder data and network resources must be tracked and monitored

11. Security systems and processes must be regularly tested

Information security:

12. A policy dealing with information security must be maintained

REQUIREMENTS FOR PCI DSS COMPLIANCE

1. Use and Maintain Firewalls:

Firewalls essentially block access to foreign or unknown entities attempting to access private data. These prevention systems are often the first line of defense against hackers (malicious or otherwise). Firewalls are required for PCI DSS compliance because of their effectiveness in preventing unauthorized access.

2. Proper Password Protections:

Routers, modems, point of sale (POS) secure systems, and other third-party products often come with generic passwords and security measures easily accessed by the public. Too often, businesses fail to secure these security vulnerabilities. Ensuring compliance in this area includes keeping a list of all devices and software that require a password (or other security to access). In addition to a device/password inventory, basic precautions and configurations should also be enacted (e.g., changing the password).

3. Protect Cardholder Data:

The third requirement of PCI DSS compliance is a two-fold protection of cardholder data. Card data must be encrypted with certain algorithms. These encryptions are put into place with encryption keys — which are also required to be encrypted for compliance. Regular maintenance and scanning of primary account numbers (PAN) are needed to ensure no unencrypted data exists.

4. Encrypt Transmitted Data:

Cardholder data is sent across multiple ordinary channels (i.e., payment processors, home office from local stores, etc.). This data must be encrypted whenever it is sent to these known locations. Account numbers should also never be sent to locations that are unknown.

5. Use and Maintain Anti-Virus:

Installing anti-virus software is a good practice outside of PCI DSS compliance. However, anti-virus software is required for all devices that interact with and/or store PAN. This software should be regularly patched and updated. Your POS provider should also employ anti-virus measures where it cannot be directly installed.

6. Properly Updated Software

Firewalls and anti-virus software will require updates often. It is also a good idea to update every piece of software in a business. Most software products will include security measures in their updates, such as patches to address recently discovered vulnerabilities, which add another level of protection. These updates are especially required for all software on devices that interact with or store cardholder data.

7. Restrict Data Access

Cardholder data is required to be strictly "need to know." All staff, executives, and third parties who do not need access to this data should not have it. The roles that do need sensitive data should be well-documented and regularly updated — as required by PCI DSS.

8. Unique IDs for Access

Individuals who do have access to cardholder data should have individual credentials and identification for access. For instance, there should not be a single login to the encrypted data with multiple employees knowing the username and password. Unique IDs create less vulnerability and a quicker response time in the event data is compromised.

9. Restrict Physical Access:

Any cardholder data must be physically kept in a secure location. Both data that is physically written or typed and data that is digitally kept (e.g., on a hard drive) should be locked in a secure room, drawer, or cabinet. Not only should access be limited, but anytime the sensitive data is accessed, it should be kept in a log to remain compliant.

10. Create and Maintain Access Logs:

All activity dealing with cardholder data and primary account numbers (PAN) requires a log entry. Perhaps the most common non-compliance issue is a lack of proper record-keeping and documentation when it comes to accessing sensitive data. Compliance requires documenting how data flows into your organization and the number of times access is needed. Software products to log access are also needed to ensure accuracy.

11. Scan and Test for Vulnerabilities:

All ten of the preceding compliance standards involve a variety of software products, physical locations, and, most likely, a few employees. Many things can break down, become obsolete, or suffer from human error. These threats can be mitigated by complying with the PCI DSS requirement for regular vulnerability scans and testing.

12. Policies should be documented:

For attestation of compliance, an inventory of equipment, software, and employees with access must be documented. Access to cardholder data logs will also necessitate documentation. It is also necessary to document how information enters your organization, where it is held, and how it is used after the point of sale.

ADVANTAGES OF PCI COMPLIANCE

At the very least, complying with PCI Security Standards appears to be a demanding endeavor. The tangle of rules and difficulties appears to be too much for even huge corporations, let alone smaller businesses. However, compliance is becoming increasingly vital and may not be as difficult as you think, especially if you have the correct tools.

According to the PCI SSC, there are significant benefits to compliance, especially when failure to comply can result in serious and long-term implications. As an example:

PCI Compliance standards imply that your systems are secure, and your customers may put their sensitive credit card information in your hands; trust leads to customer confidence and repeat business.

PCI Compliance enhances your image with acquirers and payment brands - exactly the partners your company requires.

PCI compliance is a continuous procedure that supports the prevention of security breaches and payment card data theft both now and in the future; PCI compliance implies you are contributing to a worldwide payment card data security solution.

As you work to satisfy PCI Compliance, you'll be better equipped to fulfill other regulations such as HIPAA, SOX, and others.

PCI compliance helps corporate security plans (even if it is merely a starting point).

PCI compliance is expected to improve the efficiency of IT infrastructure.

CHALLENGES CAUSED BY PCI NON-COMPLIANCE

The PCI SSC also warns of the potentially disastrous consequences of failing to meet PCI Compliance. Don't put your consumers' sensitive information at risk after you've worked hard to create your brand and protect them. By adhering to PCI Compliance, you are protecting your clients and ensuring their continued patronage. PCI non-compliance can have the following consequences:

Data that has been compromised has a detrimental impact on consumers, retailers, and financial institutions.

Your reputation and capacity to conduct business effectively will be severely harmed, not just today but in the future.

Account data breaches can result in catastrophic losses in sales, relationships, and community status; also, public organizations' share prices are frequently reduced as a result of account data breaches.

Suits, insurance claims, canceled accounts, payment card issuer fees, and government fines are all possibilities.

PCI Compliance, like other regulatory standards, can provide difficulties for firms that are not prepared to deal with the issues of protecting important information. However, with the correct software and services, data protection becomes a far more doable undertaking. Choose data loss prevention software that accurately categorizes and uses data so you can rest easier knowing that your cardholder data is protected.

HEALTH INSURANCE PORTABILITY AND ACCOUNTABILITY ACT (HIPAA)

HIPAA stands for Health Insurance Portability and Accountability Act.

In 1996, Congress passed the Health Insurance Portability and Accountability Act (HIPAA). As part of HIPAA, Congress requested laws promoting administrative ease of healthcare transactions, as well as regulations assuring patient information privacy and security. HIPAA is intended to protect personal healthcare information by enhancing security standards and enacting federal privacy legislation. It specifies the criteria for storing patient data before to, during, and after electronic transfer. It also establishes compliance rules for important company operations like risk analysis, awareness training, audit trails, disaster recovery plans, and information access control and encryption.

The HIPAA Security Rule must be followed by Covered Entities (CEs). This applies to health plans (for example, HMOs and group health plans), healthcare clearinghouses (for example, billing businesses), and healthcare providers (for example, doctors, dentists, and hospitals) who transmit or keep any Electronic Protected Health Information (EPHI). CEs shall keep reasonable and appropriate administrative, physical, and technical protections in place to preserve the confidentiality, integrity, and availability of their EPHI from any reasonably foreseeable hazards.

CEs shall take reasonable precautions to mitigate all reasonably foreseen hazards to their EPHI. They must weigh the dangers to their EPHI against their resources and business requirements. The provision applies to all members of a CE's workforce, including management and those who work from home.

A comprehensive range of security processes, rules, and procedures must be formally documented and approved by CEs. Furthermore, CEs must give regular security training and awareness to their workers, as well as change their security policies and processes as necessary.

The Security Rule's standards are divided into five categories:

- Administrative safeguards
- Physical security measures
- Technical precautions
- Organizational norms
- Policies, processes, and documentation
- Program

All departments that accept, process, store, and transmit electronic protected healthcare information (ePHI) must ensure that the Risk Management team conducts risk assessments on all applicable systems and databases used to process this data.

University Ethics and Compliance requires annual HIPAA training for all divisions and departments that handle protected health information (PHI).

All university personnel who access, use, send, or otherwise process electronic protected healthcare information (ePHI) should review university policies. The Compliance team can engage with schools and business divisions to verify that all HIPAA Security Rule regulatory requirements are met.

HIPAA COMPLIANCE AND CYBERSECURITY

In some respects, HIPAA is related to cybersecurity since it mandates covered businesses to establish different administrative, physical, and technical protections to protect the confidentiality, integrity, and availability of electronically protected health information (ePHI). These precautions are intended to prevent illegal access, use, or disclosure of ePHI as well as to reduce the risks of cybersecurity incidents such as data breaches or ransomware attacks.

Access controls, such as unique user IDs, passwords, and other authentication systems, are among the technical safeguards required by HIPAA to limit access to ePHI to only authorized personnel. HIPAA also requires covered entities to encrypt and decode electronic protected health information (ePHI) when it is transferred or stored, as well as to develop backup and disaster recovery strategies to safeguard the availability and integrity of ePHI in the event of an emergency or system failure.

Furthermore, HIPAA requires covered companies to conduct periodical risk assessments in order to detect potential cybersecurity risks and vulnerabilities and adopt countermeasures. Covered institutions must also educate their employees about the security policies and procedures in place to protect ePHI and quickly disclose any security incidents or breaches.

Overall, HIPAA regulations help to guarantee that covered entities employ proper cybersecurity measures to protect ePHI and the privacy and security of individuals' health information.

1. File Integrity Monitoring:

Obtaining HIPAA compliance is a difficult procedure, but sustaining it is sometimes even more difficult. FIM calculates the hash value of files before and after changes are made, ensuring that you always maintain control over your sensitive assets and are notified whenever a new directory or file is created, destroyed, renamed, or its content is changed. FIM also monitors the creation and deletion of files and directories.

2. Detecting Access to Systems:

You can easily detect users and systems attempting to access other systems, as well as other key contextual information such as actions taken, final status, or other entities used, such as IP addresses. Monitoring access control aids in verifying users' access to systems and resources. Logpoint can detect failed and successful logins, various login attempts, and users who are locked or unlocked.

3. Authentication and Transmission Control:

Authentication measures ensure that users are who they say they are. Password-based authentication, public-private authentication, and two-factor authentication are all examples of this.

Transmission restrictions ensure that only authorized users conduct data transfers outside of the enterprise. This necessitates the use of private key email, HTTPS file transfer, or the usage of a VPN.

HIPAA COMPLIANCE

The Health Insurance Portability and Accountability Act (HIPAA) establishes the standard for the security of sensitive patient data. To maintain HIPAA compliance, businesses that handle protected health information (PHI) must implement and adhere to physical, network, and process security measures. HIPAA compliance is required for covered entities (anyone who offers treatment, payment, or operations in healthcare) and business associates (anyone who has access to patient information and provides support in treatment, payment, or operations). Other companies, such as subcontractors and other relevant business connections, must be in compliance as well.

IMPORTANCE OF HIPAA COMPLIANCE

HHS emphasizes that HIPAA compliance is more important than ever as healthcare providers and other entities dealing with PHI transition to computerized operations, such as computerized physician order entry (CPOE) systems, electronic health records (EHR), and radiology, pharmacy, and laboratory systems. Similarly, health plans make claims, care management, and self-service tools available. While all of these electronic approaches improve efficiency and mobility, they also significantly increase the security threats associated with healthcare data.

The Security Rule was put in place to secure individuals' health information while also allowing covered entities to use innovative technology to improve the quality and efficiency of patient treatment. By design, the Security Rule is adaptable enough to allow a covered entity to implement policies, processes, and technologies that are appropriate for the entity's size, organizational structure, and threats to patients' and customers' e-PHI.

HOW TO AVOID COMMON HIPAA COMPLIANCE ISSUES

- Improper notice of privacy practices:

HHS discovered that patients were either not receiving a Notice of Privacy Practices (NPP) or that the notice was inadequate. The Final Rule modified how practitioners can use and disclose Protected Health Information (PHI) about their patients. As a result, your NPP needed to be updated. A sample NPP can be downloaded from the HIPAA Toolkit's sample policies tab.

- Timeliness and cost of providing medical records:

HIPAA requires providers to disclose access to medical and billing information upon request and as soon as practicable, but no later than 30 days. If the practitioner has the capacity to do so, copies must be delivered in the format desired by the patient. In most cases, this implies that if you have electronic medical records (EMRs) and a patient asks for a digital copy (such as a PDF), you must comply if your existing system supports it.

A provider may only charge a "reasonable, cost-based" price for copies when providing records to a patient. Charging a patient a per-page copy fee, as was common with paper records, may no longer be regarded as reasonable or cost-effective with EMRs. You may not refuse a patient a copy of their medical records because they have not paid for services rendered. Furthermore, you may not charge a fee for finding and collecting medical records in specific instances. Refer to your state's legislation regarding copying fees.

- Provide only the relevant medical record information:

According to the Minimum Necessary Standard, you must produce only those sections of medical data that are required for the purpose for which the disclosure is approved. For example, you may reveal some PHI while sending a patient to collections for failing to pay a bill. In this case, however, billing information is usually sufficient, and a provider should not divulge medical treatment records unless requested.

- Authorization issues:

These include failing to get a required HIPAA-compliant authorization or using an insufficient authorization form. A sample authorization form can be found in the HIPAA Toolkit's sample forms area.

SECURITY RULE CONCERNS

- Maintain an up-to-date risk assessment:

The first step in assuring HIPAA Security Rule compliance is to conduct a thorough risk analysis and update it on a regular basis. A risk assessment assists your firm in ensuring compliance with HIPAA's administrative, physical, and technology safeguards. It also aids in identifying areas where PHI may be compromised. If a patient files a HIPAA complaint, the government will request the most recent risk analysis. When a significant data breach happens, the lack of a risk analysis, or the lack of an up-to-date one, has been extensively mentioned as the rationale for imposing huge fines.

To aid in this compliance endeavor, the Office of Civil Rights, in collaboration with the Office of the National Coordinator, developed an online tool to guide you through the process of completing or revising your risk analysis.

- Lost or stolen data:

"Media Movement and Disposal" refers to PHI that is lost or stolen while being moved or disposed of incorrectly. PHI loss or theft accounted for 65% of breaches involving more than 500 patients' information. The majority of them were lost or stolen laptops, thumb drives, DVDs, cellphones, and other kinds of portable media, although briefcases or paper patient files were also stolen from cars or left behind in taxi cabs.

Be wary of unprotected laptops, thumb drives, or cell phones that could be stolen. Encryption may have an initial cost, but it could save you money in fines and reputational damage.

In terms of disposal, copies of medical records should be securely destroyed. Never dispose of billing information or copies of medical data in the regular trash. Also, before returning your leased digital copier, make sure to clean the hard drive.

- Monitoring and auditing:

HIPAA requires covered companies to audit their systems for intrusions on a regular basis and to have policies and processes in place for how and when that monitoring will take place. Most healthcare workers do not have access to internal information technology experts and must rely on outside contractors. Providers should raise these concerns with their contractors, as well as discuss auditing and monitoring. You could be hacked and not know it if your systems are not audited and monitored.

Concerns Regarding Breach Notification

Unauthorized acquisition, access, use, or disclosure of PHI that does not fit under one of the exemption categories is considered a breach under the Final Rule and requires notice of the impacted persons, the Office of Civil Rights, and, in some situations, the media. If the breach is committed at or by a Business Associate (BA), the BA is required to notify the covered entity. For more information on reporting a violation, visit the Office of Civil Rights website.

Concerns of Patients

The foundation of a trusting relationship between a patient and a physician is privacy and secrecy. According to studies, the public is deeply worried about the privacy and security of health information, and the HIPAA Privacy Rule has helped to alleviate some of those worries. It is critical that healthcare organizations and providers follow these rules in order to give patients the best privacy and security protection for their health information that the law allows.

CHAPTER 7

CYBER SECURITY CONTROLS

POLICIES AND PROCEDURES FOR CYBERSECURITY

A cybersecurity policy establishes rules of behavior for activities such as email attachment encryption and social media prohibitions. Cybersecurity rules are essential because cyberattacks and data breaches can be costly. Employees, on the other hand, are frequently the weakest connections in an organization's security. Employees share passwords, open malicious URLs and attachments, access unauthorized cloud applications, and fail to secure crucial information.

These rules are especially important in publicly traded corporations or organizations that engage in regulated fields like healthcare, finance, or insurance. If their security processes are considered poor, these firms face severe fines.

Even small businesses that are not subject to federal laws are expected to fulfill baseline IT security standards and may be punished for a hack that results in the loss of consumer data if the corporation is judged irresponsible. Some governments, such as California and New York, have imposed information security obligations on businesses doing business in their jurisdictions.

Cybersecurity rules are also important for an organization's public image and legitimacy. Customers, partners, shareholders, and future workers seek proof that the business is capable of safeguarding sensitive data. An organization may be unable to offer such evidence if it does not have a cybersecurity policy in place.

ESTABLISHING A CYBERSECURITY POLICY

Cybersecurity policies describe how employees, consultants, partners, board members, and other end users access online applications and internet resources, send data via networks, and practice responsible security. Typically, the first section of a cybersecurity policy explains the organization's general security expectations, duties, and obligations. Stakeholders include outside consultants, IT personnel, finance personnel, and so forth.

The policy may then include sections for various aspects of cybersecurity, such as antivirus software requirements or the use of cloud apps. The SANS Institute gives numerous examples of cybersecurity policies. A remote access policy, a wireless communication policy, a password protection policy, an email policy, and a digital signature policy are all included in these SANS templates.

Online resources that address specific legal requirements, such as the HIPAA Journal's HIPAA Compliance Checklist or IT Governance's article on writing a GDPR-compliant policy, can be used by organizations in regulated industries.

A cybersecurity policy is sometimes dozens of pages long for large firms or those in regulated industries. A security policy for a small firm, on the other hand, maybe simply a few pages long and contain fundamental security practices. Examples of such practices include:

- Rules for using email encryption
- Steps for accessing work applications remotely
- Guidelines for creating and safeguarding passwords
- Rules on the use of social media

Regardless of how long the policy is, it should emphasize the topics that are most important to the organization. This could involve safeguarding the most sensitive or regulated data, as well as safeguarding against the causes of previous data breaches. A risk analysis can suggest policy issues that should be prioritized.

The policy should also be straightforward and simple to understand. Include technical information in linked documents, especially if it needs to be updated frequently. For example, the policy may require employees to encrypt all personally identifiable information (PII). However, the policy does not have to specify which encryption software to use or how to encrypt the data.

WHO SHOULD BE IN CHARGE OF DEVELOPING CYBERSECURITY POLICIES?

The IT department, frequently led by the CIO or CISO, is in charge of all information security rules. Other stakeholders, based on their expertise and roles within the organization, usually contribute to the policy. The following are the important stakeholders who are likely to engage in policy development, as well as their roles:

C-level executives establish the critical company security demands as well as the resources available to support a cybersecurity policy. It is a waste of people's time to create a policy that cannot be implemented due to a lack of resources.

The legal department ensures that the policy conforms with government legislation and meets legal standards.

Human resources (HR) is in charge of explaining and enforcing employee policies. Human resources personnel ensure that employees have read the policy and reprimand those who do not.

Procurement departments are in charge of screening cloud service suppliers, monitoring cloud service contracts, and screening other service providers. Procurement personnel can confirm that a cloud provider's security fulfills the organization's cybersecurity requirements and that other outsourced related services are effective.

Board members of public corporations and groups are responsible for reviewing and approving policies. Depending on the needs of the company, they may be more or less involved in policy making.

Consider who is most important to the policy's success when inviting personnel to participate in policy creation. An ideal participant would be the department manager or corporate executive who will enforce the policy or give resources to aid in its implementation.

UPDATING AND AUDITING CYBERSECURITY PROCEDURES

Technology is constantly evolving. Regularly update cybersecurity protocols, ideally once a year. Create an annual review and update process that includes key stakeholders.

When analyzing an information security policy, compare the policy's guidelines to the organization's actual practices. A policy audit or review can identify regulations that are no longer applicable to current work procedures. An audit can also help identify areas where stronger cybersecurity policy enforcement is required.

The InfoSec Institute, an IT security consulting and training firm, recommends three policy audit objectives:

- Compare the organization's cybersecurity policy with its current actions.
- Determine the organization's vulnerability to internal threats.

- Assess the threat of external security threats.

An updated cybersecurity policy is an important security resource for all firms. Without one, end users are more likely to make mistakes and create data breaches. A reckless approach can cost a company a lot of money in fines, legal bills, settlements, public trust loss, and brand degradation. Creating and adhering to a policy can help avert these negative results.

IMPORTANCE OF CYBERSECURITY POLICIES

Companies are vulnerable to a variety of possible attacks on their systems and data. Many cyberattacks make use of an organization's personnel in some way, either by exploiting their negligence or duping them into action through a phishing or social engineering attack. Because of the proliferation of BYOD rules and the ability of infected devices to access corporate networks, the increase in remote work has also presented new vulnerabilities.

Cyber security policies serve to safeguard a company from cyber threats while also ensuring compliance with applicable requirements. These rules can minimize an organization's risk by instructing employees to avoid specific actions and enable more effective incident response by specifying methods for detecting, avoiding, and remediating incidents.

TYPES OF CYBERSECURITY POLICIES

There are different types of cyber security policies that can be implemented by a company. Some of the most common ones are as follows:

- IT Security Policy:

An organization's IT security policy establishes the rules and procedures for defending against cyber attacks. Acceptable use of corporate assets, incident response plans, business continuity strategies, and the organization's plan for achieving and maintaining regulatory compliance are all parts of an IT security policy.

- Email Security Policy:

An email security policy describes the authorized usage of corporate email systems in order to assist in protecting the organization from spam, phishing, and viruses (such as ransomware), as well as to prevent corporate email misuse. This type of policy may include broad guidelines for how business email should and should be used, as well as detailed instructions for dealing with questionable links and email attachments.

- BYOD Policy:

A BYOD policy establishes guidelines for personal devices used for work. These rules typically include security criteria for these devices, such as the use of an endpoint security solution, strong passwords, and a virtual private network

(VPN) when connecting to corporate networks and IT assets through an untrusted network.

HOW TO CREATE A CYBER SECURITY POLICY

Creating a cyber security policy is a multi-stage process with the following key steps:

- Determine the threat surface:

Each policy is designed to handle a specific hazard or risk to the organization. The first stage in developing a policy is to get a thorough understanding of the systems and processes that will be governed, such as the usage of personal devices for business purposes.

- Identify applicable requirements:

Corporate cyber security policies may be driven by both internal and external factors, such as company security goals and regulatory obligations (HIPAA, PCI DSS, and so on). The next step in developing a cyber security policy is to identify the requirements that the policy must meet.

- Draft the Policy:

After identifying the requirements, the following stage is to design the policy. This should be done by a team comprised of stakeholders from IT, legal, HR, and management.

- Solicit Feedback:

A cyber security policy is most effective when it is straightforward and easy for employees to understand. Soliciting feedback from employees outside the policy group can aid in the prevention of misconceptions and other problems.

- Employee Training:

Once the policy has been written, it must be promoted throughout the organization. Employees will also need to be trained on these policies in order to comply with them.

- Update the Policy on a Regular Basis:

Policies can become out of date, and their requirements can alter. They should be examined and updated on a regular basis to stay current.

CYBERSECURITY AWARENESS TRAINING

Cybersecurity awareness training is provided to teach employees about the different potential cyber dangers that can manifest themselves and how employees can recognize and remain vigilant against them, preserving an organization's and its stakeholders' data privacy. The major goal of cybersecurity awareness training is to increase employees' knowledge and comprehension of potential cybersecurity risks, as well as to help them implement measures to protect themselves and their organizations against cyber-attacks and data breaches.

POTENTIAL SECURITY RISKS FOR ORGANIZATIONS LACKING CYBER SECURITY AWARENESS TRAINING

- Attacks Using Phishing:

Employees who are unfamiliar with phishing techniques may unintentionally fall prey to phishing emails, resulting in compromised credentials, data breaches, or ransomware infestations. In cyber security, these assaults are also known as whaling because the phishing attempt is meant to maximize impact by focusing on senior/high-level executives and leadership individuals within an organization.

- Social Engineering Exploitation:

Social engineering is defined as tricking, manipulating, or influencing a victim in order to take control of a computer system or obtain personal or financial information. Employees may unwittingly provide sensitive information or provide illegal access to attackers impersonating colleagues due to a lack of awareness about contemporary social engineering strategies.

- Weak passwords:

Despite widespread awareness of the need for password protection, stolen credentials are used in 86% of data breaches revealed in the 2023 Verizon Data Breach Investigations Report. Employees may be using weak passwords or passwords for several accounts, making it easier for attackers to obtain illegal access.

- Unsecured mobile devices:

Employees who have not received adequate training may engage in insecure practices on both their personal and work mobile devices, rendering them more vulnerable to mobile-based assaults. For example, if you use the same password for your personal and business accounts, you will be more vulnerable to a cyber-attack. Furthermore, unintentionally downloading dangerous spyware onto your mobile device can render it insecure, putting the workforce at risk.

- Inadequate Incident Reporting:

Employees may not understand how to detect and process a security incident report, causing the organization's reaction to possible threats to be delayed and perhaps increasing the severity of the attack.

IMPORTANCE OF CYBER SECURITY AWARENESS TRAINING

Creating a workforce that knows and is cautious against attempted attacks is a critical component in preventing a successful cyber security attack. According to Verizon's 2023 Data Breach Investigations Report, 74% of breaches featured the human factor, while a startling 95% of cybersecurity vulnerabilities were traced back to human error in 2022. Organizations may considerably protect themselves from a wide range of cyber dangers by implementing an effective cyber security awareness training program.

Employee Cyber Security Awareness Training Is important in the following ways:

1. Identifying cyber threats:

Employees might benefit from training to become more conversant with potential cyber risks such as phishing emails, social engineering assaults, malware, and ransomware. This information enables them to recognize potential threats, take necessary safeguards, and report suspicious conduct promptly.

2. Promote secure remote work:

With remote working becoming more common in most businesses, employees must be aware of the particular cybersecurity threats that exist outside of the office. When employees operate from home or other distant locations, training ensures that these are identified and that security practices are followed.

3. Employee Empowerment:

Security awareness training enables employees to not only take an active role in cyber security within their profession but also to traverse the digital terrain safely both at work and in their personal lives. Employees who are confident in their talents will perform better and provide more security in their professions.

4. Security Incident Reporting:

It is critical to provide cybersecurity awareness training to employees so that they understand the need to report security issues to the proper team members as well as law enforcement. If staff are familiar with the security measures in the aftermath of a data security breach and respond immediately, the threats may be contained.

BENEFITS FROM CYBER SECURITY AWARENESS TRAINING

1. Savings on expenses:

While investing in cybersecurity training programs can be costly in the short term, they will save you money in the long run. With all of your employees adequately taught about the security threats that can arise as a result of a data breach, they will be more aware and able to defend themselves better if this occurs. The financial consequences of security breaches and sensitive data loss can be disastrous for an organization and are frequently irreversible. As a result, investing in cyber security awareness training upfront means you can avoid paying more money later due to an attack.

2. Security Breach Prevention:

Data breaches can be costly in terms of monetary losses, reputational harm, and legal ramifications. You can lessen the risk of a data breach and potential legal penalties by teaching personnel on best data protection practices. Understanding how to defend against a successful cyber-attack is one of the most critical skills you can teach your employees, and cybersecurity awareness training programs are the best method to learn these abilities.

3. Improved Incident Responses:

Employees who have received enough security awareness training are more likely to discover and report security events on time, allowing for faster incident response and containment. Being able to swiftly disclose, reverse, or limit the effects of an attack on susceptible data or a system means you can recover faster and keep a large portion of your vital data safe.

4. Customer Retention and Trust:

Customers who interact with a company want their data to be treated safely and protected from cyber-criminals. You will develop trust and confidence with your clients by displaying a commitment to creating a secure environment and training personnel on security issues. This can also be the tipping factor for a customer in deciding whether to do business with you or a competition.

5. Adherence to Compliance:

Compliance with your industry's norms and standards is a legal requirement, and human error can have irrevocable consequences. Offering a cyber security awareness training program ensures that you raise staff knowledge and prevent hefty penalties for noncompliance if a security breach occurs.

6. Competitive Advantage:

Organizations that prioritize cybersecurity security and provide security awareness training can earn a market advantage. This is because companies will appear more reliable and trustworthy from the perspective of customers, suppliers, and business partners because they are demonstrating their commitment to keeping stakeholders' sensitive information protected.

7. Adaptation to New Threats:

Employees are kept up to date on new and growing cybersecurity dangers by investing in a cyber security awareness training program, allowing your firm to stay on top of any emerging hazards and change security measures accordingly.

Investing in cybersecurity awareness for your company can not only help you by lowering the danger of a sensitive data breach but also place your company ahead of the pack in the digital transformation race.

HOW TO EDUCATE EMPLOYEES ON CYBERSECURITY

1. Determine Your Training Requirements:

Conduct a thorough review of the organization's cybersecurity threats and weaknesses before conducting security awareness training. Make a point of identifying specific areas where employees may be lacking in skills or where possible dangers may already exist.

2. Create a Training Plan:

Create a detailed training plan based on the assessment that describes each topic you will cover, the format in which it will be given, and the schedule for completion. This will help you keep on track when teaching staff and provide them with the most relevant and important information.

3. Establish Specific Goals:

Make sure to create specific and measurable training goals. Determine what you want your staff to learn and accomplish as a result of such a program. In this manner, you may track development by administering tests or simulating attacks to see how much staff have learned.

4. Engage Leadership Support:

To be effective, a security awareness training program must have the backing of the entire workforce. Enabling top-level management support and commitment while demonstrating the necessity of cyber security awareness training will motivate employees to attend and engage.

5. Personalize Your Training Content:

Each organization will have different digital security demands and threats. Thus, it is critical that they do not all receive the same cybersecurity awareness training curriculum. Make your content relevant to them and their security architecture by personalizing it. Include real-world examples and case studies relevant to your business and workforce to make this more approachable and to demonstrate the importance of having the correct skill set.

6. Select the Best Training Methods:

One training strategy will not work for all firms when implementing a security awareness program. To effectively engage employees, use a variety of approaches such as workshops, webinars, e-learning modules, quizzes, and interactive simulations.

7. Include hands-on exercises:

In addition to using various training methods, including hands-on exercises that allow staff to apply their knowledge in a variety of physical security scenarios. This will help to reinforce learning and boost confidence throughout the program.

8. Offer Phishing Simulations:

Conduct phishing simulations to assess employees' abilities to detect phishing attempts and respond quickly. Use these simulations as teaching opportunities to promote best practices and raise security awareness.

WHAT SHOULD CYBER SECURITY AWARENESS TRAINING PROGRAMS COVER?

1. Cyber Threat Types:

It is critical for students to understand the various sorts of cyber risks. The majority of cyber security awareness training programs include basic cyber dangers such as phishing, malware, ransomware, social engineering, and insider threats.

2. Phishing Prevention:

One of the most common security dangers that a company might face is phishing. Teach staff how to identify phishing emails, websites, and phone calls, as well as how to avoid falling prey to such frauds.

3. Password Protection:

To protect accounts, emphasize the significance of setting and changing strong, unique passwords on a frequent basis, as well as the use of multi-factor authentication. To add credibility to your claim, provide real-world examples of cybercriminals gaining access to virtual private networks.

4. Data Security:

A security strategy's major purpose is to protect data, and it is critical to train personnel on the skill set required for this. Employees should be educated on how to handle and protect sensitive information in both digital and physical media, and they should be confident in the best practices for doing so.

5. Remote Work Security:

Nowadays, the majority of companies allow employees to work remotely. As a result, it is critical to discuss best practices for secure remote work, such as the usage of VPNs and secure Wi-Fi connections. In this manner, both you and your staff can be assured that they will be safe while working in their own environment.

6. Mobile Device Security:

Mobile devices are becoming a more popular target for cyber-attacks. Address the hazards connected with mobile devices, educate them on how to protect the sensitive information that they contain, and explain the best networking practices. Make a plan in case the device is stolen or misplaced, as this can prevent unauthorized parties from gaining access to important information.

7. Identifying and Protecting Against Malicious Content:

Malware is a particularly dangerous sort of cyber-attack, so it is critical that staff understand how to properly protect their systems from infiltration. Specific training on viruses, worms, trojan horses, and spyware will offer personnel an understanding of how malware may be presented, making it easier to protect against it.

8. Reporting and Responding to Incidents:

A lot of cyber security awareness training helps to defend against cyber-attacks, but it doesn't go much further. When such occurrences occur, teaching employees which organizations or security professionals should be contacted helps protect an organization from legal ramifications. Also, instruct people on how to mitigate the harm while restoring normal operations as soon as feasible.

9. Adaptation in Response to Technological Advances:

Because the world is always changing and technology improvements are made on a regular basis, it is critical that personnel maintain their security awareness training. Instead of repeating the same procedures, offer monthly refresher training to help firms keep on top of their security rules and build a strong cybersecurity culture.

10. Data Backup and recovery:

A regular backup of data is a vital component of a cyber security awareness training plan. This protects an organization's sensitive data in the event of an attack or other form of cyber danger, allowing systems to be recovered quickly and simply if this occurs. Having the ability to restore data implies that firms may typically avoid losing clients or large sums of cash.

INCIDENT RESPONSE

Incident response is the process of responding to a data breach or cyberattack, including how an organization seeks to control the effects of such an occurrence. The goal is to handle incidents effectively in order to limit damage to systems and data, save recovery time and cost, and maintain brand reputation.

Organizations must have a clear incident response plan in place. This strategy should define what defines a security event and explain a simple process that teams can use when an issue happens.

It is also critical that firms choose a team, employee, or leader to manage the overall incident response program and carry out the plan. This team is known as the Computer Security Incident Response Team (CSIRT) at larger organizations.

IMPORTANCE OF INCIDENT RESPONSE

Uncontrolled incident activity can quickly evolve into a larger problem, resulting in data breaches, exorbitant expenses, or system failures. Organizations can minimize damages, eliminate exploited vulnerabilities, restore services and processes, and reduce the risk of repeat disasters by responding rapidly to incidents.

Organizations can use incident response to do the following:

- Prepare for the known as well as the unknown.
- Identify security incidents as soon as possible.
- Establish best practices for preventing intrusions before they cause harm.

Incident response is vital to their operations because most firms rely on mission-critical computing systems and retain sensitive information. Security events can have both short- and long-term consequences that affect the overall success of the company. Downtime and service disruption, regulatory fines, litigation fees, and data recovery costs are examples of these.

Aside from these immediate consequences, failure to effectively respond to incidents has a negative influence on the organization's business performance. Unresolved issues are linked to a negative brand reputation as well as low levels of consumer loyalty and satisfaction.

Although an organization cannot totally avoid occurrences, incident response can help to reduce the number of incidents that occur. Organizations should concentrate on preparing for the consequences of a security incident. Attackers will always exist, but with a functionally successful strategy for incident response, any business can prepare for an attack.

The cyber incident response lifecycle is divided into six stages.

The NIST's Computer Security Incident Handling Guide is the most widely used cyber incident response framework. It is divided into six stages that lead organizations through the process:

- Preparation
- Identification
- Containment
- Eradication
- Recovery
- Learning experiences

Despite the fact that each of these stages comprises complicated and interconnected actions, the documented plan should provide a simple and accurate direction that is free of jargon.

This allows stakeholders to make quick decisions and establish a course of action without having to dig through extensive technical details.

Let's dive deeply into the six stages:

1. Preparation:

An effective incident response plan outlines the steps an organization should take far in advance of a disruptive incident. The plan begins by explaining how a company might reduce the risk of a data leak.

During the planning phase, organizational data protection policies should be aligned with security goals and technology defenses. You must, at the very least, guarantee that personnel have undertaken information security staff awareness training. They should ideally also obtain incident response training. Similarly, you should conduct a system audit to ensure that your sensitive data is securely protected.

2. Identification:

The second phase of incident response planning refers to the actions taken by an organization to determine whether its systems have been compromised.

You are better able to thwart an infiltration if you can detect it quickly. Even if that isn't possible, you can speed up the reaction and reduce damage, saving you time and money.

When determining a security issue, you should consider the following:

- Who discovered the breach?
- What is the extent of the breach?
- Is it affecting our operations?
- What is the source of the compromise?

3. Containment:

The third phase discusses the procedures you should take to limit harm after you've been breached. Depending on the nature of the situation, this may imply removing the criminal hacker from your networks or isolating the already compromised data.

During this stage, examine if systems should be taken offline or removed, as well as whether there are any immediate steps you can take to close vulnerabilities.

4. Eradication:

The fourth phase of a cyber incident response plan focuses on repairing the flaw that allowed the data breach to occur. The specifics will depend on the type of occurrence, but at this point, you must determine how the information was compromised and how to eliminate the danger.

If your organization was infested with malware, for example, you would remove the bad software and isolate the afflicted areas. Meanwhile, if the attack was carried out because a criminal hacker compromised an employee's login credentials, their account would be frozen.

5. Recovery:

Once the threat has been eliminated, you can proceed to the penultimate stage of cyber event response, which is restoring your systems to operational status.

This will be more complicated in some cases than others, but it is an important element of the process and should be handled with care. Without a suitable recovery procedure in place, you may stay vulnerable to similar attacks, compounding the harm.

Once the situation has been resolved, you should test and monitor the affected systems as part of the recovery process. This ensures that the measures you implement function as planned and allows you to remedy any errors.

6. Learning experiences:

The last step in the cyber incident response plan is to assess the incident and identify areas for improvement. Everyone on your incident response team should gather to discuss whether elements of the plan worked and what challenges you experienced.

Every step of the process should be evaluated, including what happened, why it happened, what you did to control the problem, and what could have been done differently. Were there any gaps in the plan, for example, and was the documentation effective and easy to understand?

This conversation should take place between one and two weeks after the security event occurred - long enough to evaluate the scenario in retrospect but short enough to keep it fresh in everyone's memory.

The goal of this step is not to point out team members' mistakes but to ensure that inefficiencies do not recur in the future. Failures in the process indicate that either the paperwork was unclear, required steps were not described, or staff training was insufficient.

TECHNICAL SECURITY CONTROLS

Any steps made to mitigate risk through technology means are considered technical security controls. They contrast with physical controls, which are literally tangible, and administrative controls, which focus on people management. Encryption, firewalls, anti-virus software, and data backups are examples of common technical measures.

These security controls are not mutually exclusive. For example, security cameras are both a technical and a physical control. Furthermore, password management is typically used to bridge the gap between technological and administrative controls.

Security controls can also be classified according to their purpose:

- The goal of preventative measures is to avoid security issues.
- Detective controls seek to detect issues as they occur or after they have occurred.
- Corrective controls seek to lessen the impact of an incident after it has occurred.

- Deterrent controls are intended to prevent attackers from attempting an attack.
- Compensating controls can be used if another control fails.

All of the following reasons can be served by technical security controls. We'll go over some common technical controls in the section below.

1. Encryption:

Encryption is a technical safeguard that scrambles data so that unauthorized people cannot access it. Encryption converts intelligible "plaintext" into "ciphertext," which looks to be gibberish of seemingly random characters.

However, encryption is not a random process. Instead, it employs algorithms and patterns to make the data unreadable. If a person possesses the correct key, they can decrypt the data and access it.

Encryption is a defensive measure aimed at preventing unauthorized people from accessing data.

2. Firewalls:

A firewall monitors and prevents all incoming and outgoing network traffic. It is effectively a boundary between two networks, most commonly between a private network and the Internet.

A firewall, once installed, inspects all traffic entering and exiting a network. If an information packet violates the firewall's predefined rules, it can be blocked from passing.

A firewall is both a detective and a preventative technical control in that it both watches for threats and prevents them from gaining access to the network.

3. Antivirus Protection:

Antivirus software continuously monitors for dangers in the background of a device. When you download or open a new file, the antivirus software Controls it immediately for viruses and other infections.

Your antivirus software will also do a more thorough scan of your device on a regular basis. If it detects something suspicious, it will usually warn the user and ask what action they want to take. Antivirus software, like a firewall, serves as both a detective and a preventative measure.

Users used to have to install third-party antivirus software to secure their PCs. However, most consumer operating systems now include firewalls and antivirus software by default.

4. Password Management:

Password management straddles the border between administrative and technological controls. If a corporation has a clear password policy, that's an administrative control. If the corporation employs technology to enforce it – for instance, by requiring passwords to be a specific length – it's also a technological control.

Password requirements are preventative controls by nature. By requiring a password to meet a certain level of complexity, the policy prevents simple brute-force attacks from cracking the password in a matter of minutes. Multi-factor authentication is also preventative, making it considerably harder for attackers to break into someone's account.

If a password system locks users out after a certain number of attempts, it also counts as a deterrent control. If the system alerts a user via email or text that multiple failed attempts just occurred, it's also a detective control, alerting the person or organization that an attack may have been attempted.

5. Backups:

Backups are a great example of corrective security control. If a server rack goes up in smoke, you could lose key systems or data. But if you have a backup copy of the data, you can restore much or all of the information lost.

There's more than one way to backup data. Some organizations might do a full backup on a daily basis. Others might rely on incremental backups, which only backup files that have changed since the most recent backup.

Note that although backups are certainly a technical control, they may also count as administrative control if the organization has a clear backup policy in place.

6. Access Control Models:

An access control model structures who can access what is in a given system or organization. Many organizations follow the principle of least privilege when it comes to sensitive data: each user only has enough access to perform their job duties.

The most common access model is discretionary access control. Under this system, each object has an owner who can then determine what access other users have. You can read more about the different access control models in our ultimate guide.

Access control models are both administrative and technical by nature. They can even extend to physical controls as well: if a guard at a gatehouse Controls IDs against a list before raising the gate so people can pass, that's an example of access controls in action.

Access control models are largely preventative in nature. Their aim is to prevent unauthorized people from gaining access to information and resources they should not have access to.

7. Physical Security Systems:

Physical security systems often coincide with technical controls. Security cameras and motion sensors count as both. These systems can both detect and deter attacks. A camera is, by its nature, designed to spot intruders, and the presence of cameras can also discourage people from even making an attempt to break in.

Security isn't just about keeping out trespassers. A fire alarm and sprinkler system mitigates risk just as much as a security system does, qualifying it as a physical and technical corrective security control.

IMPORTANCE OF TECHNICAL CONTROLS

Technical controls perform many critical functions, such as keeping unauthorized individuals from gaining access to a system and detecting when a security violation has occurred. Because they are so critical, some people think of technical controls as being the entirety of cybersecurity, ignoring other essential elements (those captured in the other building blocks).

Technical controls must be organized in such a way that they provide protection for both data at rest (e.g., data stored on a hard drive) and data in motion (e.g., data moving across a network). A common approach for deploying controls is defense-in-depth, where controls are layered. In such an arrangement, if an attacker breaches one control, controls at the next layer continue to provide protection.

The above are just a few examples of common technical controls. The National Institute of Standards and Technology lists dozens of security controls in SP 800-53, and even their list is by no means conclusive. Any measure that attempts to mitigate risk through the use of technology qualifies as a technical security control.

ACCESS CONTROL

Access control is a data security process that enables organizations to manage who is authorized to access corporate data and resources. Secure access control uses policies that verify users are who they claim to be and ensures appropriate control access levels are granted to users.

Implementing access control is a crucial component of web application security, ensuring only the right users have the right level of access to the right resources. The process is critical to helping organizations avoid data breaches and fighting attack vectors, such as buffer overflow attacks, KRACK attacks, on-path attacks, or phishing attacks.

COMPONENTS OF ACCESS CONTROL

Access control is managed through several components:

1. Authentication:

Authentication is the initial process of establishing the identity of a user. For example, when a user signs in to their email service or online banking account with a username and password combination, their identity has been authenticated. However, authentication alone is not sufficient to protect organizations' data.

2. Authorization:

Authorization adds an extra layer of security to the authentication process. It specifies access rights and privileges to resources to determine whether the user should be granted access to data or make a specific transaction.

For example, an email service or online bank account can require users to provide two-factor authentication (2FA), which is typically a combination of something they know (such as a password), something they possess (such as a token), or something they are (like a biometric verification). This information can also be verified through a 2FA mobile app or a thumbprint scan on a smartphone.

3. Access:

Once a user has completed the authentication and authorization steps, their identity will be verified. This grants them access to the resource they are attempting to log in to.

4. Manage:

Organizations can manage their access control system by adding and removing the authentication and authorization of their users and systems. Managing these systems can become complex in modern IT environments that comprise cloud services and on-premises systems.

5. Audit:

Organizations can enforce the principle of least privilege through the access control audit process. This enables them to gather data about user activity and analyze that information to discover potential access violations.

HOW DOES ACCESS CONTROL WORK?

Access control is used to verify the identity of users attempting to log in to digital resources. But it is also used to grant access to physical buildings and physical devices.

Physical Access Control

Common examples of physical access controllers include:

- Barroom Bouncers

Bouncers can establish an access control list to verify IDs and ensure people entering bars are of legal age.

- Subway Turnstiles:

Access control is used at subway turnstiles to only allow verified people to use subway systems. Subway users scan cards that immediately recognize the user and verify they have enough credit to use the service.

- Keycard or Badge Scanners in Corporate Offices:

Organizations can protect their offices by using scanners that provide mandatory access control. Employees need to scan a keycard or badge to verify their identity before they can access the building.

- Logical/Information Access Control:

Logical access control involves tools and protocols being used to identify, authenticate, and authorize users in computer systems. The access controller system enforces measures for data, processes, programs, and systems.

- Signing Into a Laptop Using a Password:

A common form of data loss is through devices being lost or stolen. Users can keep their personal and corporate data secure by using a password.

- Unlocking a Smartphone with a Thumbprint Scan:

Smartphones can also be protected with access controls that allow only the user to open the device. Users can secure their smartphones by using biometrics, such as a thumbprint scan, to prevent unauthorized access to their devices.

- Remotely Accessing an Employer's Internal Network Using a VPN:

Smartphones can also be protected with access controls that allow only the user to open the device. Users can secure their smartphones by using biometrics, such as a thumbprint scan, to prevent unauthorized access to their devices.

WHAT IS THE DIFFERENCE BETWEEN AUTHENTICATION AND AUTHORIZATION?

Authentication and authorization are crucial to access control in security. Authentication is the process of logging in to a system, such as an email address, online banking service, or social media account. Authorization is the process of verifying the user's identity to provide an extra layer of security that the user is who they claims to be.

Importance of Access Control in Regulatory Compliance

Access control is crucial to helping organizations comply with various data privacy regulations. These include:

- PCI DSS:

The Payment Card Industry Data Security Standard (PCI DSS) is a security standard that protects the payment card ecosystem. An access control system is crucial to permitting or denying transactions and ensuring the identity of users.

- HIPAA:

The Health Insurance Portability and Accountability Act (HIPAA) was created to protect patient health data from being disclosed without their consent. Access control is vital to limiting access to authorized users, ensuring people cannot access data that is beyond their privilege level, and preventing data breaches.

- SOC 2:

Service Organization Control 2 (SOC 2) is an auditing procedure designed for service providers that store customer data in the cloud. It ensures that providers protect the privacy of their customers and requires organizations to implement and follow strict policies and procedures around customer data. Access control systems are crucial to enforcing these strict data security processes.

- ISO 27001:

The International Organization for Standardization (ISO) defines security standards that organizations across all industries need to comply with and demonstrate to their customers that they take security seriously. ISO 27001 is the ISO's gold standard of information security and compliance certification. Implementing access controls is crucial to complying with this security standard.

TYPES OF ACCESS CONTROLS

There are various types of access controls that organizations can implement to safeguard their data and users. These include:

1. Attribute-based Access Control (ABAC):

ABAC is a dynamic, context-based policy that defines access based on policies granted to users. The system is used in identity and access management (IAM) frameworks.

2. Discretionary Access Control (DAC):

DAC models allow the data owner to decide access control by assigning access rights to rules that users specify. When a user is granted access to a system, they can then provide access to other users as they see fit.

3. Mandatory Access Control (MAC):

MAC places strict policies on individual users and the data, resources, and systems they want to access. The policies are managed by an organization's administrator. Users are not able to alter, revoke, or set permissions.

4. Role-Based Access Control (RBAC):

RBAC creates permissions based on groups of users, roles that users hold, and actions that users take. Users are able to perform any action enabled to their role and cannot change the access control level they are assigned.

5. Break-glass Access Control

Break-glass access control involves the creation of an emergency account that bypasses regular permissions. In the event of a critical emergency, the user is given immediate access to a system or account they would not usually be authorized to use.

6. Rule-based Access Control

A rule-based approach sees a system admin define rules that govern access to corporate resources. These rules are typically built around conditions, such as the location or time of day that users access resources.

ACCESS CONTROL IMPLEMENTATION

One of the most common methods for implementing access controls is to use VPNs. This enables users to securely access resources remotely, which is crucial when people work away from the physical office. Companies can use VPNs to provide secure access to their networks when employees are based in various locations around the world. While this is ideal for security reasons, it can result in some performance issues, such as latency.

Other access control methods include identity repositories, monitoring and reporting applications, password management tools, provisioning tools, and security policy enforcement services.

HOW DOES ACCESS CONTROL WORK?

Access control identifies users by verifying various login credentials, which can include usernames and passwords, PINs, biometric scans, and security tokens. Many access control systems also include multifactor authentication (MFA), a method that requires multiple authentication methods to verify a user's identity.

Once a user is authenticated, access control then authorizes the appropriate level of access and allowed actions associated with that user's credentials and IP address.

There are four main types of access control. Organizations typically choose the method that makes the most sense based on their unique security and compliance requirements. The four access control models are:

- Discretionary access control (DAC):

In this method, the owner or administrator of the protected system, data, or resource sets the policies for who is allowed access.

- Mandatory access control (MAC):

In this nondiscretionary model, people are granted access based on an information clearance. A central authority regulates access rights based on different security levels.

This model is common in government and military environments.

- Role-based access control (RBAC):

RBAC grants access based on defined business functions rather than the individual user's identity. The goal is to provide users with access only to data that's been deemed necessary for their roles within the organization. This widely used method is based on a complex combination of role assignments, authorizations, and permissions.

- Attribute-based access control (ABAC):

In this dynamic method, access is based on a set of attributes and environmental conditions, such as time of day and location, assigned to both users and resources.

ENCRYPTION

At its most basic level, encryption is the process of protecting information or data by using mathematical models to scramble it in such a way that only the parties who have the key to unscramble it can access it. That process can range from very simple to very complex, and mathematicians and computer scientists have invented specific forms of encryption that are used to protect information and data that consumers and businesses rely on every day.

What is Data Encryption?

Data encryption is a method of protecting data by encoding it in such a way that it can only be decrypted or accessed by an individual who holds the correct encryption key. When a person or entity accesses encrypted data without permission, it appears scrambled or unreadable.

Data encryption is the process of converting data from a readable format to a scrambled piece of information. This is done to prevent prying eyes from reading confidential data in transit. Encryption can be applied to documents, files, messages, or any other form of communication over a network.

How does encryption work?

Encryption works by converting "plaintext" into "ciphertext," often using cryptographic mathematical models known as algorithms. To decode the data back to plaintext, a decryption key, a string of numbers, or a password generated by an algorithm is required. Secure encryption methods involve so many cryptographic keys that an unauthorized human cannot guess which one is correct, nor can a computer simply calculate the proper string of characters by trying every possible combination (a brute force attack).

The "Caesar cipher," named after Roman emperor Julius Caesar because he employed it in his private communications, is an early example of simple encryption. The method is a substitution cipher in which one letter is substituted by another letter a certain number of positions down the alphabet. The recipient would need to know the key to the cipher, such as moving down the alphabet four places and over to the left (a "left shift four"), to decrypt the coded text. As a result, every "E" becomes a "Y" and so on.

Modern cryptography is far more advanced, employing strings of hundreds (or even thousands) of computer-generated characters as decryption keys in some circumstances.

TYPES OF ENCRYPTION

There are two types of encryption algorithms: Symmetric and Asymmetric.

The same key is used for encryption and decryption in symmetric encryption, also known as a shared key or private key algorithm. Symmetric key ciphers are less expensive to develop and need less computational resources to encrypt and decrypt, resulting in less delay in deciphering the data.

The disadvantage is that if an unauthorized person obtains the key, they will be able to decrypt any messages or data exchanged between the parties. As a result, the transmission of the shared key must be encrypted with a different cryptographic key, resulting in a dependence cycle.

Asymmetric encryption, commonly known as public-key cryptography, encrypts and decrypts data using two distinct keys. One is a public key that all parties use for encryption. Anyone with the public key can, therefore, transmit an encrypted message, but only those with the private key can decrypt it.

Asymmetric encryption is more expensive to generate and requires more computational power to decrypt because the public encryption key is generally huge, ranging from 1,024 to 2,048 bits. As a result, asymmetric encryption is frequently unsuitable for large data packets.

Algorithms for Common Encryption

The following are the most frequent symmetric encryption methods:

- DES:

The US government adopted DES, an encryption standard developed in the early 1970s, in 1977. Because the DES key size was just 56 bits, it was rendered outdated in today's technological ecosystem. Nonetheless, it had an impact on the development of modern cryptography, as cryptographers worked to improve on its theories and design more powerful encryption methods.

- Triple DES:

The next generation of DES took the DES cipher block and applied it three times to each encrypted data block by encrypting, decrypting, and encrypting it again. The method raised the key size, making brute-force decryption considerably more difficult. However, 3DES is still considered insecure and has been deprecated for all software applications by the US National Institute of Standards (NIST) beginning in 2023.

- AES:

The most commonly used encryption technology today, AES, was adopted by the US government in 2001. It was created using a "substitution-permutation network" theory and is a 128-bit block cipher with keys of 128, 192, or 256 bits in length.

- Twofish:

The fastest symmetric encryption algorithm, Twofish, is used in both hardware and software. Twofish is not patented or open source. However, it is free to use. Nonetheless, it is employed in popular encryption programs such as PGP (Pretty Good Privacy). It supports key sizes of up to 256 bits.

The following are the most common asymmetric encryption methods:

- RSA:

Stands for Rivest-Shamir-Adelman, the MIT trio that first disclosed the approach in 1977. One of the first forms of asymmetric encryption was RSA. The public key is generated by multiplying two prime numbers by an auxiliary value. Anyone can encrypt data using the RSA public key, but only someone who knows the prime numbers can decrypt the data. RSA keys can be exceedingly large (2,048 or 4,096-bit sizes are typical), making them expensive and sluggish. RSA keys are frequently used to encode symmetric encryption shared keys.

- Elliptic Curve Cryptography (ECC):

It is a type of advanced asymmetric encryption that uses elliptic curves over finite fields. The approach offers the same level of protection as large encryption keys but with a smaller and more efficient footprint. On the other hand, a "256-bit elliptic curve public key should provide comparable security to a 3,072-bit RSA public key." In symmetric encryption, it is frequently used for digital signatures and to encrypt shared keys.

IMPORTANCE OF DATA ENCRYPTION

People come into contact with encryption on a daily basis, whether they realize it or not. Encryption is used to secure devices like smartphones and personal computers, to safeguard financial activities like making a bank deposit and purchasing an item from an online merchant, and to ensure the privacy of messages like email and texts.

If you've ever observed that the address of a website begins with "https://" It signifies that the website uses transport encryption (the "s" stands for "secure"). Encryption is used in virtual private networks (VPNs) to keep data arriving and departing from a device private from prying eyes.

Data encryption is critical because it protects people's privacy while also protecting data from attackers and other cybersecurity dangers. From a regulatory standpoint, encryption is frequently required for companies such as healthcare, education, finance and banking, and retail.

Encryption serves four critical functions:

Confidentiality: keeping the data's contents hidden.

Integrity: confirms the message or data's origin.

Authentication ensures that the message or data has not been altered after it was sent.

Nonrepudiation: precludes the originator of the data or message from denying it.

The benefits of encryption include data protection across devices.

Data is always in motion, whether it be messaging between friends or financial transactions. When combined with other security functions like authentication, encryption can help keep data safe while it flows between devices or servers.

- Ensures the integrity of data:

Encryption protects data so that hostile actors cannot use it to commit fraud or extort or edit crucial documents, in addition to preventing unauthorized people from seeing the plaintext of data.

- Safeguards digital transformations:

With more organizations and individuals adopting cloud storage, encryption is becoming increasingly important in protecting data while it is in transit to the cloud, at rest on the server, and while it is being processed by workloads. Google provides a variety of encryption levels as well as key management services.

- Helps meet compliance requirements:

Many data privacy and security regulations need the use of robust encryption. Healthcare data is covered by the Health Insurance Portability and Accountability Act (HIPAA), credit and debit card transactions are covered by the Payment Card Industry Data Security Standard (PCI DSS), General Data Protection Regulations (GDPR), and retail transaction data is covered by the Fair Credit Practices Act (FCPA).

DISADVANTAGES OF ENCRYPTION

- Ransomware:

While encryption is typically used to secure data, malevolent actors may utilize it to keep data hostage. If an organization's data is breached and accessed, the actors can encrypt it and hold it hostage until the organization pays to get it released.

- Key management:

Encryption is significantly less effective when the cryptographic keys used to encrypt and decrypt data are not safe. Malicious actors frequently target an organization's encryption keys in their attacks. In addition to malevolent actors, losing encryption keys (for example, during a natural disaster that damages servers) can prevent companies from accessing critical data. This is why corporations frequently utilize a secure key management system to manage and safeguard their keys.

- Quantum computing:

Modern encryption techniques face an existential danger from quantum computing. When it is complete, quantum computing will be capable of processing vast amounts of data in a fraction of the time that traditional computers do. As a result, quantum computing has the potential to decrypt current encryption. All enterprises will have to alter encryption approaches in the future by employing quantum encryption techniques. Currently, quantum computing is limited and not yet capable of breaking modern encryption standards. NIST, on the other hand, has announced its approval for four new "quantum-resistant" algorithms designed to survive quantum computer attacks.

INTRUSION DETECTION SYSTEM

An intrusion detection system (IDS) is a network security tool that examines network traffic and devices for known hostile activity, suspicious activity, or violations of security policies.

An intrusion detection system (IDS) can aid in the acceleration and automation of network threat detection by alerting security administrators to known or potential threats or by sending alerts to a centralized security tool, such as a security information and event management (SIEM) system, where they can be combined with data from other sources to assist security teams in identifying and responding to cyber threats that may slip past other security measures.

IDSs can also help with compliance. Intrusion detection measures are required by certain legislation, such as the Payment Card Industry Data Security Standard (PCI-DSS).

An intrusion detection system (IDS) cannot prevent security threats on its own. Today, intrusion detection systems (IDSs) are generally connected with or incorporated into intrusion prevention systems (IPSs), which may detect security risks and take action to prevent them.

FUNCTIONS OF INTRUSION DETECTION SYSTEM

IDSs can be software applications put on endpoints or dedicated network hardware devices. Some intrusion detection systems (IDS) are offered as cloud services. An IDS, in whatever shape it takes, will employ one or both of two major threat detection methods: signature-based detection or anomaly-based detection.

- Signature-based detection:

Signature-based detection looks for attack signatures in network packets—unique characteristics or behaviors linked with a certain threat. An attack signature is a sequence of code that exists in a certain malware version.

A signature-based system IDS maintains a database of attack signatures against which network packets are compared. The IDS flags a packet if it matches one of the signatures. Signature databases must be frequently updated with fresh threat intelligence as new cyberattacks arise and existing attacks change in order to be effective. New assaults that have not yet been evaluated for signatures can avoid detection by signature-based IDS.

- Anomaly-based detection:

Machine learning is used in anomaly detection approaches to create—and constantly refine—a baseline model of normal network activity. The system then analyzes network activity to the model and highlights deviations, such as a process using more bandwidth than usual or a device opening a port that should be closed.

Because it identifies any anomalous behavior, anomaly-based intrusion detection systems can frequently discover brand-new cyberattacks that would otherwise evade signature-based detection. Anomaly-based intrusion detection systems, for example, can detect zero-day exploits—attacks that take advantage of software flaws before the program developer is aware of them or has time to patch them.

However, anomaly-based intrusion detection systems may be more prone to false positives. An anomaly-based IDS can detect even benign activities, such as an authorized user accessing a sensitive network resource for the first time.

- Less common detection methods:

Traffic from IP addresses and domains linked with malicious or suspicious activity is blocked using reputation-based detection. Stateful protocol analysis focuses on protocol behavior, such as identifying a denial-of-service (DoS) attack by detecting a single IP address and making a large number of simultaneous TCP connection requests in a short period of time.

When an IDS detects a potential danger or policy violation, it notifies the incident response team to investigate. IDSs also log security occurrences, either in their own logs or with a security information and event management (SIEM) tool (see 'IDS and other security solutions' below). These incident logs can be utilized to improve the criteria of the IDS, for example, by adding new attack signatures or changing the network behavior model.

TYPES OF INTRUSION PREVENTION SYSTEMS

IDSs are classified based on where they are installed in a system and the type of activity they monitor.

Network intrusion detection systems:

Network intrusion detection systems (NIDSs) monitor inbound and outgoing traffic to and from network devices. NIDS is strategically positioned throughout the network. They are frequently placed immediately behind firewalls at the network's perimeter to detect any malicious traffic that gets through. Insider threats or hackers who have hijacked user accounts may also be detected by NIDS deployed within the network. In a segmented network, for example, NIDS could be deployed behind each internal firewall to monitor traffic traveling between subnets.

To prevent interfering with legitimate traffic, an NIDS is frequently located "out-of-band," which means that traffic does not pass directly through it. A NIDS examines copies of network packets rather than the actual packets. Legitimate communication is not delayed as a result, but the NIDS can still detect and report malicious activity.

Host intrusion detection systems:

Host intrusion detection systems (HIDSs) are software programs that are installed on a single endpoint, such as a laptop, router, or server. Only activity on that device, including traffic to and from it, is monitored by the HIDS. Typically, a HIDS operates by taking periodic pictures of essential operating system files and comparing them over time. If the HIDS detects a change, such as log file editing or configuration changes, it notifies the security team.

Network-based intrusion detection systems and host-based intrusion detection systems are frequently combined by security teams. The NIDS examines all communication, whereas the HIDS can provide additional security around high-value assets. A HIDS can also assist in the detection of harmful activities from a compromised network node, such as ransomware propagating from an infected device.

While NIDS and HIDS are the most commonly used IDSs, security teams may employ other IDSs for particular objectives. A protocol-based intrusion detection system (PIDS) examines connection protocols between servers and devices. PIDS are frequently used to monitor HTTP or HTTPS connections on web servers. An application protocol-based intrusion detection system (APIDS) monitors application-specific protocols at the application layer. To detect SQL injections, an APIDS is frequently installed between a web server and a SQL database.

IDS EVASION STRATEGIES

While intrusion detection systems (IDS) can detect many threats, hackers have discovered techniques to circumvent them. IDS companies respond by improving their systems to take these strategies into account. However, this has resulted in a kind of arms race, with hackers and intrusion detection systems competing to remain one step ahead of one another.

Among the most prevalent IDS evasion techniques are:

- DDoS attacks, which take IDSs offline by flooding them with blatantly malicious traffic from many sources. When the IDS's resources are overburdened by decoy threats, the hackers infiltrate.
- Spoofing is the practice of forging IP addresses and DNS records to make it appear that their traffic is originating from a reliable source.
- Fragmentation is the process of dividing malware or other harmful payloads into small packets in order to obscure the signature and evade detection. Hackers can prevent the IDS from detecting the attack by purposefully delaying packets or sending them out of sequence.
- Encryption—the use of encrypted protocols to circumvent an IDS if the IDS lacks the necessary decryption key

- Operator fatigue—intentionally creating a huge number of IDS alerts to distract the incident response team from their main work.

IDS AND OTHER SECURITY MEASURES

IDSs are not stand-alone applications. They are intended to be part of a comprehensive cybersecurity system and are frequently tightly linked with one or more of the security solutions listed below.

SIEM (security information and event management) and intrusion detection systems

Integrating IDS with SIEMs allows security teams to enrich IDS alerts with threat intelligence and data from other tools, filter out false alarms, and prioritize incidents for remediation.

INTRUSION DETECTION AND PREVENTION SYSTEMS (IDS AND IPS)

As previously stated, an IPS, like an IDS, analyzes network traffic for suspicious activity and intercepts threats in real-time by immediately terminating connections or activating other security mechanisms. Because IPSs are designed to prevent cyberattacks, they are typically installed inline, which means that all traffic must pass through the IPS before it can reach the rest of the network.

Some businesses use an IDS and an IPS as independent solutions. IDS and IPS are frequently coupled in a single intrusion detection and prevention system (IDPS), which detects intrusions, logs them, alerts security personnel, and responds automatically.

FIREWALLS AND INTRUSION DETECTION SYSTEMS

IDSs and firewalls work in tandem. Firewalls are barriers that face the outside world and use predetermined rulesets to allow or deny traffic. IDSs are frequently placed near firewalls to help catch anything that gets past them. Some firewalls, particularly next-generation firewalls, include IDS and IPS functionalities.

CLASSIFICATION OF INTRUSION DETECTION SYSTEM

Intrusion detection systems are intended for use in a variety of situations. An IDS, like many other cybersecurity solutions, can be either host-based or network-based.

- Host-Based IDS (HIDS):

A host-based IDS is installed on a specific endpoint to defend it from both internal and external threats. An IDS of this type may be able to monitor network traffic to and from the machine, view active processes, and examine system logs. The visibility of a host-based IDS is limited to its host machine, reducing the accessible context for decision-making, but it has comprehensive visibility into the host computer's internals.

- Network-Based Intrusion Detection System (NIDS):

A network-based IDS system is intended to monitor a whole protected network. It can see all traffic going over the network and makes decisions based on packet metadata and contents. Although this broader perspective provides greater information and the potential to detect widespread threats, these systems lack visibility into the internals of the endpoints that they defend.

Because of the various levels of visibility, adopting a HIDS or NIDS in isolation provides an organization's system with insufficient protection. A unified threat management solution that combines different technologies into a single system can provide more complete security.

IDS Deployment Detection Method:

Aside from deployment location, IDS solutions differ in how they detect possible intrusions:

1. Signature Detection:

Signature-based IDS solutions use fingerprints from known threats to identify known threats. When malware or other harmful content is found, a signature is created and added to the list that the IDS solution uses to examine incoming content. Because all warnings are generated based on the identification of known malicious information, an IDS can achieve a high threat detection rate with no false positives. A signature-based intrusion detection system, on the other hand, is confined to detecting known threats and is blind to zero-day vulnerabilities.

2. Anomaly Detection:

Anomaly-based intrusion detection systems (IDS) create a model of the protected system's "normal" behavior. All future behavior is compared to this model, and any deviations are identified as potential dangers, resulting in alarms. While this method can detect novel or zero-day threats, the challenge in developing an accurate model of "normal" behavior implies that these systems must balance false positives (incorrect warnings) with false negatives (missed detections).

A hybrid intrusion detection system employs both signature-based and anomaly-based detection. This allows it to detect more possible assaults with a lower error rate than either system alone would.

IDS VERSUS FIREWALL:

Firewalls and intrusion detection systems are both cybersecurity solutions that can be used to defend an endpoint or a network. However, their objectives are vastly different.

An intrusion detection system (IDS) is a passive monitoring device that detects possible threats and generates alerts, allowing SOC analysts or incident responders to analyze and respond to potential issues. An IDS offers no genuine endpoint or network protection. A firewall, on the other hand, is intended to serve as a safeguard. It analyzes network packet metadata and allows or restricts traffic depending on predetermined rules. This establishes a barrier through which specific types of traffic or protocols cannot flow.

A firewall is more like an Intrusion Prevention System (IPS) than an IDS because it is an active protection mechanism. An IPS is similar to an IDS in that it actively inhibits recognized threats rather than simply generating an alarm. This adds to the capability of a firewall, and many next-generation firewalls (NGFWs) include IDS/IPS. This allows them to impose specified filtering rules (firewalls) as well as identify and respond to more complex cyber threats (IDS/IPS). More on the IPS vs IDS dispute can be found here.

CHOOSING AN IDS SOLUTION

An intrusion detection system (IDS) is an important part of any organization's cybersecurity strategy. A simple firewall serves as the foundation for network security, but many sophisticated attacks can bypass it. An intrusion detection system (IDS) adds another line of security, making it more difficult for an attacker to obtain unnoticed access to a company's network.

It is critical to carefully analyze the deployment scenario when picking an IDS system. In some circumstances, an IDS may be the ideal solution for the job, whilst an IPS with integrated security may be a better alternative in others. Using an NGFW with IDS/IPS functionality provides an integrated solution that simplifies threat detection and security administration.

Check Point has a long history of producing intrusion detection and intrusion prevention systems that deliver a high level of threat detection with very low mistake rates, allowing SOC analysts and incident responders to easily identify actual threats.

PHYSICAL SECURITY

Physical security is simply the protection of your people, property, and assets. This involves the physical safeguarding of equipment and technology, including data storage, servers, and employee computers.

Physical security is often sarcastically referred to as "guards and gates," however current physical security systems include a variety of aspects and procedures, such as:

- Where are your weak points in terms of site layout and security configuration?
- What is the most vulnerable?
- Critical area visibility, incorporating lights and video cameras
- Access control ranges from simple locks to keypads and biometric access
- Perimeter security is the "guards and gates" component of physical security.
- Motion sensors, cameras, and tripwire alarms are examples of intrusion detection devices.
- Power, fire, network connectivity, and water infrastructure protection

- Staff training and incident response: do your workers know how to handle an issue, and do you have a plan in place for an emergency response?

As you can see, the physical security examples above cover a wide range of topics, touching on every part of a facility and its functions. Some physical security plans are influenced by environmental factors, such as your site layout, while others are influenced by behavioral factors, such as staff training. To return to the definition of physical security, successful protection of people, property, and assets necessitates a variety of physical security techniques.

- **Unauthorized entry:**

Unauthorized entry involves tailgating, social engineering, and gaining access through stolen passes or codes. Physical security breaches occur at the initial point of entrance to your site, conceptually. If unauthorized people get access, it is only a matter of time before other physical security problems emerge.

- **Theft and burglary:**

Businesses have many valuable assets, ranging from equipment to paperwork and personnel identification cards. Because of what they store on their premises, some businesses, such as jewelry or technology stores, are especially vulnerable to physical security concerns such as theft. A wealth management organization, for example, stores incredibly important information. Despite the fact that their assets are significantly different, both businesses are great targets for criminals.

- **Vandalism:**

Some businesses face the threat of having their property destroyed or tampered with. This can be tied to a company's location; for example, if your business is next door to a bar or nightclub, alcohol-related vandalism may be a common occurrence. Vandalism can also be driven by ideology, as when activists inflict physical damage to a business's property, such as smashing windows or flinging paint.

These are a few examples of high-level physical security risks. Physical security concerns particular to your sector and region will be discovered as you undertake a risk assessment of your own organization.

METHODS AND TECHNIQUES OF PHYSICAL SECURITY

There are many different sorts of physical security measures, but the four primary ones are deterrence, detection, delay, and response. These tiers of physical protection begin with Deter and go inwards until, if all previous levels are breached, a response is required.

Levels of physical security

Physical security measures aimed at deterring intruders are known as deterrence measures. Tall perimeter walls, barbed wire, clear signs declaring that the property has active security, commercial video cameras, and access controls are common ways. All of these are intended to send a clear message to thieves that trespassing is not only difficult but also highly likely.

- Detect:

Detection works to catch any intruders who get past the above-mentioned deterrence measures. Some criminals may sneak up behind an employee, a practice known as tailgating, or they may find a means to scale barricades. A physical security mechanism that can identify their presence promptly is critical in these instances. There are numerous sorts of physical security systems that you are likely aware of. CCTV cameras, motion sensors, intruder alarms, and smart alerting technology such as AI analytics are examples of physical security controls. If an intruder is discovered quickly, security personnel can prevent them from proceeding and, if necessary, alert police enforcement.

- Delay:

You'll observe that some physical security devices serve several functions: they can both discourage and detect. Many of the physical security measures mentioned above are also useful in delaying intruders. Access control systems demand credentials to unlock a locked door, slowing an intruder and making apprehending them easier.

- Respond:

Having the technology and systems in place to respond to intruders and take action is critical for physical security, but it is sometimes underestimated. Communication systems, security guards, designated first responders, and mechanisms for closing down a site and contacting law enforcement are examples of response physical security measures.

Physical security controls can take several forms, ranging from boundary fences to guards and security camera system recorders. Many physical security components serve multiple purposes, and when multiple measures are coupled, they are extremely effective at stopping or intercepting intruders and illegal activity.

PHYSICAL SECURITY CONTROL TECHNOLOGY

There is a vast array of physical security instruments and cutting-edge technologies available under the four basic types of physical security control categories.

In recent years, physical security systems have grown by leaps and bounds, providing superior protection at affordable prices. Physical security equipment is now using cloud technology and artificial intelligence for even smarter real-time processing.

Automated physical security components can serve a variety of purposes in your overall physical security system. You may want to use access control technologies to check entry and exits for physical controls. Proactive intrusion detection is possible with video security and access controls that work as a single system.

One of the nice things about physical security technology is that it is scalable, allowing for flexible implementation. If you are experimenting with physical security equipment, you could start with a limited number of cameras, locks, sensors, or keypads to evaluate how they operate. However, significant government cameras, access control, and security equipment are most likely required for a more robust strategy for assets such as municipalities and should be developed accordingly. Physical security systems can capture important data for audit trails and analysis when connected to the cloud or a secure network. It can also be used to convince stakeholders of the benefits of your physical security approach.

Consider how different types of physical security instruments will interact while developing your physical security investment strategy. Choosing physical security devices that work together seamlessly will make things much easier, especially during the soak testing period. Many physical security firms now adhere to universal standards such as ONVIF, allowing devices from many manufacturers to connect considerably more smoothly than in the past. Other specialized requirements, such as FIPS-certified technology, should be considered while examining your investment strategy.

- Video security:

Today, video surveillance technology is a critical component of many physical security plans. CCTV has come a long way since the days of recording analog signals to tape. So is internet connectivity - thanks to fast network connections and the cloud, high-quality video transmission is now faster than before.

Video surveillance is essentially a detection type of physical security control. It is possible to detect suspicious activity in real-time by using a live link and smart cameras. They can also be used to deter intruders because the presence of cameras around a property deters criminals from attempting to break in.

There are numerous types of security cameras available to meet a wide range of needs and circumstances, such as city surveillance cameras utilized in low-light situations. Alternatively, varifocal lens cameras are ideal for targeting certain small spaces in a corporate scenario. Analog cameras are still a cost-effective alternative for many physical security measures, and while the technology is older, they have advantages over more modern counterparts in some circumstances. HD analog security cameras are a popular option because they combine the best of both worlds: low-cost hardware and high-quality footage.

IP cameras use cutting-edge technology to transmit high-quality video over an internet connection via ethernet security camera connections. These cameras contain a plethora of intelligent functions, such as motion detection and anti-tampering. This means you get data not only about what's happening around your site but also about the cameras themselves. IP cameras come in a variety of models, depending on the type of footage you need to record.

Fixed IP cameras, as the name implies, have a fixed viewpoint. This may appear to be a limitation, but most cameras only need to focus on one important area at a time. Fixed IP cameras are an excellent solution for both indoor and outdoor applications, and versions are available for both. These cameras can work in a variety of lighting settings. These cameras, which are available in both bullet and dome formats, may provide wall-to-wall and floor-to-ceiling coverage. As a result, there are also suitable security options like elevator cameras. If vandalism is a physical security problem, certain models are especially intended to be vandal-resistant.

If you require 360-degree views, pan-tilt-zoom (PTZ) security cameras are an excellent alternative. These allow you complete control over what you view in a certain area. They are designed to be adaptable in a variety of lighting circumstances and to provide long-distance views. Look for cameras with low latency, which deliver footage with little delay.

Panoramic IP cameras are an excellent choice if you require 360-degree views throughout the clock. They are continually filming from every angle. If you need maximum visibility in certain areas, these could be an excellent addition to your physical security plan.

Some environments are more difficult and necessitate a particular solution. Ruggedized cameras that can withstand blasts and severe temperatures are available for industries such as oil and gas plants. Ruggedized cameras are particularly useful in harsh outdoor environments, such as busy ports where water and humidity can damage equipment.

Examples of Physical Security Challenges

Many firms are unable to make an effective physical security expenditure due to budget constraints. Failure to budget for an effective physical security system, on the other hand, might lead to physical security problems over time. Some physical security methods are more expensive than others; for example, hiring security guards can be costly, especially if a large number of them are required to watch a site for extended periods of time. Furthermore, more modern physical security hardware, such as high-end video cameras and access control systems, will necessarily be more expensive. However, failing to implement those safeguards might expose a company to a variety of physical security concerns, which can be equally costly.

Staff shortages might also put physical security systems under strain. Even with the most advanced physical security equipment, organizations require staff to manage larger systems and make judgments about how and when to intervene. Many firms had recruitment shortages in the aftermath of the coronavirus outbreak. Inadequate personnel to perform your physical security plan might strain morale and cause operational challenges. Even if you are able to hire new employees, if they are not well trained in the physical security technologies you use or your company's physical security rules, this might create bottlenecks that expose you to risk.

Physical security technology improves business security, but if not properly integrated into a wider physical security system, it can cause more difficulties than it solves. A critical consideration is how your physical security devices interact and feed information back into your physical security system. If your gadgets are incompatible or improperly integrated, crucial information may be lost. Using devices that meet ONVIF camera physical security criteria is one method to reduce the likelihood of this happening. ONVIF is a set of standards designed to allow many various forms of physical security devices to connect smoothly, regardless of manufacturer. Go to the section on physical security planning in this handbook for more information on how to integrate technology into your physical security system.

Physical security management can be a logistical difficulty when securing a large business network. Keeping track of several moving pieces at once is difficult when you have a number of connected sites to safeguard. If you are dealing with any of the concerns listed above, managing several sites will only make matters worse. Because no two locations are identical, your plan must be flexible enough to suit each site's unique physical security risks and vulnerabilities in addition to executing a company-wide physical security policy.

Physical Security Planning

Physical security plans demand input from all areas of your company. Physical security measures do not occur in a vacuum; they have an impact on all aspects of your day-to-day operations. Many of the examples of physical security in the guide below will show how they affect your company's finances, regulatory status, and operations. An effective physical security planning strategy is highly researched, holistic, and includes all of your departments and functions. You will learn how to apply physical security best practices at every stage of your physical security plan, from risk assessment to implementation, in the following:

1. Performing a risk assessment:

You can't authorize any physical security investment unless you know what physical security measures are required. This is why a thorough risk assessment is such a great asset: once completed, you can return to it, add to it, and utilize it to alter your physical security systems over time.

Trying to figure out where to start might be intimidating. If you lack the knowledge or time to conduct this yourself, there are many physical security businesses that specialize in risk assessments and penetration testing. You can also hire a physical security company to advise you on how to carry out the process efficiently.

Consider your most prevalent physical security risks and vulnerabilities first. Consider which physical security breaches might occur in your firm at each stage using the Deter-Detect-Delay-Respond categories above. Identifying any exposed ports of entry, as well as any places of interest or high value, is the most obvious place to start.

Check to discover whether your organization has any previous documented physical security breaches. Your insurance company will have records of previous claims, and previous physical security management may have kept track of previous instances. This is also the time to communicate with stakeholders and other departments; the risk assessment stage is when expectations are defined, and team participation is necessary for the overall success of your project. Don't forget about any department: from senior management to physical security in IT, every team has something to offer.

Look into your website thoroughly. Keep no stone untouched, and keep in mind that not all physical security measures necessitate cameras, locks, or guards. Poorly lit places, for example, may require cameras, but merely improving lighting conditions will make a huge impact on how appealing that area is to thieves. Examine both high-traffic and low-traffic areas; both are vulnerable to intrusion because criminals can slip by unobserved in a crowd or when no one is there. These are the locations where identifying and delaying invaders will be crucial.

With this knowledge, you can begin to plan where to place physical security components and redundancy networks. A redundancy network is essential since any physical security control may fail. A backup network will safeguard you from any physical security threats in these circumstances.

2. Examine your current operations and resources:

All of the information gleaned from your risk assessment will assist you in determining which physical security controls to acquire and apply. The scope of your project will be determined by the resources you already have. For example, if you intend to put additional IP cameras over analog cameras and smart access controls, you must first determine whether you have the internet speed to handle streaming all of this data. You should also ensure that you have enough server space to store all of the data generated by these physical security devices.

Then there's the matter of whether you want to monitor your security in-house or outsource it to a physical security provider. One fundamental question is space – do you have adequate on-site space for a security operations center (SOC)? You'll also need to assess whether your current crew can manage extra data streams from more devices or whether you'll need to hire more people. Outsourcing this duty can alleviate some operational stress, but depending on your sector, you must determine whether physical security policies and compliance require you to keep data confidential.

This is the time to think about what physical security tools you want, what you need right away, and what your long-term physical security plans are. It will be much easier to deal with stakeholders on financial approval if you have a solid plan in place.

3. Commercial and operational authorization:

You will now submit your strategy for business approval. The main goal during this phase is to reach an agreement on a financially sustainable plan that does not compromise physical security and exposes you to risk.

As stakeholders and other interested parties evaluate and suggest changes to your plan, make sure to create a fresh risk matrix for each iteration. This allows you to refer back to previous versions to ensure that no physical security threats are missed. Documenting each stage in writing ensures that you and your stakeholders are on the same page so that there is accountability for how your physical security solutions work later on.

Prepare yourself for a situation in which you will have to compromise. In such cases, examine the places where you are unable to allocate as many resources as you would want and see if there is a workaround. For example, if lighting conditions are improved, an apparently dangerous dark region may not require specialist thermal cameras. Alternatively, instead of hiring a huge staff of operators to handle alerts, investigate if your present team can handle the additional burden with the help of smart analytics.

4. Putting in place physical security policies and procedures:

Your physical security plan is finally ready for deployment, thanks to stakeholder support. This is the stage at which processes, protocols, and internal physical security policies are defined in greater detail.

At this stage, you should complete the Respond components of your physical security system. Establish incident response points of contact, such as who is accountable for threat verification and when to alert law enforcement. This is also the time to finalize issues like how to manage after-hours monitoring and when to arm and disarm your location.

This is also the time to confirm KPIs and write down any stakeholder expectations. Once your physical security measures are in place, engage with stakeholders to discuss how you plan to satisfy their expectations, as well as how the "settling in" process will function. Set up check-in calls with stakeholders in the first few months to keep them updated on how physical security threats are being managed and how your plan is performing.

5. Best Physical Security Practices:

Some physical security best practices should be followed when your physical security system settles in and grows over time. Accountability should be the cornerstone of your growing plan: who is responsible for every aspect of your company's physical security? Create a physical security guide or playbook that everyone can refer to, and that can evolve with your facility.

Physical security examples in your playbook should include the following:

A list of all the components that you employ (for example, cameras, keypads, and passcodes)

A list of all of your device configurations

Objectives agreed upon and how to achieve them

Protocols and configurations for redundancy networks

Physical security policies for testing and maintenance on a regular basis

Any local, national, or international physical security standards or laws you adhere to, as well as renewal dates

A guide like this not only keeps everyone on the same page but is also an excellent resource for any new hires. By putting all of your critical information in one place, you will avoid physical security hazards as well as compliance issues.

FACILITY SECURITY

Facility security is the process of safeguarding your physical space, hardware, and software against illegal internal and external forces. It takes into account techniques for access control, inventory management, visitor management, and maintenance records.

Facility security entails ensuring that all of the company's security requirements are followed on a regular basis. It entails prioritizing the security and security of everyone in the office, from employees to suppliers to visitors.

It entails monitoring daily activities such as entry and exit, video surveillance, and other security-related devices. It also entails evaluating closed-circuit television footage, ensuring security compliance, and monitoring employee access to restricted and protected areas.

COMPONENTS OF FACILITY SECURITY

Facility security comprises several components that organizations must address in order to protect their assets.

The following are the primary components of facility security:

1. Equipment and Procedure:

Personnel are critical to maintaining a safe and secure environment, but they are not the only thing to consider. There is extra equipment and procedures, but their utility is limited by the security team's ability.

It is critical to follow certain rules while safeguarding locations that store expensive or hazardous commodities. To make it more difficult for an intruder to steal valuables, keep sensitive locations and things as physically separated as possible. However, the security policy of a facility may necessitate the concentration of high-risk places under tighter surveillance.

Access control, monitoring, detection, communication, and incident response devices may be required. Controlling who has access to a building can be as simple as installing locks or as complex as utilizing biometric scanning equipment that detects a person's fingerprints or iris. The most frequent type of surveillance technology is cameras.

Other detection tools, such as motion detectors and sirens, can also be used.

Provide a mechanism for employees to communicate with one another and with the headquarters. They should also be able to contact outside providers in the event of a major security breach or other emergency.

2. Audits and Critical System Checklist:

Audits are objective evaluations of a firm or other organization; in this case, they analyze potential threats to the security of a building and its operations. They present an in-depth examination of the facility security guide and its effectiveness in practice. They evaluate a building's security and make recommendations for improving safeguards against unauthorized entry and disruptive incidents.

Facility management and security personnel may assist audits by providing information on the facility's technology components. They can also conduct timely audits during the site development process.

As a result, not only will the building's layout be more accommodating to your requirements, but it will also help prevent any hazards during construction. In addition, the auditor will search for security problems and code breaches related to the facility's vehicles, fire control systems, electrical components, and heating, ventilation, and air conditioning (HVAC).

The auditor will examine the automation systems and their interface with the public and emergency communications as part of the facility security communication component. After completing a building security audit, transmit the findings and the following action plan to the appropriate authorities and individuals. In light of the audits, update the facility security guide; communication is critical to this process.

3. Assessment of Attacks and Threats:

It is critical to realize that the nature of the assaults and threats that a facility faces might vary greatly depending on its intended purpose and contents. Use the findings of the research to improve existing security procedures and develop new ones to address detected vulnerabilities.

Once the security system is in place, the best way to keep any threats at bay is to construct a facility maintenance checklist and run through it on a regular basis to look for any faults that could jeopardize the building's security.

4. Security Countermeasures:

Many companies are looking to the future of technology integration in security to tackle both current and potential threats. As internet use and other types of digital communication have become more common in the workplace, the costs associated with modems, lines, and cable installation and maintenance have fallen.

It gives managers greater flexibility in selecting how to distribute resources, what to outsource, and how much to spend on operations. Monitoring can be centralized in one area (such as a network or laptop), making it easier to keep track of large and complex systems.

The capacity to monitor and respond from a distance expands the possibility of collaboration and adaptability. However, the internet offers another possible access point. If an intruder gains access to the facility's server system via the Internet, they may have access to sensitive data and information.

Extra identifying information may be useful in an emergency or in the event of card theft. Biometrics can assist in bringing order and legitimacy to the security industry.

Facility Security Solution:

You can use a variety of facility security solutions to secure the security of your staff and equipment.

1. Access Management:

Access control is an essential component of any comprehensive security solution. You can restrict who is permitted to enter your property and which portions they can access when inside by establishing a high-quality access control system at entry points.

Another option is to install an intruder alarm system, which will sound an alarm if an unauthorized person enters your property.

2. Video Surveillance and CCTV:

CCTV and video surveillance systems are also essential in protecting your facility from external and internal dangers. When installing a CCTV system, keep the following things in mind:

High-definition (HD) cameras, which are now standard on all reputable CCTV systems, capture crystal-clear footage. It is also critical to consider night monitoring and supplemental illumination for areas with low vision at night.

Remove any potential weak points on the building's perimeter and within it. Internal theft is just as serious as exterior theft, especially when it includes valuable items or private information. Security specialists should always be engaged for a comprehensive examination to assist you in developing the best defense because they are trained to find holes that most people overlook.

Because today's technology is so advanced, a human monitor isn't always required. When motion is detected, sophisticated CCTV and video surveillance systems may notify you and begin capturing footage immediately.

3. Fire protection:

Because of their relevance, many of us are familiar with fire protection systems such as fire detection and alarms, as well as different suppression systems such as sprinklers. That is why it is critical to ensure that all of your plans are in perfect operating shape.

Furthermore, they should provide suitable security precautions for the activities that take place there; for example, industrial facilities and chemical labs face significantly more intricate issues and significant fire security risks than offices or schools.

4. Security Integration and Growth Monitoring:

Cutting-edge security solutions may assist you in confronting these issues and protecting your personnel and property. You can manage all of your security systems from one location, streamlining operations and saving money on person-hours spent managing the various systems independently.

ENVIRONMENTAL CONTROLS

Environmental controls are measures that are put in place to protect your organization's information and resources from environmental damage. This could include (but is not limited to) floods, earthquakes, fires, or extreme weather conditions.

The key point here is to understand that even a single control failure (such as a malfunctioning smoke detector) can cause a total disaster, destroying key assets (such as servers and every piece of equipment stored in a data center) and, in the worst-case scenario, endangering the lives of employees or anyone else nearby.

Environmental controls can be complicated and changeable. Given that they must all function properly and be closely monitored, the person in charge of their design and operation must have sufficient experience and authority to take a holistic risk-based approach and create a clear set of rules to ensure the necessary level of protection.

THE ENVIRONMENTAL CONTROLS AND THREATS:

As previously said, there are numerous environmental controls, each of which might be highly complicated and full of variables. While it is critical to understand each type of control and the type of protection it provides, it is also critical to understand whether or not it applies to the environment that it is supposed to protect.

Environmental Controls fall into several categories that can be useful:

- Management (Administrative) Controls:

These are the Policies, Standards, Processes, Procedures, and Guidelines that will aid in the creation of a clear set of rules for approaching environmental control issues.

Physical controls include controls such as locks, doors, and walls. While they appear to be more focused on access control, they should also protect against natural environmental threats. The use of fireproof doors and walls to protect data centers is an excellent example.

- Technical (Logical) Controls:

Logical controls can aid in monitoring environmental aspects and responding to incidents when they occur.

Moisture detection systems, fire/smoke detection systems, fire suppression, environmental control systems, uninterruptible power supply systems, wet or dry pipes, and motion and sound detectors are just a few examples.

These controls can also be organized into different types:

- Administrative (directive) controls:

The primary goal of any type of administrative control is to ensure proper behavior. If we limit this to environmental protection, a good example is stating that no food/drink/smoking is allowed in restricted areas.

- Preventive controls:

These include any sort of measure designed to prevent an environmental issue from happening. For example, controlling access and having security cameras in restricted areas can greatly reduce the chance of an environmental incident.

- Deterrent controls:

The goal of Deterrent Control is to reduce the likelihood of a vulnerability being exploited without actually reducing the exposure. This type of control is used basically to discourage the violation of security policies, mostly by employing warnings of consequences for security violations.

- Detective controls:

Detective controls are used to identify unwanted or unauthorized activities or situations. These can involve the use of practices, processes, and tools that identify and possibly react (becoming a corrective control) to specific triggers. For environmental controls, a simple example is using a data center temperature sensor or smoke detector.

- Corrective controls:

This type of control acts once an unwanted or unauthorized activity or situation is detected. Using a previous example, once a detective control such as a smoke detector identifies the presence of smoke, it can trigger a corrective control such as an automated fire suppression system, which, depending on how it was designed, can use inert gases or other chemical agents to extinguish a fire.

- Recovery controls:

Whenever an incident happens, the implementation of recovery controls is necessary to return to a normal operating state. For instance, the automated fire suppression system used in the previous example must be resupplied with inert gas. Also, action should be taken to understand why a fire started and work on a way of preventing it from happening again.

Whenever selecting the categories or types of controls that are required to ensure a proper level of protection, the determining factor is the type of threats that may affect the physical environment being protected. These may come in the following types:

- Natural / Environmental threats:

These are the consequences of natural phenomena such as earthquakes, blizzards, floods, storms, hurricanes, fires, and snow/ice. In most cases, they are bound to the geographic location of the facility. It is quite obvious that there is little to gain from using controls for specific situations (i.e., earthquakes, hurricanes) if the facility is not in a geographical location that has a record of such natural phenomena occurring. It is also important to pay attention to the facility's surroundings. For instance, if a neighboring company stores lots of fuel, it increases the chance of a fire that may affect your environment.

- Man-made threats:

There is no lack of man-made threats that can effectively affect environmental security, from simply disgruntled employees that may try to enter restricted areas, employee errors, industrial espionage, arson, acts of sabotage, hazardous/toxic spills, chemical contamination, vandalism, theft and even cases of usage explosives, including acts of terrorism. Each of these threats can affect companies independent of where they are physically located.

ENVIRONMENTAL CONTROLS

- HVAC:

In most data centers, this is an abbreviation that one will not miss, and it stands for Heating, Ventilating, and Air Conditioning. This is a system that plays a very important role in keeping the environment at a constant temperature.

This is a very complex system that calls for high-level engineering and science, and one can barely design it by one's self. It is also important that the HVAC system is properly integrated into the fire system so that in case of a fire, the cooling system does not circulate oxygen to feed the fire. In terms of the Heating, Ventilating, and Air Conditioning perspective, one's data center should be separate from the rest of the building. With overheating being a huge issue in a data center, one needs to ensure that such temperature changes do not affect the whole building but only the data center section.

Other systems include closed-loop systems and positive pressurization. The air in one's building is constantly recirculated in a closed-loop system, so no outside air is drawn in to chill the structure. When one opens the door, the air inside the building rushes out immediately, especially if there is a fire and one wants to get rid of the smoke.

- Fire detection:

It is obvious and obvious that water should not be in close proximity when working in an area with many computers and power equipment. This means that in such a setting, water-based fire suppression devices should be used sparingly.

Fire detection is also highly significant since it gives a sound foundation for the probable cause, making it easier to suppress it. Make certain that smoke, fire, and heat detectors are placed in your data center.

There are several approaches that can be taken when dealing with a fire with water. One way is the dry pipe method, in which the water pipe is entirely dry and, in the event of a fire, the pipe fills with water to the necessary pressure and extinguishes the fire. The wet pipe system allows for fast discharge of water in the event of a fire alarm.

There is also the preaction suppression method, in which the pipe is filled with water and has the right pressure but will not switch on until the temperature reaches a specified level, causing this system to activate.

Fire suppression can also be accomplished by the use of environmentally safe chemicals. This means that, in addition to water, there are numerous other choices for fire control.

- EMI shielding:

Electromagnetic interference is a typical problem that develops when multiple computers are placed in close proximity to one another. For example, if a radio is placed near a computer, one may notice electromagnetic interference radiating directly into the computer via the heat sinks, circuit boards, and cables, among other interfaces. When one opens a computer, one notices that there is a lot of metal shielding on the case itself or wrapped around the machine itself to prevent part of the electromagnetic interference from reaching into one's environs. Metal shielding should never be removed since it stops radiated signals from entering other components and gadgets in one's environment.

- Hot and cold aisles:

When we talk about hot and cold lanes, we often refer to how our data centers are engineered, that is, which racks and in which direction our servers are placed. For example, in one's data center, one may find servers placed in various racks and on raised floors beneath. Cold air is flowing in and blowing up through the floor holes beneath the raised floors. The fans suck cold air into the server racks and push it through the system in this manner. There is also a back of the server where all of the hot air from the server escapes and is drawn to the top of the building by the air conditioning systems, where it is cooled. For best efficiency, we should have cold corridors where all the cool air is pulled through and hot aisles where the hot air from the computer systems may be directed to the top of the building for recirculation.

- Environmental monitoring:

Once all environmental control systems, such as cold and warm isles, have been installed, it is our obligation to ensure that we determine whether our installation has an influence on the temperature. To determine whether or not an effect is occurring, we must monitor the temperature over time to ensure that whatever we are cooling is operating effectively and functionally. For example, one should verify that increasing the temperature does not result in an increase in the expenditures incurred.

In most situations, the cooling systems are just turned on and off without being monitored for any changes. In this instance, it is critical to have a thermometer that can be regularly watched and monitored. It can also be used to track information such as humidity and daily temperature variations.

With the use of such a thermometer, one should be able to see various temperature trends during various time intervals. It is also possible to discover that different times of the month have varied temperature recordings, which could be related to the level of CPU utilization. Higher CPU utilization results in greater heat generated. With these logs available, one can subsequently examine them and perform some analysis on the operation of one's cooling system, such as determining if there is an appropriate quantity of humidity in one's environment.

Video monitoring is another type of environmental monitoring. In this instance, one might elect to have one's own closed-circuit television, which is a component that can be used in-house to gather movies and data from one's cameras. Such video devices can be used to protect one's valuables. This is a typical feature in supermarkets and retail centers.

When installing such cameras, it is important to consider their location. You can choose to place them inside your building to watch your assets or outside to monitor individuals in the parking lot. It is also important to examine the size of the area to be monitored, as some cameras have a broad field of vision while others have a tiny field of view. It is also important to consider the lighting of the area to be monitored. If the region has limited lighting, it may be necessary to install special cameras that can monitor even in low-light situations, such as at night.

One should also ensure that their video monitoring system is correctly integrated with other security monitoring systems and devices so that their video system interacts properly with other intrusion systems for proper information capture.

- Temperature and humidity controls:

Temperature control in a data center can be difficult. This is because if one's systems become too hot, they may collapse, and if they become too cold, one may waste a lot of money on one's cooling system. Contrary to Google's proposal, most data centers are often very cold, with an 80-degree temperature in the cold aisle working well for all of one's systems.

The amount of moisture in the atmosphere, on the other hand, is referred to as humidity. Too much moisture in the air can cause corrosion of one's systems; hence, having cooling systems helps remove such moisture. If the humidity is too low, static discharge may occur, which can be hazardous to computers and other sensitive electronic components.

HARDWARE SECURITY

Hardware security is the protection of physical devices against risks that might allow unauthorized access to company systems. Hardware security is a subdomain of enterprise security that focuses on securing all physical devices, machines, and peripherals. Physical security, such as guards, closed doors, and CCTV cameras, can provide this protection. It can also take the shape of a specific hardware component, such as an integrated circuit, which performs cryptographic tasks to protect the hardware against security flaws and deflect attackers. Simply defined, hardware security entails physical device or operation protection rather than security programs such as antivirus.

Hardware security, in terms of 'physical' security, mainly means securing on-premise systems from natural or human interference or destruction. This is especially important as attacks on computing and non-computing connected devices, such as machine-to-machine (M2M) or Internet of Things (IoT) environments, become more common as their popularity grows.

A device that scans employee endpoints or monitors network traffic, such as a hardware firewall or proxy server, is a popular type of hardware security. Hardware security modules (HSM) – devices that produce and help manage cryptographic keys for enterprise system authentication and encryption — are also used to create device-based hardware security. These hardware technologies enable businesses to add an extra degree of security to sensitive infrastructures.

While software-based solutions exist to secure practically all corporate environments, hardware-based security is recommended in designs that are responsible for the connectivity of a significant number of hardware devices.

When the hardware receives inputs, executes code, or performs any activity, security holes can be exploited. Any device that connects to a network, whether directly or indirectly, must be secure. Attackers might target even seemingly insignificant systems, such as a smart lighting solution, to disrupt work.

To guarantee seamless daily operations, critical hardware such as servers and staff endpoints require strong security measures. Threat actors can also operate from within an organization; therefore, developing and enforcing a sound internal hardware security policy is just as critical as developing a strong external security strategy.

ENTERPRISE HARDWARE THREATS

The list of components includes firmware, basic input-output systems (BIOS), motherboards, network cards, Wi-Fi cards, hard drives, graphics cards, systems-on-a-chip, and servers. An organization is the sum of its hardware devices, and each of them has its own set of vulnerabilities, starting at the component level. As a result, enterprise-level hardware security is critical but complicated.

1. Outdated firmware:

Not every company in the 'smart devices' segment is an expert in IT security. Local producers of IoT and IIoT components such as smart HVAC, connected RFID access, and plant robots, for example, may deliver software riddled with bugs and other security issues. Inadequate patch management can result in additional hassles and the emergence of new vulnerabilities. Firmware updates that are timed to coincide with the release of new security patches can aid in the security of sensitive hardware ecosystems.

2. Inadequate encryption:

An increasing number of enterprise equipment are becoming IP-enabled. However, not all of them are connected to a network and use the proper encryption protocols. For the security of operational technology devices connected to a network, encryption for both data at rest and data in motion is critical. An attacker who connects to the network can acquire information that is not properly encrypted, but an unsecured device can be taken and its data easily accessed.

3. Unsecured local access:

Hardware supporting IoT and IoT applications is frequently accessible via an on-premise interface or local network. Companies, particularly smaller ones, may fail to properly configure or safeguard these local access points. This exposes the enterprise hardware environment to the acts of hostile actors who can easily gain access to and tamper with company systems.

4. Unchanged default passwords

The 'default password' on most workplace devices can and should be changed. Even firms that implement cutting-edge software security may fall short when it comes to hardware security. For low-cost IoT devices and turnkey hardware, personnel may continue to use the default passwords.

Often, the password is inscribed on the device itself, making it accessible to anyone having physical access to it.

5. Vulnerable customized hardware

Many organizations rely on custom-built hardware solutions. Corporate data centers, for example, and tailored systems for heavy engineering and scientific applications use purpose-built chipsets that enable them to produce specified results. Manufacturers frequently fail to assess the security posture of these custom chips and devices as thoroughly as they would for gear that serves more common applications.

6. Backdoors

A backdoor is a hidden weakness that is frequently purposely inserted during the device's manufacturing stage. Threat actors can use backdoors to bypass authentication processes and acquire root access to a device without the owner's knowledge. Hardware backdoors are far more difficult to plug than software backdoors, which can be quickly patched. Attackers can use them to install malware or insert harmful code into the system.

7. Eavesdropping

Eavesdropping attacks occur when an unauthorized entity gains access to hardware and records its data. An eavesdropping attack can be carried out even if the attacker does not have a constant connection to the hardware. For example, in the case of a card skimmer put into an ATM or a PoS terminal, the attacker periodically accesses the device to obtain a copy of its information. Eavesdropping attacks can be launched by introducing a malicious program into a compromised device, granting illegal access to data, and even establishing a protocol for the data to be relayed to the attacker at regular intervals.

8. Modification attacks

Modification attacks interfere with a device's natural operation and allow bad actors to circumvent hardware operating boundaries. A modification attack goes one step beyond an eavesdropping attack by altering the communication that a device uses.

Malware software is either inserted into a hardware component or existing vulnerabilities are exploited. The unauthorized party can then launch a man-in-the-middle attack, allowing them to receive and change packets before transmitting them to the intended recipient. Modification attacks sometimes involve unauthorized alterations to integrated circuits or the introduction of hardware Trojans.

9. Triggering flaws

To interrupt normal system behavior, attackers 'trigger' or 'induce' hardware problems. Fault injections that are specifically tailored to grant illegal rights or leak data might jeopardize system-level security. These attacks can have a cascading effect on connected devices that rely on the compromised hardware to function normally.

To carry out a successful fault attack, the attacker rarely requires precise knowledge of the targeted equipment and its flaws. However, implementing countermeasures against fault attacks necessitates a thorough understanding of the attack vector on the part of security teams. This can be difficult because the mechanics of both fault injection and propagation must be understood and resolved for every available weak point without data loss or disruption of operations.

10. Counterfeit hardware

Counterfeit hardware is a constant problem that allows attackers to easily target organizations. Devices that are constructed or modified without the permission of the original equipment manufacturer (OEM) may be intentionally infected with backdoors and other vulnerabilities. Attackers can then exploit these weaknesses at a reasonable moment to initiate illegal operations and get malicious access to enterprise systems.

WHY IS COMPUTER HARDWARE SECURITY IMPORTANT FOR BUSINESSES?

Computer hardware security is required by businesses to secure sensitive data and systems against malicious assaults, unlawful access, and other dangers. It also aids in the protection of the hardware against damage or destruction, allowing the company's operations to continue uninterrupted.

Furthermore, computer hardware security can assist firms in maintaining network integrity and preventing data breaches, which can result in significant financial and reputational losses.

Computer security is divided into two categories: software security and hardware security. Software security is concerned with safeguarding system software components such as stored data and data in transit. Hardware security, on the other hand, entails protecting the physical hardware from potential threats.

Limiting access to only authorized individuals ensures the security of the hardware, which can be accomplished by paying an Internet Service Provider (ISP) for this service.

However, relying on an external provider can pose security problems; thus, many firms are now establishing their own ISPs. In this manner, they have direct control over the security of the corporate server.

Nodes are critical components of any computer network, serving as distribution systems or communication endpoints that connect devices to the network. As a result, businesses may implement the security measures indicated above to protect the network's security.

The hub is a critical network device that is responsible for exchanging data between connected computers. It acts as a network gateway and must be kept in a safe position away from high-traffic areas to avoid tampering.

CHAPTER 8
IMPLEMENTING A GRC PROGRAM

CREATING AND LEADING A SUCCESSFUL GOVERNANCE, RISK, AND COMPLIANCE (GRC) TEAM

Establishing and building an effective GRC team is unique to each organization because the firm's vision, values, and mission statements are determined by its overall strategic goals and objectives. There are parallels that influence GRC functionality and performance, with important drivers being the buy-in of the leadership team (board down) and the firm's personal and cultural commitment.

GRC Management

The US Army's 'Be, Know, Do' leadership paradigm is straightforward and practical, and it can assist boards and senior management in influencing and creating a culture that allows GRC to develop and succeed. Although boards and senior leadership teams should be aware that certain characteristics facilitate and others inhibit and destroy GRC success. If an organization's culture does not promote principled performance, then all of the people, processes, and technologies put in place to manage ethics and compliance issues will be ineffective.

GRC functions should have the autonomy to act in the best interests of the firm's sustainability, even if it involves major disagreement with board members or senior management team members. ESMA has emphasized that the compliance function should be independent for investment firms, that the "compliance officer and other compliance staff act independently when performing their tasks," and that "where senior management deviates from important recommendations or assessments issued by the compliance function, this should be documented accordingly." As a result, the approach to developing an effective GRC culture should focus on facilitating the inclusion of board and senior management, remaining independent, providing advice and support on regulatory matters, staff training, day-to-day assistance to the firm, and developing new policies and procedures within the firm. The GRC leader's ultimate goal is to widen the leadership team's intellectual capital while also bridging gaps in the GRC team's knowledge, skills, and understanding.

A GRC practitioner must be able to create and articulate the firm's GRC agenda in order to gain management buy-in. As a result, the GRC function must first examine the firm's compliance, risk, and governance concerns before developing a clear plan to unleash the GRC function's potential in the business. When working with important stakeholders, the GRC function must engage in a way that inspires trust, confidence, and proactive risk management.

As a result, the firm's GRC culture should be consistent with its mission statement, vision, and values. The culture of a company must guarantee that 'good' leadership is recognized alongside practitioners' technical skills and commercial understanding. Culture is a crucial enabler of GRC's success. Thus, a GRC leader must have a comprehensive understanding of an organization's drives as well as the restrictions and shortcomings that would stymie change.

A GRC function must establish an internal control framework and be capable of determining, designing, or assessing adherence to GRC concerns across this framework. GRC must have a plan to examine the controls inside a vertical (i.e., a business line) while reviewing it. The identification of high-impact areas, control deficiencies, and the implementation of a roadmap to educate, train, raise awareness, and mitigate cultural issues enables GRC practitioners to obtain senior management buy-in through value-add management information, allowing decisions to be made and validating a strong GRC culture.

DEVELOPING THE GRC AGENDA

When developing a firm's GRC agenda, GRC practitioners can adopt a simple three-stage method - review, respond, and monitor.

1. Examine how controls are developed to mitigate the highlighted risks, as well as control documentation and the use of control libraries.

2. Control effectiveness is addressed by regulating the control maturity profile within set risk appetites and tolerances.

3. Monitor control assurance, reporting the current state of the control environment to governance (i.e., the board and appropriate committees).

When creating the GRC agenda with the board and senior management, taking a pragmatic approach to what can be done and the risks encountered builds the building elements of trust inside a firm, including communication, support, respect, fairness, predictability, and competence. These foundational pieces enable a GRC function to work effectively toward the achievement of a strong, culturally-led GRC framework.

GRC PROGRAM IMPLEMENTATION

The following are seven suggestions for successfully developing a GRC framework that leads to a comprehensive GRC program across your organization;

1. Determine the worth of implementing a GRC platform:

Understanding the true benefit of GRC implementation is critical for finding existing GRC tactics in many domains of activity. It also allows you to decide which processes are operational and should be included when building a unified system.

Similarly, you can eliminate redundant or unneeded data, technologies, or assets that lower value and may impede the centralized process. From there, you may prioritize your company's most profitable assets and work to improve them in your GRC plan.

2. Develop a GRC Project Roadmap:

A clear objective that highlights the framework's major GRC functions is required for narrowing the scope of your strategy. These outcomes should be the product of ongoing collaboration among all stakeholders in order to suit the demands of each department. Understanding the potential benefits of a successful CRM strategy can help you predict your outcomes.

Here are some of the advantages of a strong GRC framework:

- Improved alignment between all departments and broader corporate objectives,

- Ensures that all forms of risks are mitigated; such risks include financial, legal, strategic, operational, and cybersecurity risks are among them.

- Faster decision-making surrounding business processes and procedures

3. Conduct a gap analysis

After collecting pertinent information on your current GRC process, you must determine the following for each:

- Process maturity
- Data quality
- Operational gaps

Consider the following factors:

- Determine whether data is missing or duplicated.
- Determine the existence of duplicate or redundant procedures.
- Identifying automation or removing manual workflows

4. Determine and reconcile stakeholder expectations

Although it is often forgotten, your entire organization must be on the same page with your GRC implementation plan. Each department is involved in a well-planned GRC initiative. All major stakeholders should be given the opportunity to comment on your idea.

In general, there are two major steps to obtaining organizational alignment:

The first step toward obtaining organizational approval is to align executive team members on critical issues such as budget and execution dates. Before taking any additional actions or making any necessary modifications, you must ensure that the rest of the organization is on board with your plan.

Approach the problem from the top down, Once you have gotten executive permission, you must execute realistic and well-communicated change management practices in all other business divisions. For example, it is reasonable to anticipate some opposition to your suggested modifications. Departments frequently have long-standing processes and procedures that will need to be phased out gradually.

To facilitate a smooth transition, send informed updates to each team on a regular basis, alerting them of key changes and how they will affect their jobs. Make a clear mechanism for all team members to share any concerns, recommendations, or other important remarks that may be required to adjust your approach.

5. Lay a solid framework for the GRC's plan.

For your GRC system to be practical and adaptive, a sufficient foundation must be established. Because of the dynamic nature of the cyber-dangers landscape, the continually evolving cyber threats and vulnerabilities, and the severe implications of data breaches, these elements are critical for IT GRC.

Financial institutions and healthcare organizations must devote even more attention to ensuring that their risk-management methods are suited to the regular legislative changes that affect their businesses.

6. Collaborate with a GRC solution vendor.

Implementing a GRC program from the ground up necessitates the unification of information silos, constant upgrades, and the usage of manual processes such as spreadsheets. Many of these pain points can be alleviated by using a CRM platform, allowing you to focus your implementation efforts on higher-level responsibilities.

You must use caution, as you would with any third-party provider, to ensure that your chosen GRC product meets compliance requirements and does not expose your firm to extreme security risks.

The appropriate GRC technology should provide a return on investment (ROI) in the form of cost and time savings.

Here are some key questions to consider while selecting GRC software:

- Is it simple to use/friendly?
- Is it based on fully automated workflows?
- Is it possible to customize it? For example, custom reporting
- Is it scalable?
- Do its features perform tasks with the detail you require? E.g., in-depth risk analysis.
- Is it compatible with other third-party software?
- Are the costs factored into your budget?

7. Make your GRC strategy consistent:

One of the most important characteristics of a strong CRM strategy is its ability to match the demands of the entire organization. While each department will have its unique set of criteria, a reference foundation should be available. You can standardize your control structure, for example, by implementing an industry standard, such as NIST 800-53 or ISO 27001.

8. Manage and evaluate your GRC approach:

Launching your new GRC program is a process that takes time and effort. Once implemented, you must ensure that your strategy may mature and develop in accordance with your business objectives.

All teams should maintain thorough and dated records of their GRC requirements, including significant changes such as the introduction of new technology.

These reports can be used as a reference during frequent stakeholder meetings to ensure that your entire business is on the same page with the overarching strategy. To ensure compliance management, an audit should be performed at least once a year. You should then prioritize any compliance issues that need to be addressed.

RISK EVALUATION AND MITIGATION

A cybersecurity risk assessment necessitates determining an organization's primary business objectives and identifying IT assets that are vital to accomplishing those objectives. This includes detecting cyber attacks that may harm these assets, calculating the likelihood of such attacks occurring and the impact they may have, and, in general, developing a comprehensive picture of the threat environment for specific business goals. This helps stakeholders and security teams to make educated decisions about how and where to apply security measures to minimize overall risk to levels acceptable to the enterprise.

How to Conduct a Cybersecurity Risk Assessment:

There are various aspects to a risk assessment, but the five basic steps are scope, risk identification, risk analysis, and documentation.

Step 1: Establishing the scope of the risk assessment

The first step in conducting a risk assessment is establishing what comes within the scope of the evaluation. It might be the entire corporation, but because most businesses are too vast, it is more likely to be a business unit, a location, or a specialized aspect of the firm, such as payment processing or a web application. It is critical to have full support from all stakeholders whose activities are covered by the review since their input will be critical in determining which assets and processes are most important, identifying risks, assessing impacts, and defining risk tolerance levels. A risk assessment specialist may be required to assist them with this resource-intensive activity.

Anyone involved should be conversant with risk assessment languages, such as probability and impact, so that everyone understands how the risk is expressed. ISO/IEC TS 27100 presents an overview of cybersecurity ideas for individuals who are unfamiliar with them. Before conducting a risk assessment, it is worthwhile to review standards such as ISO/IEC 27001 and frameworks such as NIST SP 800-37 and TS 27110, which can assist organizations in conducting a structured assessment of their information security risks and ensuring that mitigation controls are appropriate and effective.

Various regulations and laws, like HIPAA, Sarbanes-Oxley, and PCI DSS, require firms to do a formal risk assessment and frequently include guidelines and ideas on how to augment them. When performing an evaluation, however, avoid using a compliance-based checklist approach because compliance does not always imply that a company is not at risk.

Step 2: Identifying cybersecurity risks

2.1 Determine assets:

You can't safeguard what you don't know about. Therefore, the next step is to identify and inventory all of the physical and logical assets that fall within the scope of the risk assessment. When identifying assets, it is critical to identify not only those considered the crown jewels of your organization – the critical assets for the business and likely the main target of attackers – but also those that they would like to take control of, such as an Active Directory server or image and communications archive systems, to use as a rotation point to expand an attack. Making a network architecture diagram from the asset inventory list is a great approach to see interconnection and communication pathways between assets and processes, as well as network entry points, making the next threat detection step easier.

2.2 Identify threats:

Threats are tactics, approaches, and procedures utilized by threat actors that can cause damage to an organization's assets. To help identify potential dangers for each asset, use a threat library, \ which will give you high-quality and up-to-date knowledge on cyber threats. Security provider reports and recommendations from government organizations like as the Cybersecurity and Infrastructure Security Agency can be a great source of knowledge on new dangers in certain industries, vertical and geographical regions, or specific technologies.

Also, evaluate where each asset is positioned in the Lockheed Martin cyber attack chain since this will help identify the sorts of security they need. The cyber-attack chain maps the steps and targets of a typical real-world attack.

2.3 Identify what might go wrong:

This task requires outlining the effects of an identified threat exploiting a vulnerability to target a range of assets. For example:

Threat: An attacker conducts SQL injection

Vulnerability: not fixed

Active: Web server

Consequences: Private consumer data was taken, resulting in regulatory fines and reputational damage.

By summarizing this information in simple scenarios like this, it is easier for all stakeholders to grasp the risks they face in connection to important business objectives and for security teams to determine relevant actions and best practices to deal with the risk.

Step 3: Assess risks and potential consequences.

It is now time to assess the possibility of the risk scenarios outlined in Step 2 occurring, as well as the impact on the company if they do. Risk probability – the potential that a given threat is capable of exploiting a given vulnerability – should be assessed in a cybersecurity risk assessment based on the detectability, exploitability, and repeatability of threats and vulnerabilities rather than historical events. Because of the dynamic nature of cybersecurity risks, probability is not as closely related to the frequency of prior events such as floods and earthquakes.

The evaluation of probability on a range of 1: Rare to 5: "Very likely" and impact on a scale of 1: negligible to 5: "very serious" produces the risk matrix shown below in step 4.

The level of damage to the organization produced by the consequences of a threat exploiting a vulnerability is referred to as impact. In each scenario, the impact on secrecy, integrity, and availability should be measured, with the highest impact utilized as a final score. This component of the evaluation is subjective, which is why the involvement of stakeholders and safety specialists is critical. Using the SQL injection as an example, the privacy impact note would most likely be classified as "Very severe."

Step 4: Determine and prioritize risks:

Each risk scenario can be classified using a risk matrix like the one below, where the risk level is "Probability Impact." Our sample risk scenario would be classified as "very high" if the chance of a SQL injection attack was assessed as "probably" or "very likely."

Any scenario that exceeds the agreed-upon level of tolerance must be prioritized for treatment in order to return it to the company's risk tolerance level. There are three options for doing so:

Avoid. If the risk surpasses the advantages, stopping an activity may be the best choice if it means not being exposed to it any longer.

Transfer: Outsource certain operations, such as DDoS mitigation or obtaining cyber insurance, to other parties to share some of the risks. In general, first-party coverage only covers costs paid as a result of a computer incident, such as notifying customers of a data breach, but third-party coverage would include the cost of financing a settlement following a data breach, as well as penalties and fines. It will not cover intangible costs such as intellectual property loss or brand reputation damage.

Reduce: Implement safety controls and other risk-reduction measures to keep the probability and impact, and hence the degree of risk, within the agreed-upon risk tolerance level. The relevant team should be tasked with adopting measures to decrease unacceptable risks. Dates for progress and completion reports should also be established to keep the risk owner and treatment plan up to date.

However, no system or environment can be made completely safe. Thus, there will always be some danger. This is known as residual risk, and it must be publicly embraced as part of the organization's cybersecurity plan by key stakeholders.

Step 5: Record all the risks:

All risk scenarios recognized in a risk register must be documented. This should be evaluated and updated on a regular basis to ensure that management always receives an up-to-date report on its cybersecurity threats. It should include the following items:

Identification data

Risk scenario

Existing security controls

Current risks level

Treatment plan: the treatment plan consists of planned activities and a timeframe for reducing risk to an acceptable level of risk tolerance, as well as the commercial reason for the investment.

Progress status: the status of the treatment plan's implementation

Residual risk is the level of risk that remains after the treatment plan has been implemented.

The individual or group in charge of ensuring that residual risks remain within the tolerance level is known as the risk owner.

A cybersecurity risk assessment is a vital and continuing endeavor. Thus, time and resources must be made available to improve the organization's future security. It will have to be repeated as new cyber threats develop and new systems or activities are implemented, but doing so the first time will create a repeatable procedure and model for future reviews while minimizing the likelihood of a cyberattack negatively affecting business objectives.

RISK ASSESSMENT COMPONENTS AND FORMULA

Before making big modifications to your security, it is critical to conduct a thorough risk assessment. While there are other methods for assessing safety, none is as successful as a thorough risk assessment that considers all three risk aspects.

When evaluating risk in this method, a successful security program, the likelihood of a threat, and the consequences of an unwelcome criminal or terrorist incident should all be considered. Here are some definitions to help you understand how a formula works and what happens when a part of it is left out.

1. Threat:

An event can negatively affect an important asset through a criminal or terrorist act. People, property, currency, business continuity, intellectual property, and reputation are just a few of the essential asset categories. People can be threatened by violence at work, with or without weapons.

2. Determining the threat level:

As part of the formula, you will assess the history of security issues and the nature of the business to determine the possibility that an unhappy customer may harm the receiver. If the corporation, for example, is a law practice dealing with exclusion, the probability of violent attacks may grow. When a stranger loses their house, they may become enraged at the office.

3. Cyber Vulnerability Assessment:

A vulnerability is a flaw in a company's capacity to defend critical assets against an attack. Vulnerability is synonymous with susceptibility in a risk assessment.

4. Vulnerability or security effectiveness determination:

When identifying a vulnerability, it is necessary to have a fundamental understanding of what constitutes an appropriate physical security attitude toward typical threats. Hiring a certified safety professional may be beneficial in obtaining the best results from a safety risk assessment, but it is not required. Organizations should routinely investigate dangers, vulnerabilities, and repercussions to avoid assessment or undue influence by vendors who advocate products.

5. Consequences:

Consequences can be defined as the extent to which an incident will have a negative influence. The table below illustrates how a company could create a consistency model to assess security threats. Although the dimension of the repercussions for human safety is easily established, the other dimensions of the impact must be specified at the start of the safety risk assessment because they are highly personal to each business.

According to a model of staff injury outcomes, deaths, hospitalizations, time-lost injuries, first aid, and no injury are listed in descending order of importance. A company's financial impact will need the development of its model. $100,000 can be terrible for one organization while being nothing more than an insurance deduction for another.

Threats against important assets can be easily translated into a specified scenario for your organizational audience, resulting in a threat assessment. In your risk assessment, you will evaluate the risk based on this scenario. Let's say, for instance, "an angry customer in the hall hurts a receptionist."

- Threat Assessments:

A threat assessment can help you evaluate whether criminals or terrorists are interested in generating security difficulties at your firm. This will mostly concentrate on the first component of the formula, as seen below.

6. Vulnerability Assessment:

The US government requires a number of counter-terrorism activities known as vulnerability assessments. In a vulnerability evaluation, only two of the three risk formula parts will be examined. Given that the danger level has reached the highest level, the company will be required to increase the effectiveness of its security by lowering susceptibility and identifying strategies to mitigate effects, such as building business continuity plans or improving emergency response protocols. Incidents and threat levels are overlooked in vulnerability evaluations, resulting in excessive security investment.

7. Business Impact analysis:

Business impact analysis is another frequent methodology employed in some businesses, and it entails identifying the most crucial assets and developing resilience around them, sometimes in the form of business continuity plans. The whole range of hazards may not be included in Business Impact studies, resulting in spending that would not have been indicated otherwise.

8. Security audits:

Security audits are the simplest methodology to implement since they verify that all security measures that are expected to be in place are in place and working properly. Security audits will look to see if security measures are effective and if vulnerabilities are effectively mitigated. Security audits have a place in analysis landscapes, but they are not risk assessments and are unlikely to uncover unknown vulnerabilities.

The security assessment approach can be divided into numerous categories. It is impossible to use the phrases threat, vulnerability, and risk interchangeably or synonymously. The most effective way to decide whether a security system is appropriate is to consider all three risk elements: threat, vulnerability, and consequence. If you want to establish whether your security measures are adequate and prevent potential hazards like failing to comply with the OSHA General Duty Clause or being sued for premises liability, a risk assessment is the best method.

RISK MITIGATION

The application of policies, tools, and procedures to limit the possibility and impact of a successful cyber assault is known as cyber risk mitigation. It is a crucial practice that helps guide risk control and mitigation decision-making and allows your firm to be protected while meeting its business objectives.

- A cyber risk mitigation strategy enables your company to answer the following questions:

- Do we have an inventory of all of our assets?

- Do we know which assets are most important?

- Is it possible for us to see our whole assault surface in real time?

- Can we rank our vulnerabilities in terms of business criticality and risk?

- What is the scope and effectiveness of our cyber security controls?

- What are our vulnerabilities to prospective breaches and attacks?

- What policies, technologies, and procedures should be put in place to provide cyber resilience?

What are the difficulties in mitigating cyber risk?

Cyber risk mitigation can be difficult because many firms need more real-time visibility into their cybersecurity posture in light of network evolution and a shifting threat landscape. They frequently need to learn what assets they need to safeguard, where and how they may be compromised, or whether proper security controls are in place. Even when measures are in place, security professionals are only sometimes convinced that they will be successful against a variety of threats.

Another area for improvement is speed. Because many risk identification and mitigation processes are still manual, most security teams are unable to recognize and respond to threats in a timely manner. Another reason firms may struggle to mitigate cyber risk effectively is the need for more resources.

EXAMPLES OF RISK MITIGATION

To gain a better understanding of risk mitigation, consider these real-world examples of controls or processes and procedures that we employ in our daily lives to prevent certain hazards from occurring. Please keep in mind that the following examples are intended to provide background in order to understand better how mitigating activities operate; because everyone's circumstances and needs differ, these should not be construed as personal advice:

- Reducing financial risk:

To survive on a daily basis, we require money. We also need money to be prepared for the potential of a major life event necessitating a huge sum of money, as well as for when old age prohibits us from earning money through work. To maintain our financial security, we may opt to:

- Maximize retirement fund
- Maintain a liquid savings account for an emergency fund.
- Pay in cash for everything to ensure that you don't buy something you can't afford.

- Risk mitigation in personal relationships:

Positive personal relationships bring fulfillment into our lives, and we must actively maintain the quality of those relationships to keep them from falling apart. Here are some examples of nurturing initiatives:

- Showing kindness and respect for loved ones
- Calling, sending cards, and visiting on a regular basis
- Severing relationships with individuals who do not treat us well (to make more time for those who do)
- Reducing the likelihood of health problems:

We must take adequate precautions to ensure it because our health is the cornerstone of our existence. While there are an endless number of techniques to improve our health and reduce the chance of significant issues, the following are only a few of the most prevalent mitigation activities:

- Drinking enough water (the amount advised for our body size)
- Avoiding harmful behaviors such as smoking, drinking, and eating processed meals
- Exercise on a regular basis

You may or may not formalize your mitigating actions, depending on how important particular aspects of your life are to your total identity and well-being. Saving money, fostering relationships, and being healthy come naturally to certain people and do not require a planned plan to stay on track.

Making a budget sheet, filling a calendar with social engagements, or adhering to a prescribed diet are all important for others.

STRATEGIES FOR MITIGATING CYBERSECURITY RISKS

Organizations now have no choice but to embrace proactive cybersecurity risk reduction because the possibility of a cyber-attack is nearly guaranteed. These are the eight most important ways to reduce cyber-attacks on your IT network:

1. Risk assessment:

Prior to implementing your risk mitigation approach, your IT security team should undertake a cybersecurity risk assessment to identify any vulnerabilities in your organization's security policies.

A risk assessment can identify your organization's assets as well as the security controls that are currently in place. A risk assessment can also assist your IT security team in identifying vulnerabilities that could be exploited and which should be addressed first. Security ratings are a simple way to assess your company's and third-party providers' cybersecurity posture. Real-time security ratings are also available.

2. Set up network access controls:

Following the identification of high-priority problem areas and the assessment of your assets, the next step is to implement network access controls to assist in limiting the danger of insider attacks. Many businesses are turning to security systems like zero trust, which assesses trust and user access permissions on an as-needed basis based on each person's job role to reduce the likelihood and impact of threats or attacks caused by employee neglect or a lack of cybersecurity best practices. This reduces both the threat and the impact of a security breach or attack caused by employee negligence or a lack of cybersecurity awareness. Endpoint security has become a rising problem as the number of connected devices on a network grows.

3. Maintain a constant eye on network traffic:

Cybersecurity risk can be efficiently reduced by taking preemptive measures. Every day, roughly 2,200 cybercrime attacks take place, needing continuous monitoring of network traffic as well as an organization's cybersecurity posture. Rather than attempting to detect and respond to new risks manually, employing tools that provide a comprehensive picture of your IT ecosystem at any point in time can provide a comprehensive view of your IT ecosystem. Security staff can then discover and respond to new risks in real time.

4. Create an incident response plan:

One of the most important components of a company's cybersecurity strategy is its incident response plan. It must be broad enough to allow all members of the IT security team and non-tech staff to understand what to do in the event of a data breach or an attack. Because avoiding data breaches is becoming increasingly challenging, your organization must have an incident response plan in place. Having an incident response plan in place helps your organization respond quickly and efficiently when faced with a breach.

5. Reduce your attack surface:

Surveying all of a company's access points, weaknesses, and sensitive information can reveal its security posture and threat landscape. A company's attack surface can include firewalls, software updates, online applications, and staff. The correct interpretation of entry-point intelligence can help firms detect and mitigate vulnerabilities throughout their operations.

6. Keep up with patch updates:

Threat actors can swiftly exploit unpatched vulnerabilities. Today's cybercriminals are aware of this because many software suppliers deploy patches on a regular basis. An efficient patch management schedule can assist your IT security team in keeping ahead of attackers by letting them know when your service or software vendors will release patches.

BEST PRACTICES IN GRC PROGRAM MANAGEMENT

- Accept an Iterative Approach:

Recognize that due to the complexity and number of parties involved, achieving a perfect GRC solution on the first try is difficult. Prepare to examine and change components of your approach on a frequent basis, particularly given the dynamic nature of risk and compliance management, which demands constant monitoring and adjustments.

- Encourage Collaborative Teamwork:

Form a diversified project team for GRC implementation, including representatives from all levels of your organization, from senior to junior. Because of this diversity, choices are comprehensive and inclusive. It also promotes effective communication among team members and eliminates duplication of work, which is a major goal when implementing GRC.

- Make Effective Communication a Priority:

To avoid misunderstandings about the aim and impact of GRC implementation, establish clear and open communication channels throughout the organization. This is especially important in areas where workflows will be directly impacted and where staff changes may occur as a result of improved processes. Internal communication that is effective ensures that GRC is perceived as a positive step forward rather than a possible concern.

- Policy Implementation:

Consider policies to be more than just a list of tasks. Policies act as guidelines for the organization's data management and handling. Transform these policies into concrete practices, and monitor and assess them on a regular basis to ensure their relevance and efficacy in protecting your firm.

- Allocate Enough Resources:

Avoid the common misunderstanding that a GRC system can be implemented without significant financial and personnel resources. To properly manage GRC, ensure that the essential resources are accessible and that a clear plan for their optimal utilization is in place from the start.

HOW TO DEVELOP A SUCCESSFUL GRC PROGRAM

Risk management and compliance are evolving as risks become increasingly complex and difficult to control. A continually changing risk landscape necessitates swift adaptation to new legislation, rising threats, and other variables that imperil operations. To manage these difficulties effectively, more than just having a governance, risk, and compliance (GRC) program that evolves and matures with the organization is required. However, establishing such a program can be difficult, and corporations may be unsure where or how to begin.

A "crawl, walk, run" method allows a company to begin its journey toward increased risk maturity.

Phase 1: Crawl

The initial stages of GRC maturity are the most basic. Immature GRC initiatives often employ either ad hoc or policy-based decision-making. Ad hoc judgments are inherently reactive; without systems to guide them, leaders consider, act, and move on to the next problem. This strategy is based on a "hero" mentality, with a few people taking rash actions. These rash decisions are frequently the result of customer complaints, queries from governance agencies, or audits. Ad hoc risk management decisions are solely concerned with putting out flames.

Decisions based on policy are the first modest step out of the vicious circle of reactive risk management. This decision-making technique shapes an organization's risk tolerance. The key to success in this early stage of GRC maturity is to think about people, processes, and technology in that order. Moving from spreadsheets and emails to more agile GRC software will improve your risk posture, but only if senior leaders' buy-in and solid processes are developed to supplement robust technology.

Setting standards and norms for an organization's risk management approach necessitates an understanding of the needs and viewpoints of stakeholders in various sectors of the business. Demonstrate to these stakeholders that you want to collaborate with them to get better results. Knowing what risk means to each department will aid in breaking down organizational silos and influencing policy formulation.

After establishing some early policies, you may be inclined to implement them all at once. Instead, concentrate on creating risk policies before attempting to implement them. After you've earned the trust of your executives and employees by listening to them, educate them on the company's risk profile. Take measures to reinforce or build business continuity plans for each department, analyze the effectiveness of existing controls, and introduce any new controls that are required through testing and implementation processes.

Consider concentrating your efforts on a single department, maybe the one at the center of a cyber event that sparked your interest in more proactive risk management measures.

Phase 2: Go for a walk

The "walk" phase comprises decisions based on risk models as well as system-driven decisions.

Decisions based on risk models

When organizations devote time and attention to their risk management program, they pursue risk-model-based decisions. They select a risk model, such as the NIST or ISO27005 model, and begin an inventory of all the hazards in their organization.

Some CEOs audit their entire organization using a risk model. Your model should provide either quantitative or qualitative outputs regarding your risks, depending on its maturity. You'll examine the likelihood of a risk, how existing risk-mitigation procedures affect the risk, and whether you have critical vulnerabilities. You can then delve deeper to analyze and rank weaknesses.

Most executives identify more hazards than they can manage and must prioritize their efforts. The simplest fixes should be implemented first. A risk that demands as much (or more) effort and money to mitigate as it does potential consequences will be lower on your priority list.

Decisions based on systems

This strategy entails connecting systems, eliminating spreadsheets, and sending data into GRC software. When you can draw incidents from other apps, your GRC system will surface insights that can help you make better decisions. You will be more agile in accepting vs reducing risks, utilizing security scorecards and threat assessments to gather data. This serves as a "alive system" to supplement risk models and risk management on a larger scale. You'll automate workflows, replacing humans with machines to boost speed, agility, and efficiency, all while collecting more and better data to drive continuous development.

Phase 3: Exercise

Although this phase may be aspirational for some firms, it promises risk-driven decision-making fueled by machines, integrations, and code. When risk drives everything, strategic benefits emerge.

Risk analysis and risk quantification are used at this maturity level to assign financial value to hazards. However, not every risk is worth the time and effort required to establish a quantitative indicator. Many programs begin with the most high-value risks in order to have a deeper understanding of those big-ticket hazards.

Reduced cyber risk is a top goal for businesses in 2023. By quantifying cyber risk, you'll be able to better comprehend and disclose the magnitude of the damage your organization could face in the absence of an effective cyber risk program. You'll catch leadership's attention if you communicate cyberrisks in commercial terms (monetary worth). Nothing motivates leaders like the prospect of a significant financial loss.

One Thing at a Time

Building and establishing a risk program may appear to be a difficult task, but you must begin somewhere. Using the "crawl, walk, run" method, take one little step at a time. Put policies in place early on, and educate line-of-business leaders on their risks as you go. Remember to consider people, process, and technology, with people as the cornerstone. Apply these ideas to create a complete and effective risk management program that is tailored to the needs of your firm.

CHAPTER 9
SUSTAINING YOUR GRC PROGRAM

Gone is the days when GRC was, at best, a back-office function and, at worst, the department of "No." Today, GRC is a powerful and positive force for the business, one that not only helps stakeholders maintain organizational credibility and protect brands but also strengthens performance. Companies are under increasing pressure to demonstrate high levels of performance, and a strong GRC program can make all the difference.

ELEMENTS OF A STRONG GRC PROGRAM

The business drivers of GRC have altered in recent years. GRC has become a significant instrument for firms to drive growth and profitability, rather than only compliance or even downside risk management. The aim is to develop a mature, long-term GRC program that covers the following elements.

1. The Big Picture of Risk:

The capacity to provide comprehensive visibility into both present and emerging risks is the hallmark of a successful

GRC program. Organizations want to know how risks interact across the company, as well as with controls, legislation, and policies. They require risk reports that are relevant, timely, and insightful.

It begins with the creation of an integrated framework of risk and control data that multiple GRC functions can use to ensure alignment and consistency. An integrated framework contextualizes risk by connecting it to corporate objectives, processes, controls, and important risk measurements. As a result, risk intelligence improves, allowing management to balance risks and opportunities better.

2. A Bold Tone at the Top:

A GRC program's effectiveness, like any other business endeavor, is heavily reliant on the "tone at the top" and how well it is conveyed throughout the firm. This, in turn, necessitates well-written and constantly updated policies and procedures so that staff understand exactly what is expected of them.

Another critical component is to ensure that GRC operations are deeply integrated into company systems and processes rather than managed as separate or distinct projects. The more widespread GRC is, the better employees will be at embodying the firm's risk and compliance vision in their day-to-day decisions and activities.

3. Collaboration and Integration:

The advantages of integrated GRC are widely known: increased risk visibility, improved coordination, and increased efficiency. However, although it has improved over time, the level of integration among GRC tasks remains a serious challenge globally.

Many firms still conduct their risk, compliance, and audit departments in silos, with little or no data sharing. As a result, they wind up duplicating work, raising expenditures, and needing a clearer picture of risk. A better way would be to implement an integrated GRC strategy that is supported by a strong GRC solution that allows the company to manage all of its GRC initiatives on a single platform. Both the GRC program and the solution should improve collaboration and cohesion among GRC roles, processes, activities, and information.

Organizations can consider forming a specialized group of people with cross-functional knowledge who can bring together multiple teams and departments and enable easy coordination among them to push this endeavor. Finally, the performance of a GRC program is heavily reliant on the level of communication and collaboration among teams.

GRC Integration Has An Effect On Organizational Confidence:

According to the OCEG 2017 GRC Maturity Survey, organizations with integrated GRC strategies have a higher level of confidence that their governing bodies (e.g., board of directors) are receiving the appropriate level of risk and compliance detail to aid in the establishment and achievement of organizational objectives.

4. Well-Defined Roles, Responsibilities, and Processes:
GRC responsibilities and reporting lines are evolving as C-level jobs grow. In many companies, for example, the compliance function, which previously reported to the Chief Legal Officer (CLO), now reports to the Chief Risk Officer (CRO). Similarly, GRC operations that a small group of people formerly controlled has now become a top corporate priority.

With all of these changes, firms must identify their GRC goals and objectives, break them down into tactical actions, and align each of those phases with the applicable activities or departments. This systematic approach clarifies everyone's duties and responsibilities while also boosting responsibility.

Another important component is training. With GRC standards evolving, GRC experts must maintain their skills and knowledge up to date in order to deal with the changes ahead.

5. GRC is ingrained in organizational culture.

As millennials go up the corporate ladder, their perspectives, attitudes, and approaches to work are altering how firms operate. Social media, mobile, and the cloud have all become popular office tools. The new styles of labor require agility, adaptability, and a "never-say-die" mentality, but GRC issues must not be overlooked.

Companies must consider how to incorporate GRC into their organizational culture while adapting to millennial working styles.

According to Aberdeen Group's 2017 report "Manage Risk Efficiently with Integrated GRC Solutions," users of GRC solutions are 4.1 times more likely than non-users to identify and track audit risk.

6. The Correct Information at the Correct Time

Business leaders must make choices faster than ever before in the face of increased geopolitical uncertainty, cyber-attacks, and rapid regulatory changes. They must be able to swiftly extract meaningful insights from vast amounts of data and apply those findings to improve corporate planning and strategy. The most critical consideration is speed. Today, strong tools for data visualization, analytics, and reporting are available, allowing business units to make quick, risk-aware decisions that drive performance.

7. Technology and tools that work

A really successful GRC program is enabled by technology as much as it is by people and processes. Automation is one of the most significant advantages of a GRC technology solution; it increases efficiency and lowers expenses. A GRC system can also assist businesses in improving cross-functional collaboration on GRC operations and transforming raw GRC data into actionable intelligence.

In an increasingly mobile, social, global, and virtual business world, the emphasis must be on simplifying GRC programs and attaining a high level of agility. Companies must be able to quickly adapt and respond to a volatile business landscape, changing regulatory environment, and ever-changing context of how business is done. Technology plays a critical role in accomplishing this goal.

TECHNOLOGY'S ROLE IN GRC

Governance, risk, and compliance (GRC) management is being transformed by technology. As firms become more sophisticated and global, the demand for effective GRC procedures and technologies is greater than ever. Technology is assisting firms in better managing GRC procedures and ensuring compliance with applicable rules and regulations.

GRC Automation

Automation is one of the major ways that technology is altering GRC. Organizations can benefit from automation by streamlining GRC operations, reducing manual errors, and improving accuracy. Organizations can also use automation to identify and address any risks and compliance issues quickly.

- Improved risk management:

Organizations can employ technology to identify possible risks and establish risk-mitigation measures. Technology also helps firms monitor and track risks more effectively, ensuring that they are managed in a timely and effective manner

- Improved compliance management:

Companies can utilize technology to guarantee that they comply with all applicable rules and regulations. Organizations can also use technology to identify and remedy potential compliance issues swiftly. Technology can also assist firms in better tracking and monitoring compliance activities to ensure compliance with applicable laws and regulations.

HOW TO USE TECHNOLOGY TO INCREASE GRC EFFICIENCY

Using technology to increase cybersecurity GRC efficiency protects an organization's data and infrastructure. Organizations may increase their GRC efficiency by employing technology to automate procedures, streamline workflows, and provide improved visibility into their security posture.

1. Automation of procedures:

Automated programs can monitor networks and systems for vulnerabilities, detect malicious behavior, and notify administrators of any unusual activity. This can assist firms in identifying and responding to possible threats more rapidly, lowering the chance of a data breach or other security disaster.

2. Workflow automation:

Using automated tools to optimize workflows and procedures is another approach to use technology to increase GRC efficiency. Automated tools can be used to automate data gathering and processing, as well as report results. This can assist firms in promptly identifying and addressing any possible risks or compliance concerns, lowering the time and resources required to manage GRC.

3. Increased visibility:

Utilizing technology can also assist firms in improving insight into their security posture. Automated programs can monitor and track system and network changes, as well as detect any unusual activities. This can assist enterprises in promptly identifying and responding to possible attacks, as well as ensuring the security of their systems and networks.

THE ADVANTAGES OF AUTOMATING GRC PROCEDURES

Automation of cybersecurity GRC (Governance, Risk, and Compliance) processes can be a wonderful method to improve an organization's security. Automation can help businesses improve their security posture, decrease the risk of data breaches, and maintain compliance with industry requirements.

- Improves security posture management:

One of the primary advantages of automating cybersecurity GRC activities is that it can assist firms in better managing their security posture. Automation can assist businesses in identifying potential security threats and vulnerabilities and taking the appropriate steps to mitigate them.

Automation can also assist firms in continuously monitoring their security posture, ensuring that any modifications or updates are swiftly noticed and rectified. This can assist firms in staying ahead of potential threats and reducing the likelihood of data breaches.

- Ensures that industry regulations are followed:

Automation can assist firms in quickly identifying areas of noncompliance and addressing them. This can help firms avoid costly fines and penalties while still maintaining their reputation and customer trust.

- Saves both time and money:

Automation can assist organizations in streamlining their security procedures, hence lowering the time and resources required to manage their security posture. This allows firms to concentrate their efforts on other aspects of their operations, such as innovation and expansion.

Technology can assist firms in better managing their Governance, Risk, and Compliance (GRC) operations.

Technology can make monitoring and managing GRC procedures more efficient and cost-effective.

Automated GRC processes can assist in reducing the risk of human mistakes and ensure regulatory compliance.
Technology can give firms real-time visibility into GRC operations, allowing them to identify and handle any possible issues swiftly.

Organizations can use technology to streamline their GRC operations, allowing them to focus on more strategic objectives.

Technology can help firms manage their GRC operations more effectively, resulting in increased efficiency, cost savings, and compliance.

Chapter 10

GRC IN ACTION

In the previous chapters, we've discussed GRC, how important it is to organizations, and how it can help you achieve your goals and keep your organization safe. Now, let's look into a company that adopted the GRC framework and how it helped them.

This Fiserv GRC case study includes:

The Fiserv Environment

Fiserv was started in 1984 and now employs over 19,000 people across 200 locations worldwide.

Fiserv is a global provider of information management and electronic commerce systems for the financial services industry, providing clients with integrated technology and services. It offers five types of technology solutions:

- Payments
- Processing services
- Risk and Compliance
- Customer and channel management
- Transforming data into usable business insights

Banks, credit unions, mortgage lenders and leasing organizations, brokerage and investment firms, and other enterprises are among the company's more than 16,000 clients globally. Fiserv assists these companies in addressing difficulties such as customer acquisition and retention, fraud prevention, and regulatory compliance.

Fiserv adopted a formal GRC strategy in 2008 "because it was the best way to manage through a thicket of simultaneously occurring changes in our business and regulatory environment," according to Murray Walton, senior vice president and chief risk officer.

According to Walton, the company's business strategy has shifted in recent years from a holding company to an integrated operational model, resulting in more complexity in the organization and the solutions it offers clients.

"The external environment has also changed, and today we face more government regulation and non-government standards, such as [PCI DSS]," said Walton. "Navigating all these challenges at the same time required a much more structured approach to governance, risk, and compliance than our previous spreadsheet-driven methods."

Prior to implementing the framework, Walton described his company's environment as "diversity on steroids." "We had different perspectives on what risk assessment and monitoring entailed." We had different perspectives on what was required or expected, as well as different methodologies and procedures. As a result, we had an immense problem in attempting to construct a picture of our company risk and compliance."

UPGRADING RISK MANAGEMENT PROCESSES

The company's GRC emphasis is now on risk assessment, compliance monitoring, policy administration, and remedy tracking. Fiserv is regulated by the FDIC as if it were a bank because it provides technology solutions to the financial services industry.

"It has been critical to our regulators and clients since the 2008 market collapse that we have rigorous processes in place to identify, understand, control, remediate, and monitor our risk and compliance posture," says Raji Ganesh, Fiserv vice president of risk and compliance.

To tackle that challenge, the corporation recognized the need to modernize its procedures and tools, as well as standardize its approach to GRC throughout an enterprise where decentralization previously reigned.

Fiserv launched its program update with the understanding that it would require a technology solution to support its goals. "But we were concerned that the technology solution could drive the program rather than the other way around," Walton said.

Some market solutions look to be dogma-driven. Someone believes they have all the answers and has a one-size-fits-all approach to risk and compliance management."
The corporation desired software that addressed as many regulatory and third-party criteria as possible. "If we only needed to be compliant with Gramm-Leach-Bliley or HIPAA or some other single regulation," Walton says,

"flexibility would be less of an issue." "But all those [regulations], and more, matter to us."

Fiserv meticulously designed its GRC program to match the demands of the organization, and then it chose the technology to support that program. Managers chose RiskVision after researching other alternatives in the industry. So far, they are satisfied with the technology, which they believe has transformed the risk-management program.

"RiskVision has empowered our risk-management staff to operate on a higher, more strategic plane," Walton said. "Previously, our team spent a disproportionate amount of time manually collecting and manipulating data." The process of establishing a baseline awareness of our risk profile absorbed the majority of our available horsepower, leaving much too little time for analysis and problem-solving."

According to Ganesh, the software has enabled Fiserv to "turn our paradigm on its head," allowing her team of former risk tacticians and figure crunchers to move into increased roles as risk strategists, allowing them to have a far higher impact on the firm.

"It allows us to get beyond that almost clerical use of people," she said. "The system is very good at that [number crunching]." It has shifted our people's attention from minutia to the broader picture."

Captured Advantages

The program automates operations such as data gathering, aggregation, workflow, and reporting that previously occupied the majority of this team's time. "They can primarily focus on deeper analysis and engagement that leads to more effective remediation and control of the risk in our organization," says Ganesh, now that they have useful, organized output from the system.

Fiserv additionally benefits from the GRC software's workflow and configuration management components.

"In a complex enterprise like ours, inputs and approvals may be needed from multiple units within the company to complete a single assessment," Ganesh said.

Producing a risk profile the previous way would have needed seven to ten additional staff members and cost Fiserv an additional half-million dollars.

"RiskVision workflow management speeds up our processes and eliminates file sneakernet movement." In addition, he claims that "organization and hierarchy changes that previously required many hours of manual effort to implement are now a simple matter of system configuration that takes only minutes."

The GRC system's basic reports and data export function, which lets the firm build reports using tools of its choosing, also makes reporting easier, according to Ganesh.

The software enables Fiserv to create a dashboard for managers that displays a color-coded image of where risk exists in the enterprise. "It makes it abundantly clear that this is where you ought to be focusing on remediation efforts, investments, policy, people issues," Walton said.

"Rather than spending all that time figuring out where the risk is, we now get that intelligence from the system and can spend more time addressing what we've found."

The company estimates that it would have taken around six months using Fiserv's old manual procedure to develop the type of thorough risk profile it currently gets from the software over three months. The earlier system would have also necessitated the hiring of seven to ten additional employees and would have cost Fiserv an additional half-million dollars.

Another advantage is the improved credibility the enterprise risk management team has garnered through contacts with management, regulators, and board members. "We have much broader, deeper, and better-presented data than ever before," Walton said.

"I can now engage with any of my team's constituencies with greater authority and confidence, and this has strengthened all of these key relationships."

Fiserv has benefited from knowing how other business users of the program have successfully managed GRC processes because it has contacts with them. Ganesh is a member of a product advisory group, and she and Walton have taken advantage of official and informal opportunities to communicate with other Agiliance consumers.

"Although every company is different, the journey to maturing the risk management function has common elements, whatever your business," according to Ganesh. "We have appreciated the opportunity to interact with others who are at different points on the maturity curve and who have already figured out how to meet a challenge that is new to us."

GETTING OVER OBSTACLES IN GRC IMPLEMENTATION

Because Fiserv faced a variety of issues during its GRC deployment, exchanging best practices and seeking assistance from more experienced GRC practitioners was very beneficial.

For example, when the organization implemented a new comprehensive information security standards program about a year and a half ago, another rule set for GRC was produced.

"So now we were adding another layer to our control policies, and we needed to learn how to build that" into the program, according to Walton.

"We didn't anticipate this need, but we could talk to others and our Agiliance advisers, who recommended a policy-management module that links directly to existing RiskVision content." It saved us months of research and at least a couple hundred thousand dollars."

It is critical to remember that GRC is a process that is aided by technology, and businesses should avoid relying just on the software.

According to Walton, building a consistent understanding of the logic, discipline, and terminology of professional risk management was an even greater problem for Fiserv.

"Fiserv was formed through the acquisition of more than 140 companies over the past 26 years, and until a few years ago, most of our business units operated with considerable autonomy," Walton said. "They managed risk the same way they always had, with varying degrees of maturity and sophistication prior to 2007." We achieved disparate results due to a lack of standard systems and processes across our organization."

According to Walton, the value of a packaged solution is that it does not skip steps. "It enforces a rigorous, process-driven approach to risk management that is inherently missing in the kind of homegrown, paper-based processes we used before."

The RiskVision installation has been generally successful due to extensive user training within the organization, as well as the tool itself anticipating that users may approach the system with varied degrees of understanding.

"Essentially, there's a lot of help built into the tools, and the user interface is solid," Ganesh said. "In fact, Agiliance was willing to take our suggestions and incorporate them as core product functionality."

"We chose an implementation path that included a lot of professional services support," Ganesh explains because the program was new to everyone. "This enabled us to launch our product on time, with no surprises and excellent user support." We scored a home run with RiskVision because usability was one of our most carefully weighted selection criteria.

The most difficult part of GRC implementation was security. "Because we have so many business units and a complex hierarchy, the ability to set user permissions at a granular level is very important to us," Walton said. "We utilize a 'least privilege' security model, and it has taken time for us and Agiliance to fully develop this functionality."

Walton believes that two linked factors are working to make having a strong GRC strategy and software deployment more of a must for many businesses.

"First, we seem to be in an era of re-regulation, and every new regulation brings new compliance obligations," he said. "Second, contract and vendor-management processes are being used more frequently to shift the onus of compliance obligations onto vendors."

From a vendor's standpoint, there are situations when it makes commercial sense to accept contract stipulations from a prospective client that involve exceptional or extra risk. "We believe that the better we understand our existing risk profile, the more intelligently we can evaluate nonstandard client terms," Walton goes on to say.

"When we agree to unusual requests, we must also be able to monitor our compliance." This is a significant benefit of our RiskVision deployment. It enables us to take chances that we would never consider if we were flying blind."

Walton, like many industry experts, believes that it is critical to remember that GRC is a process supported by technology and that businesses should avoid relying just on the software.

"An effective risk-management program is part of an organization's quest for self-awareness," Walton said. "Beginning with technology rather than process risks allowing the tool to define the program rather than supporting it." Before you can pick which technology is best for your needs, you must first examine your company's assets, vulnerabilities, and risk tolerance."

Only once a corporation understands these fundamental concepts will it be able to determine how a GRC software solution will fit into its risk-management program.

THE LESSONS LEARNED FROM THE PROCESS

The more decentralized the organization, the more complex the GRC implementation. Basics such as technical project management and network preparation should be noticed.

Your current risk-management team may be concerned that implementing GRC software would eliminate their positions or change their job functions in ways that will force them to work outside of their comfort zones or skill sets. Please work with your GRC software vendor and its user community to help your team comprehend the new system's chances for professional advancement and other potential benefits.

Don't try to employ every feature of your GRC solution on the first day. Begin modest, uncomplicated, and focused, with a clear vision of the desired outcome. Develop into your system.

Consider your GRC system to be a torch that shines into your organization's dark cabinets. You'll be astonished at how much better your risk and compliance fact base and reporting capabilities are right away after implementing your new system. You'll also be amazed at how difficult it is to figure out how to use your newfound knowledge to improve risk management in your firm.

FUTURE TRENDS IN GRC

You are aware that GRC has developed and will continue to do so. However, there are key principles and areas on which you should concentrate going forward. Let's look at some of the GRC trends that, according to G2, might help your firm adopt a proactive approach to transforming risk into a competitive advantage.

Trends in governance, risk, and compliance

GRC issues require a resilient and agile culture.

Resilience is the ability to rebound from adversity, such as a breach or a disruption in operations, and get back in the game. You should ask the following questions:

- How quickly can I recover from a traumatic event?
- How soon can I re-establish processes and operations?
- How quickly can I identify and contain a risk event when it is still small?

Agility is about looking ahead, anticipating potential risk scenarios, and assessing how they may affect your firm. Can these scenarios present chances for your company?

So, what should you expect?

There is only one certainty: you cannot eliminate all dangers. Fostering a culture of resiliency and agility, on the other hand, will enable your organization to be proactive and quick to respond when issues arise.

How can GRC support your resilience and agility?

Many tedious and time-consuming procedures, like as risk assessments and compliance reporting, are automated by GRC systems. This will allow you to devote more attention to strategic efforts.

A centralized GRC platform would allow you to more effectively identify, assess, and prioritize risks. This allows you to make better-informed decisions and respond to threats with greater speed and agility.

GRC systems can help businesses stay on top of changing legislation and standards by providing real-time compliance information. This would allow you to avoid fines or legal penalties and respond promptly to regulatory changes.

A GRC platform gives you and management a consolidated view of your risk and compliance position, allowing you to make better-informed decisions. This allows you to respond to risks and difficulties more quickly and effectively, boosting your resiliency.

The CIO's Changing Role

Risks are no longer classified as low, medium, or high. For risk management experts who struggled to link their assessments with real-world business choices, the traditional method of doing things simply wasn't cutting it.

As a result, the CIO's job has been revised. They are increasingly taking on more responsibility for risk management and business choices, as well as conveying any pertinent information to the board.

Third-party risks are becoming increasingly important.

To properly manage third parties, three actions must be taken:

Consistent process review: By thoroughly evaluating all contracts and enforcing agreements, you may use GRC software to improve efficiency and speed.

Prioritization: You must be able to distinguish and prioritize among vendors. Criteria can be created based on the business environment and requirements.

Use the information: The above information will assist you in short-listing the best vendor with the least amount of risk exposure and monitoring it throughout the project. Follow these steps to accomplish this:

Rank each third party in terms of your relationship and key needs.

List the data and levels of authorization for each vendor.

Create a full analysis of the consequences of any incidents.

Use this information to keep a close eye on your chosen dealer.

Third-party risk evaluation and scoring is provided by a number of systems, including SecurityScorecard and RiskRecon. We have integrated these two solutions into our StandardFusion risk management platform due to the rising demand for third-party risk management in GRC.

Regulations are becoming more stringent.

The most recent GRC developments reveal an escalation in the discussion of environmental, social, and governance (ESG). It is also a good idea to investigate whether incorporating ESG into your GRC program might provide you with a better understanding of your risks.

Cyber dangers are introduced by hybrid work.

Although hybrid employment improves flexibility, it also adds risk to your organization. However, because remote work is here to stay, you must understand how to maximize productivity while minimizing hazards.

Remote work has a corresponding impact on cyber threats since remote employees use personal devices to access your network. However, some solutions, such as installing multi-factor authentication and providing effective employee training, can improve security and eliminate some vulnerabilities.

CONCLUSION

Numerous advantages are made available by an integrated GRC program developed and managed appropriately. These advantages include enhanced governance, excellent risk management, and improved compliance. As organizations strive to achieve their goals in a world that is becoming increasingly disruptive, an integrated approach to governance, risk, and compliance (GRC) is no longer merely a recommended practice; rather, it is an organizational necessity.